FATTY BATTER

How cricket saved my life
(then ruined it)

Michael Simkins

EBURY
PRESS

For Mum

And Dad

3 5 7 9 10 8 6 4

Published in 2007 by Ebury Press, an imprint of Ebury Publishing

Ebury Publishing is a division of the Random House Group

The Random House Group Limited Reg. No. 954009

Addresses for companies within the Random House Group
can be found at www.randomhouse.co.uk

A CIP catalogue record for this book
is available from the British Library

The Random House Group Limited makes every effort to ensure that the
papers used in our books are made from trees that have been legally
sourced from well-managed and credibly certified forests. Our paper
procurement policy can be found on www.randomhouse.co.uk

Printed and bound by Mackays of Chatham Ltd
Interior design by seagulls.net

Front cover photograph of the author by Fred Wackett
Inside front cover photograph of Harry Baldwin copyright holder unknown
Inside back cover photograph of the author copyright holder unknown
Page 161: Extract from 'To John Berry Hobbs on his seventieth birthday'
by John Arlott, 1952, copyright © *The Cricketer* magazine

ISBN 9780091901509

Contents

Acknowledgements

My thanks to everyone who has helped me, by accident or design, in the writing of this book. My special thanks to Andrew Goodfellow, Tony Morris, Mari Roberts, Verity Willcocks, Caroline Newbury, Hugh Osborne and Jonathan Coy for their encouragement and patience and, lastly, my family and friends, without whom, I suspect, none of the enclosed would have been possible. Certain names and locations have been changed. My apologies in advance to anyone who feels they may have got a dodgy decision...

This is how bad it is.

By some fantastic coincidence of the natural world it's possible for anyone with a full set of teeth and a working upper palate to make the sound of a cricket ball hitting a bat. That unique sound, like the tock of a grandfather clock mixed with a large, overfed trout being released into a lazy stream from a height of about eight inches above the water on a golden, sunlit afternoon.

'The sound of summer', as it's often called.

And because it's so evocative I make it all the time. Standing at the checkout in Tesco, in rehearsals for a play, or in those few blissful moments after my wife and I have made love, and we're lying there enjoying the sense of mutual triumph against middle-aged odds. Even as Julia is reaching for my hand across the sheets and framing the words to express her crowded emotions – something like, 'Jesus, I didn't think you still had it in you' – I'll drift off into some reverie, perhaps knocking up in a net on a Wednesday evening, or playing in a proper match against deadly rivals, or even the unexpected call-up for England for the crucial Ashes decider at the Oval.

I'll imagine the bowler trundling in, the sweep of his arm arcing over, that hard red ball hurtling towards me, and then my shot, perhaps a luscious cover drive or a disdainful pull. Whichever it is, as Julia's fingers are touching mine across the creased bed linen, my tongue will automatically slide to the vertical, finding the warm wet roof of the mouth, tightening like the trigger of a gun; and before I can stop myself ...

And her fingers will freeze. Or the checkout girl will stop feeding the washing-up liquid past the scanner; or the director of the play will turn his head, convinced I'm tutting in derision at his musings about the importance of symbolism in Shakespeare's verse. And I have to try and explain that it wasn't criticism that just issued forth from my lips, it was an exact vocal replica of a handsome lofted drive into that canopy of trees in the distance.

But of course they don't believe me. So I'm condemned, like some sporting Tourette's sufferer, to make these curious clucking sounds throughout the day with the constant gnawing knowledge that sooner or later I'm going to startle or upset those around me. Believe me, it's a living hell.

Unless, of course, the ball clears the pavilion and sets a new record for the longest hit ever made at the Oval, beating Dickie Dodds's gigantic sixer in the Whitsun bank holiday fixture there in 1956 ...

FIRST INNINGS

One Short

There I am.

Down there. The one standing at the far end of the playground between the two duffel bags acting as goalposts.

No, not him, that's my opposite number, Anthony Hall. Try the other end, by the railings. The one with the plastered-down hair and the scarlet cheeks. The one with his pully tucked into the top of his shorts. The one with the chafe marks on the inside of his thighs, with kneecaps the colour of self-raising flour.

The one who's carefully unwrapping the chocolate bar.

I've been frozen in that pose for some while. The game hasn't been up my end for a bit so there's a chance to concentrate on the thing I'm really interested in. Which isn't standing in goal in a rain-soaked playground during a game of sock football, waiting for the next opposition attack. Rather the unfurling of this new addition to the shelves of my dad's sweetshop: Cadbury's Walnut Crinkle.

Walnut Crinkle. Until now I'd thought it was only something you caught at the swimming baths. But Dad has been persuaded to take two dozen of them this morning by the Cadbury's rep on a special trial offer, so I've got a couple on me. One for now and one for later.

This is the reason – one of the reasons – why Gordon Banks keeps goal for England whereas I only keep goal in the lower playground of Middle Street Primary School in Brighton. The other reason is that with Eusébio bearing down on him in a World Cup semi-final, Gordon Banks would keep his eye on the ball, whereas I would get whacked in the forehead because I'd be too busy gazing longingly at the packet of chocolate digestives underneath the subs bench. Were I to look up now I'd see our playground's own version of Eusébio already barely twenty-five feet away in the shape of ten-year-old Michael Lowe. But of course I'm not looking up. I never do.

Michael Lowe is our star player. His father is PE teacher at the technical college and spends his weekends teaching his son to sail their mirror dinghy on the river Adur. Michael Lowe can swim, life-save, and trains each Saturday morning with Sussex under-twelves cross-country squad. He can take an impromptu ball made up of socks and rubber bands bandaged in yards of Sellotape and dribble it effortlessly between forests of thundering juvenile feet, before darting clear of the scrum and racing like a greyhound to the far end of the playground, where all that stands between him and yet another goal is me. The one who's just about to take a big, deep bite out of a chocolate bar on which Cadbury's are pinning their hopes for increased market share in the confectionery and mixed boilings market for 1966, the one whose only claim to sporting excellence is the ability to down a family-size bottle of R Whites Cream Soda in under a minute.

In between us is everyone else. People whose aspirations are to be as similar as possible to Michael Lowe and as different as possible from Michael Simkins: the Nigels, the Stevens and Barrys, the ones with a modicum of athletic prowess, the ones with a distinguishable waistline, the ones who can get on a speak-your-weight machine without it requesting only one at a time please ...

I'm joking. Of course I am. I wish I weren't. They've just installed one on the pavement outside the Home & Colonial in Gardner Street and it didn't say, 'One at a time please,' it said, 'Your current weight is eleven stone three pounds,' which, when you're ten years old, is a lot worse, particularly when amplified in a rich BBC accent to a gaggle of sniggering teenagers.

All those other Michael Lowe wannabes trying to back-heel the sock ball out from the foetid drain in which it has temporarily lodged think by touching the hem of his shorts they can become like him. That's why Michael Lowe has all the friends he can handle whereas I've only got the kid in the far corner, the other goalie, Anthony Hall. Although we're nominally on opposite teams, he and I are in fact on the same side. In reality it's the two of us versus the other forty-two players thrashing and charging about in the middle of the playground.

My teeth fasten on the thick, thick outer shell of the bar. With any new taste sensation this is always the best moment: a second to savour the unique feeling of enamel pressing into milk chocolate, and then the bite, in this case severing the walnut from the crinkle in one easy motion. This is the best moment, the second before the act, the delicious half-second before—

A wet sock encased in Sellotape, which has only recently been retrieved from a drain, hits me between the eyes at 30mph.

The bar is dashed from my lips by the force of the blow and drops into a puddle. Meanwhile the compressed sock has ricocheted off my forehead back into the path of the still-advancing Michael Lowe who retrieves it, nutmegs his opponent, jinks inside two other defenders and cannons it past me into the railings, narrowly missing my left eye in the process.

'You spaz!' somebody shouts. 'Why didn't you kick it?'

One of my team-mates retrieves the sock and trots back to the centre circle. 'Pillock,' he says as he passes. I can already feel an ugly welt starting to erupt above my nose.

The taste sensation is now a dog-turd smear in the goalmouth. Michael Lowe's plimsoll marks are on it. Welcome to my world.

No Ball

What it is about men and sport?

Why do we all have to be winners or losers? Why is one's entire worth measured only by whether one can kick a ball, throw a punch, leap a hurdle, or, in the case of speedway, blind thousands of innocent spectators by hurtling round a cinder track on a bike with no brakes.

We go to speedway once a month as part of our Sunday afternoon out, Dad steering our huge tank of a Rover along the coast road, Mum humming along to *Two-Way Family Favourites*, with me wedged between my two elder brothers in the back. Geoff, being already at secondary school and thus anxious to distance himself from his kid brother as much as possible, buries his head in his train-spotting magazines for the whole journey and won't speak, while Pete, being nearly twenty years older, brings along one of an assortment of various-shaped girlfriends, who crams in with us.

Each race is exactly the same, the same blokes hurtling round and round in endless circuits, at the end of which nobody knows who's won because they all look identical, and in any case everyone's been blinded by grit. The people who attend the meetings all wear anoraks and elastic-sided shoes and talk about nothing except carburettors and fuel consumption and how you can improve the performance of the Ford Cortina without extensive reboring.

Dad has a love of speedway because his own father took him to see it in the 1930s. But that was different. That was at places with glamour, like White City and Manchester Bellevue, not a stretch of waste ground near Polegate. Between races there used to be spectacular displays to keep the crowd entertained while they waited for the St John Ambulance men to divvy out the eye drops, daredevil exhibitions in which men in bathing trunks dived off high boards into tubs of lighted petrol. If they'd do that sort of thing at Arlington I might just look up from my bag of Nut Brittle. But they don't. Instead they have the Alfriston town band sitting in a semi-circle in the middle of the track playing the theme tune to *World of Sport*.

Which brings me to wrestling. Mum's best friend Ida Wackett sometimes gets free seats for bouts at the Essoldo Sports Hall, and occasionally takes Mum and me along with her. Mum and Ida aren't the same as the real die-hards who congregate front row ringside with their stockings rucked around their ankles and continuously stuff Spangles into their mouths. Those are the real fans: the ones so caught up in all the drama that they don't even bother to check which flavour they've unwrapped.

Mum isn't one of those women, of course she's not, she just likes to let her hair down once every so often. So we sit in a freezing-cold cinema for several hours as a procession of pasty-faced men in sagging bathing trunks execute an endless series of well-rehearsed moves and throws. The wrestlers are always either goodies or baddies. The goodies are distinguishable by the fact they're 'carrying an injury', as the announcer always informs us beforehand. Dave Roberts has agreed to fight tonight despite the fact that he's 'carrying an injury', perhaps a strapped calf muscle or a bandaged ankle in case we don't know where to find it.

The baddies, on the other hand, know exactly where to find it. Some arrive wearing cheetah-skin dressing gowns, such as Adrian Street, or mysterious masks, such as Kendo Nagasaki, while the Wild Man of Borneo is so terrifying and uncontrollable that he has to be brought from the dressing rooms to the ringside in a specially constructed bamboo cage on wheels.

It's all a con of course. Mum and Ida Wackett go for a drink in the bar after the programme is finished, and all the baddies wander in for a pint, now without their disguises and looking like mechanics or greengrocers. The mysterious Kendo Nagasaki from the far Orient has a fondness for salted peanuts, while the Wild Man of Borneo is really called Ron and owns a small builders and decorators somewhere near Walsall.

In any case, if I wanted to spend my free time watching fat, pasty-faced individuals in sagging pants I could just look in the mirror in the comfort of my own bedroom. Why should I want to pay for the privilege?

And then of course there's football.

Everybody loves football. The Beatles love football. Harold Wilson loves football. If you don't love football, you don't really exist. With the World Cup final at Wembley only weeks away you're expected to reel off the names of the current England players on demand. Our sweetshop is selling World Cup bubble-gum cards so the shop is full from morning to night with kids spending their parents' life savings in order to obtain the last few outstanding cards and complete the set.

I try to tell them how bubble-gum manufacturers operate but they won't listen. Of course none of them can find number 67, Ralph Coates of Burnley – that's because they aren't print-ing any. That way the manufacturers ensure you keep buying their bubble gum day after day, only to have your heart broken when you find that you've just acquired your fifty-third Gary Sprake of Leeds. These are just the sorts of nasty little tricks you learn about when your dad runs a sweetshop. But the kids in the playground won't listen to me. As far as they're concerned I'm a dangerous misfit because I can't play football and I don't have a football hero.

'Baggsie I'm Peter Osgood. Baggsie I'm Roger Hunt. Baggsie I'm Bobby Tambling, or Ralph Coates, or Alan Gilzean. Who are you baggsieing, Spaz?'

'Um ...'

'Who are you baggsieing then, Spaz?'

The questioner is Jimmy Greaves of Tottenham Hotspur. He's a kid with ginger hair who lives in a detached house in Westdene and whose dad is something high up in the legal system. Jimmy Greaves has only two ambitions, to become a solicitor like his father and to ingratiate himself with Michael Lowe by humiliating any kid in the class who's an easy target.

'Who is it? Are you baggsieing Greedy Pigg from the *Dandy*?'

'I'm baggsieing—'

'Is it Billy Bunter?'

'No, I'm—'

'Fatty Arbuckle, is that who it is?'

'It's Oliver Hardy!' shouts someone from the perimeter of the group. It's Jack Charlton of Leeds. Raucous laughter from the entire England squad rattles the surrounding schoolroom windows. If Alf Ramsey could see the sort of thing that goes on when his back is turned he'd fire the whole lot of them. But he can't see. Nobody can. Because if you don't like sport you're off the radar. If I had a Walnut Crinkle for every time this has happened to me I'd be as big as a house.

I forgot. I already am.

But on Saturday 4 June, it's all about to change.

Wide

Benjamin Alfred and Peggy Irene Simkins, Confectioners, Tobacconists and Newsagents, is situated just off the seafront and sells all the usual things you'd expect from a sweetshop: chocolate bars, loose sweets and boxed assortments, as well as a variety of other goods and comestibles for the local community – cigarettes, newspapers, crisps, ice cream, greetings cards, chemist's sundries, gift wrap, ladies' stockings and hairnets. We also stock seasonal favourites: fireworks, Easter eggs and Christmas items such as selection boxes and the Sooty and Sweep chocolate smoker's set.

But the summer is our busiest time. Particularly the summer of 1966. The recent spell of warm weather means Brighton is gorged with trippers and holidaymakers, and with England about to host the World Cup finals an air of febrile excitement hangs in the air, resulting in record takings in the shop. With Mum and Dad working from first light till the *Nine O'Clock News* weighing sweets and making up vanilla cornets, I have to make my own entertainment, which is why I've spent the morning at Anthony Hall's house playing with his Chad Valley slide projector.

It's fast approaching noon, that tiny thirty-minute oasis when they both get to wolf down a hurried meal in the parlour before returning to shop duty. They're expecting me to join them. I've got to be back on time for dinner or there'll be the usual carry-on. And I'm late.

Up the street, past Dranse's second-hand clothes store, past Reece's transport café with its huge glistening slab of butter in the window, past D'Arcy's electronics, past Fred and Ida Wackett's photography studio and finally in through the shop door with its sign saying *Open, especially for Craven 'A'*. These are the runway lights of my daily life, the markers that guide me home, the signposts that define my routine and assure me that the Soviets haven't dropped the bomb yet.

I clatter in through the front, where our assistant Vi Hacker is weighing out a quarter of American Hard Gums. She gives me a friendly smile, black and rotten teeth framed by two stripes of garish red lipstick. In through the counter hatch marked 'Private', past the greetings cards, past the toffee tubs and the snuff, past the fizzy-pop stand and the Milk of Magnesia until I reach the sweet shelves. A deft flick with my left hand and within seconds I'm unwrapping a bar of Toblerone.

That's the one good thing about living in a sweetshop. Mum and Dad are so busy running the premises that they don't seem to notice how many sweets I eat. And although Toblerone were expecting big things from their new taste sensation, it hasn't exactly been leaping off the shelves since the weather turned warm.

Right turn and I'm in the inner sanctum, the rear parlour, the epicentre of my universe. Dad is sitting at the table with his dog-eared copy of William L. Shirer's *The Rise and Fall of the Third Reich* on the table in front of him, the only book he ever reads. Except it lies unopened.

'Dad—'

'Shhhhh. I'm watching the cricket.'

I've heard about cricket. Dad often watches it during his brief lunch-break when it's on telly in the summer. Someone bowls a ball to someone else who hits it with a bat, after which everyone stands round pontificating. A cross between rounders and *Does the Team Think?*.

Dad has liked cricket ever since he was a little boy. His own childhood hero was a famous batsman called Jack Hobbs, whom his own dad used to take him to see at the Kennington Oval when he was a kid. One of Dad's favourite stories is how he once got Jack Hobbs's autograph, and how to this day he regrets his decision a few years later to swap it for a balsa-wood glider. I think he made the right decision. Personally I'd rather have the test card on. At least you get some jolly oompah music.

With no sign of Mum or dinner, I break off a triangle with my teeth and settle down in the chair by the TV set, allowing Tobler's exotic medley of milk chocolate, crushed almonds and honey to churn gently in my mouth.

And then I see him.

At first it's almost impossible to make him out. He looks like nothing more than a large white bed sheet moving in the dark interior of the pavilion behind the serried rows of slumbering middle-aged men outside.

But there he is again. Moving with purpose and at some speed in the dim interior, just a snatched glimpse of a large gelatinous object between a bloke in a panama hat and another with horn-rimmed spectacles. A flash of sunlight reflecting off freshly Windolened glass as doors are thrown open, and he lumbers out of the darkness of the pavilion and down the steps.

He barrels down, two at a time, his huge stomach wobbling up and down each tread like a giant blancmange, the flesh straining against the flimsy buttons of his cricket shirt. He seems an amalgamation of every fat kid who has ever sat in the corner of a school changing room having gym shoes thrown at him by his classmates.

People this shape and size don't appear on professional sport. They appear on programmes like *Tonight* and *South Today*, where they describe to a smirking interviewer how they've got into the *Guinness Book of Records* by breaking the world record for the number of boiled eggs eaten at a single sitting.

But he reaches the middle of the pitch, leans stiffly down to flick away a blade of grass from the crease, holds his bat carefully in front of the wicket and looks up at the umpire before gesturing with two fingers. In the distance the bowler, a huge black man with a dazzling smile, steps forward as if about to start a slow rumba, and next thing he's hurtling forward, his body charging across the turf as if shot from a cannon.

Another triangle slips into my mouth. I've not even bothered to unwrap it properly, and a large sliver of silver foil churns around, looking for one of my many fillings on which to unleash its deadly cargo. There can only be one winner here. Any minute now the bloke out there on the pitch is going to have a cricket ball wedged halfway down his throat, there's going to be blood and the spitting out of teeth, and men in gym shoes running on with bottles of TCP and bandages. I want to avert my gaze, but I can't. It's like watching a road accident. You know it's disrespectful to look but somehow you're mesmerised. I squint through splayed fingers. A whirl of the arms and the ball swinging through the air.

He rocks back, swivels on a huge ham bone of a right leg, rolls his wrists and, just as the ball is going to bury itself in his skull, his bat makes contact and the ball sails high, high into the sky and finally lands over the boundary, in among a load of spectators who scatter like pigeons to avoid being hit. A middle-aged bloke in a checked cardigan holds it briefly aloft in the stands in a gesture of triumph.

And as he waves the ball high above his head, the piece of silver foil, borne effortlessly on a ribbon of saliva, finds my deepest nerve ending in a bottom left premolar and deposits its sharp electrical charge.

Pull

By the time Colin Milburn has disappeared back into the pavilion I've learnt my first cricketing statistic. England's new batting hero can hit ninety-four runs in less time than it takes a kid of ten to eat a Toblerone followed by a plate of fish in parsley sauce. I may be only ten, but I can spot a role model when I see one. He's not only fantastic at sport, but is obviously no stranger to a tub of Quality Street.

I'm still there, watching throughout the afternoon. And again after tea. And slowly, session by session, ball by ball, I begin to get drawn into the whole unfolding ceremony. I haven't a clue what's going on, but bit by bit it starts to piece together like one of those jigsaws my Auntie Lena buys me for my birthday.

Luckily I've also got Dad to hand. Over the next couple of days he explains a bit more in between mouthfuls of congealing cod or burnt stewing beef. The nuances, as he calls them. Things like why it's good for fast bowlers like Ken Higgs to have such huge backsides, why they put in an extra close fielder for the new batsman, and why, when somebody takes a wicket, all his teammates simply amble up and shake him by the hand as if he's just delivered a speech at the TUC conference.

There are other people to help out. The BBC commentators of course, Brian Johnston and John Arlott: they fill in some of the blanks with the occasional observation. Dad tells me that he served in the war with Johnston during the Allies' final push into Germany in 1945 and that they used to knock around together. But when his wartime mate describes the West Indies captain

Gary Sobers as possibly the greatest cricketer who has ever played the game, Dad's jaw tightens and he reminds me that he saw Jack Hobbs at the Oval in the 1920s and knows the truth.

There's another commentator on hand, a bloke who sweats a lot and is always fiddling in his jacket pocket as he speaks as if he's looking for his car keys. But Peter West doesn't seem to know any more than me, confining his observations to either, 'My goodness,' or, 'My word.' I reckon I could manage that.

With each session I understand a little more. What a declaration is, why it's important to save a follow-on and why you can't be out leg before wicket playing a shot if the ball pitches outside the leg stump. It's not long before my jigsaw has become all four corners, a complete edging, some sky and an outline of that tricky foliage on the left. I just need to get into the main part of the picture and I'm there.

Slowly the landscape of my days changes. A couple of Thursdays later Anthony Hall pops into the shop to ask if I'd like to see his *Famous Waterfalls of the World* slideshow. I tell him I can't, I've got to see whether Graveney and D'Oliveira can survive Hall and Griffith with the new ball. On the Saturday my other friend, a boy called Stephen Emery, offers me a go with his new Johnny Seven space gun. I apologise but explain that I'm currently detained by John Snow and Brian Close who are mounting a rearguard.

I'm repaid for my loyalty when in the next match Milburn hits a spectacular quick-fire hundred, at one point depositing Wes Hall's fastest balls into the Mound Stand. But by then Anthony Hall has stopped calling round, and Stephen Emery has gone on holiday to Wales. Mum now thinks I'm watching too much television so tells my middle brother Geoff to do something to get me out of the house. But even his unprecedented invitation to a day's train-spotting isn't enough to lure me out.

How quickly things change. A mere month ago I would have given away my most treasured possession, my set of American Civil War bubble-gum cards, including the extremely rare 43,

Death On The Spikes, to be allowed to hang round with Geoff and his mates on the luggage trolleys at the end of platform three, talking about loco sheds and boiler diameters and eating pork pies all day. But now I've got something else.

I've got Colin Milburn. But I've also got his mates Jim Parks, Geoff Boycott and J.T. Murray. And all the others. Not only the other England players but the West Indians. Until now the only coloured people I've seen on TV are the Black and White Minstrels in white toppers and spangly jackets.

June turns into July, and there's a gap of several weeks before the next Test match at Leeds. A different sporting occasion hoves into view, and nobody else seems bothered that the cricket has temporarily stopped. They're all too caught up in what's going to happen at Wembley.

I'm not. I'm missing the cricket. And with no Test match scheduled for a couple of weeks, Dad suggests I might like to go along and see my local team in the flesh. Sussex County Cricket Club have their ground a short bus ride away from our shop, out at the county ground in the adjoining borough of Hove, and are due to play a three-day fixture on the same weekend as the World Cup final. Dad thinks it would be all right for me to go by myself to see some live cricket as long as I'm back in good time. I'm given the bus fare, some sandwiches and a pound note in case I get into difficulties and need a taxi.

So while the rest of humanity settles down for a date with destiny, I find myself on the top deck of the number 6 bus to Portslade via Norfolk Square, for a date with Sussex versus Gloucestershire in a middle-of-the-table clash in the county championship.

Bye

My first day at Hove is like watching one of those interludes the BBC broadcast between programmes. Like the kittens playing with the ball of wool, or the potter moulding the clay on the revolving wheel, it's as if I'm watching the same event over and over again. And yet, like the potter's wheel, the endless repetition is itself curiously comforting.

Sussex versus Gloucestershire starts promptly at 11.30 on the Saturday morning. The players outnumber the spectators. A couple of them I recognise from the telly: wicketkeeper Jim Parks with his broad smile and crinkly hair, and the more brooding figure of opening bowler John Snow, who seems to spend much of his time idly kicking at the grass with his boot as if imagining some dark violence he'd like to perpetrate on Gary Sobers.

Speedway it's not. By noon most of the handful of spectators are asleep. Even those still awake aren't watching, and most of the kids in the crowd are already playing their own impromptu games behind the stands. A couple of old blokes in faded denim yachting caps sitting a few yards away from me spend the whole of the first two hours setting each other quiz questions from their *Playfair Cricket Annuals* without once looking up at what's happening on the field.

The thin one asks the chubby one which Hampshire batsman was born in Chippenham, Wiltshire, and then the chubby one asks the thin one which Leicestershire batsman made his debut last year against Derbyshire at Burton-on-Trent, and then the thin one asks the chubby one how many of the Kent playing staff have surnames beginning with L. When a wicket falls they look up in irritation as if a group of protesters had wandered into their living room.

The others around them aren't much better. Some are doing the crossword, others are carefully decanting warm tea out of tartan thermos flasks into plastic cups as if conducting some important nuclear experiment, while a couple of old gents are staring blearily at nothing in particular, their straw hats tipped over their foreheads and empty claret bottles rolling round on the cement beneath their seats. One woman a few rows ahead of me spends nearly the entire two-hour session of play in the morning trying to scoop a drowning wasp out of a tea-filled china saucer.

The Gloucestershire tactics seem to be to bore Sussex to death. At one point the entire game stops for over five minutes while a spectator is summoned back to her car to lay a blanket over her windscreen to stop it reflecting the sun into the batsman's eyes. Yet everyone seems perfectly happy to wait: Jim Parks even offers one of the umpires a Fox's Glacier Mint during the hiatus.

By half past twelve I've already eaten my sandwiches. When the second wicket falls, that of a cherubic farmer-type called David Shepherd whose girth makes Milburn look malnourished, I decide to seek out fresh supplies. This entails asking my neighbours if I can squeeze past. They withdraw their legs without looking up or drawing breath.

'Which currently serving first-class umpire once completed six stumpings in a single match while playing for Worcestershire against Scotland?'

It's all strangely hypnotic: the slow inexorable progress of each over, the desultory applause, the footling questions, the rattle of the numbers flipping over in the score box, the aimless loafing between overs, the fact that you can wander off for twenty minutes without missing anything. There are no nasty surprises like a wet sock hitting you in the face or cinders scorching your cheeks. Just the occasional clapping of hands, the flapping of deckchairs in the breeze and the distant cry of gulls from the seafront.

There's something welcoming about it too. The bloke wandering among the crowd selling the early edition of our local paper winks at me as he ambles by. The lady selling scorecards in the little booth by the club shop wishes me good morning when I walk past, while a passer-by points out that I might want to retie my shoelace in case it causes me to trip. And although the only food outlet is a dilapidated shed next to the front gates, it has rock cakes, sausage rolls and slices of fruitcake. What's more, I'm the only customer.

As I'm sitting at one of the tables working my way through a McVitie's blackberry and apple pie, I spot a gaggle of kids hanging round the back doors of the adjacent pavilion. It becomes apparent they're waiting for players' autographs. In a moment of rash daring I decide to join them to try my luck, and no sooner have I done so than Gloucestershire wicketkeeper Barry Meyer pops out for a fag. When he goes to sign my score-card he points out my biro has stopped working, but he merely asks another kid if he can borrow his and happily continues; what's more, the kid offers his pen without complaint even though he's just spotted the Sussex twelfth man Don Bates a few yards away searching for something in his glove compartment.

Later in the afternoon I'm back in the café enjoying a pork pie and a bag of Potato Puffs when through an open window on the first floor of the pavilion I hear Gloucestershire captain John Mortimore making a phone call to the bookies to put a quid each way on Pride of Place in the 4.30 at Wincanton. Just then a huge cheer goes up from the field of play. Given the crowd's reaction to previous wickets I can't imagine what could possibly have happened to provoke such passion, unless John Snow has skewered Arthur Milton to the sight screen with a cricket stump. And when I reach the top of the steps the scene is indeed exactly as I left it.

Then I realise the reason for the outburst. England, who apparently had been trailing 1–0 in the World Cup final, have levelled the score. Several spectators have transistor radios discreetly stationed in their holdalls, and word has got round of Hurst's equaliser. Up in the players' box I can see David Shepherd pumping his arms furiously in the air in triumph, while John Snow is calling for confirmation to a spectator in the front row of the pavilion. Only the two blokes in the yachting caps seem not to have noticed.

I wonder if fifty miles up the road Nobby Stiles is asking the bench if Mike Bissex has reached his half-century yet? It seems unlikely. But in any case it's time I got back home. At this rate I'll be lucky to catch the second half. As I squeeze back along the row for a second time the chubby one pipes up again.

'Which current England batsman was born in County Durham to a mining family?'

'That's Colin Milburn,' I answer before I can stop myself. The two of them turn to look at me for the first time in the day.

'That's right, young man,' says Chubby.

That proves my only successful answer in the subsequent stream of cricket teasers on which I'm allowed to eavesdrop, and by the time I finally wrench myself away from Chubby and Thinny, Gloucestershire are all out, England have scored again at Wembley and I'm feeling decidedly peckish. As I leave the ground I decide to pop into the club shop by the main gates, and five minutes later I'm the proud owner of my own copy of the *Playfair Cricket Annual* and a carton of Paynes Poppets.

By the time I've got back home, the football is into extra time, Geoff Hurst has scored his second and third goals and the house is in bedlam: Geoff and Pete have opened a tin of Watney's Party Four and Dad is doing his Hitler impression, brushing his hair over to one side and goose-stepping up and down with a black plastic comb held underneath his nose. He only does that on special occasions.

I try to join in with their mood of celebration by fetching a

Toffee Cup and a bottle of limeade from the shop, but the fact is my enthusiasm is slightly forced. I'm already longing for the world I've just left, the world of Tupperware sandwich boxes, tartan thermoses, requests not to move behind the bowler's arm and halting announcements over the public address about the supporters' club coach leaving for Canterbury at 8.30 on Wednesday from in front of the Tate Gates.

On the Monday following our nation's historic win I'm back at Hove again for the second day. And again for the third. The game meanders to a draw, but by the end of the match I feel at home there. The woman who sells the scorecards is called Brenda, the paper vendor answers to the name of Wally, and the two blokes in the denim hats, Roger and Len, have even allowed me to set them some of my own questions. One of them offers a ritual token of acceptance into the sacred tribe by sharing with me a piece of home-made bread pudding.

By now I've learnt all the fielding positions and the rules regarding follow-ons. I also know the entire Sussex team by sight and have most of their signatures in my new autograph book. After the game I'm allowed briefly into the pavilion where the blazer worn by K.S. Ranjitsinhji, the Maharajah of Nawanagar and Sussex's most illustrious player, hangs in a battered case on the wall, like some religious relic. I gaze in awe for several minutes. I briefly wonder if I'm expected to light a candle.

As I sit on the bus home, flicking through my *Playfair Cricket Annual*, I realise that for the first time ever, sport has made me very, very happy. And as for this book – it's crammed with enough information and useless statistics to keep those blokes in the denim hats going for ever.

In fact, I must try to get along for the next home match, if only to ask them who was the only Test-match cricketer ever to be hanged for murder.

Cuts

The first time it happens is a week later.

There's been a power cut and Mum has had to improvise for our midday meal. There's no cricket at Hove and the next Test match has yet to begin, so I pass the time by staring deep into the inky blackness of the TV screen, trying to imagine my new heroes still flitting back and forth. It offers nothing more in return than a distended reflection of our tiny parlour.

Instead of Gary Sobers and John Snow, there's me with a head the size of a bowling ball swinging twenty-foot legs back and forth on a giant's chair, and far off in the distance Jimmy Clitheroe sitting at a nursery table scrutinising a copy of *The Rise and Fall of the Third Reich* the size of a postage stamp.

What must it be like to have to bat against someone like Wes Hall, bounding in at you in the gloom of a London evening? How must it feel, standing there with only bat, pads and a mop of tousled hair for protection? I close my eyes and imagine Wes Hall turning at the end of his run-up, before breaking into his long, menacing approach to the wicket.

Thus I fail to spot Mum's long, menacing approach to the parlour with a hastily arranged cold collation. I'm so busy being lost in Hall's gathering pace, limbs flailing, his right hand gripping the gleaming ball, a pure vision of hostility and purpose, that I barely register Mum gathering her breath, depressing the door handle with her left bottom cheek and lumbering in, her hands gripping an oval-shaped walnut-veneer dinner tray with brass handles (a gift to retailers from Keillers Coconut Macaroons), a vision of irritation and stress. I can see Hall's silver crucifix swinging wildly from a chain round his neck, but I am not alert to the blood-stained handkerchief knotted round Mum's left hand after an encounter with our new Kwick-a-kut can opener, provided with the compliments of Bewley's pipe tobacco. Hall is in a murderous mood. He's not the only one.

He reaches his delivery stride, his great fast bowler's feet throwing up clouds of dust and chalk, and releases the ball – just as Mum reaches my chair and releases my lunch onto my lap.

It's a bouncer, one of those balls that lands halfway down the pitch and rears up at your throat. There's only one way to play a bouncer, to swivel on one foot and hit the ball just inches from your nose.

And at that moment of impact my tongue instinctively finds its way to the roof of my mouth and makes a noise I didn't even know I could make, a noise not dissimilar to the ticking of a clock, or a large overfed trout being released gently into a stream. Or somebody hooking a ball for six off the fastest bowler in the world on an August evening.

Mum swivels round instantly. 'What did you say?' she demands.

Lord's has vanished. It's five to one on a Monday afternoon, and I'm back with Dad, the Third Reich and what I instantly recognise as two huge sweaty slabs of Plumrose Chopped Ham and Pork staring up at me, along with most of a can of Heinz Russian Salad, bits of white potato and lurid green peas and flecks of diced carrot bound together with a glutinous syrup of salad cream.

'Are you tutting at it?' Mum is staring across the room at the plate of food on my lap with the look of a basilisk.

'No, I—'

'Did you just tut at that doings?' Mum means food. 'Doings' is an all-purpose expression she uses when she's tired and anxious and can't think of the precise word.

'No, I—'

'You did. I heard you.'

No, Mum, I didn't tut. I don't know what I did. Or at least, I do know what I did, but it would take too long to explain that what she thought was an expression of distaste was actually an instinctive vocal accompaniment to hooking Wes Hall for six into the Mound Stand.

'You cheeky young beggar.' Mum trudges back across the carpet to where I'm sitting. 'You can go bloody doings then.'

Hungry.

With a single sweep of her huge forearm she gathers up my plate, slams it down on the empty tray and lumbers out of the room. 'That boy is getting above himself,' she says as she disappears back down to the kitchen.

Dad smiles sheepishly across at me and turns to a new page. Chapter 26: 'The Great Turning Point'. He picks up his dinner knife, carefully lifts one of his own slices of ham substitute, places it gently on a paper serviette and lays it down in my lap. With that he lifts a forkful of Russian Salad to his lips, tips it gingerly into his mouth and returns to the relative peace and tranquillity of Hitler's advance towards Stalingrad.

That's what facing Wes Hall must be like. A bit like facing Mum when there's been a power cut, she's slit open her hand on the tin opener, she's spent twenty minutes cobbling together a meal and you've just turned your nose up at it.

Primal fear.

Stumped

In any walk of life one needs a mentor, someone who provides you with the break you need in order to follow your dream. At first sight Mr Fitchit seems an unlikely candidate.

He has greasy hair and the sickly pallor of the middle-aged man with money worries. His shoes may be polished but the tell-tale mud marks on the back of his trousers show what he's been using as a cleaning cloth. His spectacles are bound together at the bridge with sticking plaster and he has dirty fingernails. And yet his visit to our shop, barely a fortnight after my first sight of cricket, is to become a seminal moment.

The season is nearly over. The holidaymakers have returned home, the West Indies have won the series 3–1, and our ice-cream fridge now has nothing left in it except Mum's varicose vein cream. With winter only a couple of months away, Mr Fitchit, the south-east sales rep for Waterhouses of Leeds, is trying to persuade Dad to place an order for his firm's famous Invalid Butter Toffees – and he's come laden with free gifts in order to secure the deal.

Free gifts are the traditional form of bribery for sales reps. In addition to the Kwick-a-kut can opener, in recent months we've been given gravy boats, steering-wheel covers, handsome statuettes and door chimes. Even now we're trying to find room for a Colibri Monogas table lighter from Rothmans, which apparently holds enough lighter fuel to last for up to three years. Mum won't have it in the house in case there's a malfunction of the sparking mechanism and it takes out most of central Brighton.

Mr Fitchit is passionate about Invalid Butter Toffees. More than that, he's desperate. He assures Dad that Invalid Butter Toffees are all the go up north. But Dad reads the trade papers and he knows the truth. Nobody wants a sweet with the word 'invalid' on it any more. It's old-fashioned, a throwback to rationing and Spam and make-do-and-mend. People aren't interested in that sort of thing nowadays.

'I wouldn't normally ask you to put in an order as a favour, Mr Simkins, but if you could see your way to taking even a single box, it would help me enormously with my district manager. We're going through restructuring at the moment and … ' His voice tails off miserably before piping up again. 'I'm reliably assured that there's going to be a major television campaign fronted by George Chisholm. And of course we would look to thank you for your commitment to our range of products by offering you and Mrs Simkins a free gift as a token of esteem for your continuing loyalty.'

If he offers a Monogas table lighter he's sunk.

He rummages in his briefcase and pulls out a crumpled leaflet showing a jolly dad on the beach whacking a ball enthusiastically with a plastic cricket bat, while all round him his delighted children leap in the air to catch it.

'It's a family cricket set,' says Mr Fitchit. 'Guaranteed suitable for garden or holidays on the beach. Proper stumps, a soft ball and a half-size cricket bat, all made in hard-wearing durable plastic with a lifetime guarantee. It comes in its own netting bag with easy grip handles and a scorebook.'

Dad looks across at me. He's seen me over the last couple of weeks watching the Test matches, asking how many England need to win and asking for the bus fare to revisit the county ground at Hove. Maybe he feels that anything that gets me interested in arithmetic and exercise is worth encouraging. Or maybe he's just one middle-aged man looking for an excuse to help another middle-aged man whom he can see is terrified for his future.

'Would you like a cricket set?' My grin says it all. 'All right,' he says, turning to Mr Fitchit. 'Just one box, though. Two dozen, no more. We'll see how it goes.'

Mr Fitchit and I smile victoriously. I've got my first cricket set. And Mr Fitchit's still got a job.

The beach cricket set proves a godsend. A marbled pink and white plastic bat made in Taiwan with a welt along the handle that could split elephant hide is not ideal to begin my career with, of course it's not, but it gives me my first taste of the real thing. Most nights between the end of the rush hour and closing time, Dad and I play impromptu Test series between England and the West Indies, him always the bowler from behind the counter and me always the batsman in the well of the shop. An inventory of complex rules and regulations to denote runs and wickets evolves as we go along.

In addition Dad shows me how to fill in the tiny paper scorebook. It's a laborious process, having to put the bat down between each delivery to fill in the grids with the minute information necessary – dot balls, wides, singles, maiden overs, fall of wickets and runs per stand – but with each session I become more adept. What's more, my half-term marks in arithmetic leapfrog me from twenty-sixth in class to seventh.

We have other interruptions to deal with of course, pitch invasions being the commonest. A customer we call Chimneypot Charlie because he spends his days on the opposite pavement talking to an imaginary character up on our roof disrupts play for about ten minutes each evening for half of Old Holborn and a Mint Cracknell, and on one occasion Ernie Black, who owns the dirty book shop in Gardner Street, causes an entire session of play to be cancelled with reminiscences of his recent caravan holiday to Porthcawl. But there are other, glorious evenings as well, evenings when not a single customer comes in for the entire twenty overs in the last hour. Slowly, week by week as the nights draw in, my eye gets keener, my hitting cleaner, my stats neater and the sweet spot sweeter.

The rules of shop cricket are complex. A nudge into the crisp boxes at third man counts as a single; a clip past the soft-drinks dispenser next to them at backward point counts as two, as does a hit into the loose toffees at cover. A lofted drive over their heads into the Raspberry Ruffles at deep extra is a boundary, as are the ciggie shelves at long on and long off, although I avoid them as there's always the chance of Dad intercepting and taking a smart return catch.

I soon learn to work the ball squarer, using lots of bottom hand, round towards the ice-cream fridge at midwicket. In fact, the cross-batted smear soon becomes my most productive shot. Dad does all he can to encourage it as the fridge hasn't been defrosted for nearly three years and the lid won't close properly, so any scuffs or dents only strengthen his pleas to Walls for delivery of a new model. Through square leg into the revolving ladies' stockings display is three, and fine leg offers a single down to hairnets and sleepnets, or a couple if it reaches gift wrap. Anything hit into the window and demolishing Dad's seasonal displays is automatically Out without Dad having to give any reason.

Yet by November, shop cricket is beginning to pall. I'm painfully aware that a half-size beach cricket set is a long way from the real thing, and however much I try to imagine myself batting at Lord's I can't escape the reality that backward point is corn plasters, fly slip is Andrews Liver Salts and my wicket is merely a greetings-card stand, with slip and gulley 'Good Luck In Your New Home' and the wicketkeeper 'Sorry You're Leaving'.

I'm desperate for something more in which to lose myself, something which will allow my imagination to roam free, something which will make me feel more like my heroes on the screen.

And then a new boy joins our class at school and he's given a seat next to me. I'm not yet quite eleven, and I'm about to be exposed to experiences for which I'm tragically unprepared.

* * *

A big burly eleven-year-old kid with a mop of sticky-up hair you could clean the toilet bowl with, Kevin Draper has attended five different schools in as many years because his dad is a captain in the army and keeps getting posted to new bases. The first time he sits next to me he tells a long joke about a woman defecating into a policeman's helmet, and when I fail to correctly guess the location of the punchline he moves onto an even more involved one which relies for its comic value on the unlikely happenstance of the heroine of the story being christened Shaggerarder. But this is just the beginning. He's about to unleash far more profound influences into my life.

It first occurs one lunchtime when I notice he's fumbling under the desk in his trousers. I try to concentrate on the *Playfair Cricket Monthly* I'm reading, but I'm aware that his right hand is joggling something on the desktop. It's becoming impossible to ignore what he's doing.

'What are you reading?' he asks after a pause.

'A profile of Brian Crump.'

'Have a look at what I'm doing.'

'I don't want to.'

'Go on. Have a look.' He takes my hand and places it on something. It feels cool and hard. 'Like it?' he asks.

'It's all right.'

'Push it up and down.' He takes my fingers in his and kneads them gently.

'Like this?'

'Yes, yes, don't stop, that's it.'

'How long do I do it for?'

'Till I say stop. Oh hang on. That's it. Finished. That happened fast. Now it's my turn. Here we are.'

My fingers have been gripping a small six-sided metal roller. Now he pulls a second cylinder from his trousers and pushes it across the desktop. It rattles across the wood and when it comes to rest Kevin scrutinises the writing on the topmost side. 'Caught,' he says triumphantly. 'You're out, caught for forty-five. Not bad for a first go. My turn to bat. See if I can beat your score … '

We exchange the tiny rollers and he begins pushing his back and forth as I've just done, though in his case with more assurance, more consistency; he's obviously been doing this a lot. He rolls a three, then a two. On and on his score mounts up. Finally it comes to rest on 'Owzthat' again, and I roll mine as instructed to see if he's out. But I push it too hard and it falls off the edge of the desk onto the floor.

'Run out,' I whisper hoarsely, peering down. Curiously, there's a strange excited energy to my voice.

'It doesn't count if it's fallen off,' says Kevin. 'Not on the field of play. Throw again.' The second time it settles on 'No Ball'.

'Bad luck,' he says gleefully. 'On we go … ' But the sound of a pair of women's buckle shoes tramping along the lino outside alerts us that our headmistress Mrs Turnbull is returning. He gathers up both rollers, puts them in a little blue tin and slips them inside his desk just as the door opens. I never knew he was capable of such dexterity.

'Now remember,' he whispers, 'you're forty-six on first innings, I'm seventy-five still batting. That's a lead of twenty-nine. We'll carry on tomorrow … '

And that's it. My first encounter with the Owzthat pocket cricket game, available in all good sports and games shops. Kevin assures me it's all the rage in his brother's school, that there are leagues, knockout trophies, even entire Test series. But as I'm walking home that evening I find myself thinking it's not like the real thing at all. In fact, it's about as much fun as doing sums. Ludicrous really, pushing tiny rollers back and forth and pretending that it in any way simulates real cricket. A complete waste of time.

Mind you, a lead of twenty-nine on first innings isn't much. Not at all.

And Kevin wants to continue tomorrow. If I could get an appeal first thing, before he's settled into his stride, got his eye in, it might be possible to rack up, say, seventy or eighty on my second innings, which would leave him a nasty little thirty or forty to get on the final knock – particularly on a wearing surface like the desktop. I've noticed there's a nasty worn patch where a previous incumbent has scratched the words 'Valerie Goodwin smells' with a penknife. That's bound to take spin.

I'm fooling myself. Kevin's rolling technique is too smooth, too practised, and he scores a further sixty-eight. It's a humiliating defeat by an innings and plenty. But Kevin tells me not to worry. He promises another match the next day, my World XI versus his. I've got the evening to come up with my team. There's even talk of different coloured biros and proper averages.

That night the burdens of selection weigh heavily on my mind and it's nearly midnight before I drift off. But at least I've come up with a side that represents strength and depth in all aspects of the game. Apart from myself and Colin Milburn, my middle order boasts Henry VIII, Dan Dare, The Saint, The Man From UNCLE and the Wild Man of Borneo. The bowling attack, too, offers variety. Captain Hurricane from the *Valiant* and Alf Tupper from the *Victor* will be taking the new ball, and on the basis that Afro-Caribbeans are naturally gifted at the game I've also included Al Jolson. Dad is wicketkeeper.

Kevin's team, by contrast, reflects his parents' influence. The entire team is comprised of military leaders of the Second World War, including Rommel, MacArthur, Alanbrooke, General Patton, Field Marshal Montgomery and Dwight Eisenhower.

The result is, of course, a foregone conclusion. Al Jolson trying to out-strategise Marshal Zhukov was a non-starter. I lose by an innings. The ignominy of watching Colin Milburn dismissed in each innings for single figures, both times to Admiral Yamamoto, proves the final straw.

I spend that evening picking over the bones of the contest. Where am I going wrong? I want to have another go but I'm uneasy about being dragged further into Kevin Draper's orbit. Then I have a flash of realisation. I don't need Kevin Draper. I don't need anyone. I can play this game by myself. In fact, it's much the best way. If I represent both teams I need never be disappointed. I can have Milburn score a double century in every innings if I want. And what if he does fail? It'll just be my little secret.

By six o'clock the next evening I'm preparing my own series of international fixtures. I've got my own exercise book, my own coloured biros, my own averages tables and run charts and boxes for putting down individual partnerships, and, most importantly, I've got my own set of rollers. There they are, nestling in their tiny blue tin, shiny and new, and only 2s. 6d. from Kilroy Sports and Games at the bottom of our road.

With an Owzthat tin I'm never going to be lonely again.

Stifled Appeal

The condition of autism is one that medical science is still endeavouring to unlock. One of its most obvious features is that individuals afflicted by the condition seem to obtain comfort and structure from carrying out the same meaningless and repetitious activity for hours on end.

Callard to face. Bowser the non-striker. It's a two. That takes the total to 134 and Callard to 34.

Symptoms of autism include a lack of awareness for the feelings of others, little social communication and a preference for the autistic's own closed world in which some order and control can be maintained.

'*What do you make of his innings today, Brian?*'

Many children with autism are solitary, self-isolating and self-stimulating. No danger of that with me. I've got Brian Johnston and Peter West with me in my bedroom.

'*Well, he's playing marvellously, Peter, though umpires Pickup and Penguin seem to be checking for bad light. It's getting pretty dark out here, and December isn't the ideal time of year to be playing a match in this country.*'

Callard again. It's an appeal.

'*High drama here, Peter. Everyone's gaze is at the umpire, he's having a long look, it might take a moment as the other roller seems to have gone under the bed ... *'

It's Christmas Eve, about eight in the evening, three months sixteen days since my first encounter with Kevin Draper.

Christmas Eve, normally the most exciting night of the year, a time for families, for friendships and for an economy-size tub of Cheese Footballs. And downstairs in the lounge the party is in full swing. Uncle Percy has just won Pin The Tail On The Donkey, brother Pete has followed it up with a medley of Cole Porter songs on our upright piano, and as the Glamorgan opening bowler runs in again to bowl to Callard the sound of Mum and Dad doing their party piece, an affectionate if slightly slurred rendition of 'The Sunshine of Your Smile', drifts up the stairs and under my bedroom door.

I'd never normally miss this. I love seeing my parents at play, Mum with her annual cigarette in one hand and a glass of Warninks Advocaat in the other, warbling away in a shrill but substantial treble, Dad kneeling beside her with a red hankie draped round his head in tribute to John Hanson, meandering his way through an uncertain but optimistic harmony. It's the only time in the year when both of them can forget about the shop for a few hours and let their hair down.

I'd give anything to be down there with them now, surrounded by Geoff and Pete and all our uncles and aunts among the music and chit-chat and racy jokes, watching the twinkling tree lights reflecting in the sherry decanters, cocooned in the aroma of panatellas and tangerine peel and the sound of the munching of Twiglets.

So why am I up here in the eaves of the house, alone in my bedroom with only Brian Johnston, Peter West and a one-bar electric fire for company?

'*I think most pundits agree that the blame lies firmly at the door of Kevin Draper, Peter.*'

Over the past twelve weeks my life has been changed by Owzthat. The fact that it's completely taken over my life can be traced back to that afternoon with Kevin. It was he who drove me here today, up here with my own games, my own teams, my own leagues and records and highest stands, my own fixtures between Glamorgan and Derbyshire at Sofia Gardens.

'*It was certainly a seminal moment, as important in the development of the game as when overarm bowling was introduced ...*'

It hasn't turned out how I intended. My early experiments involved a couple of trial matches between England and the West Indies, using all the players I've seen on the telly and copied in the shop: Milburn, of course, and Cowdrey and Barrington to follow, down through Titmus to Higgs and Brown against the West Indies team starring Sobers, Kanhai, Gibbs, Hall. With only myself to answer to, I was looking forward to Milburn scoring a stack of runs.

Except he didn't.

He made nought, three, nought and nought. Maybe it was my inexperience with the rollers, or the threadbare state of my bedside rug, but the fact remains he had a disaster. As did most of the England batsmen. With each failure the chasm widened between the world I was trying to engineer and real life. In real life Milburn scores forties and fifties. In the Owzthat world he was dangerously near to being asked if he'd ever thought of retraining as a plumber. On his dismaying last failure I even thought of joggling the carpet to shake the roller onto the next edge to simulate a dropped catch. But no. Once I start cheating ...

Even worse than all my heroes failing with the bat, all the rabbits, the useless ones, the ones who are specialist bowlers and who aren't supposed to be able to bat at all, keep scoring double hundreds. Ken Higgs, for instance, whom I had coming in at number ten in the batting order as he does in actual life. As well as having the largest backside in cricket, Higgs has a batting average of five. In my bedroom between 16 October and 21 November he makes 134, 289 and 212. Suddenly Shaggerarder bowling to Yamamoto seemed realistic by comparison.

Callard again. It's another two.

That's why I had the brainwave of inventing my own players. If I was the only one who knew who any of them were, we'd all be free to create our own destiny. There would be no real-life parallel world with which to compare them. I may not be able to share in Milburn's triumphs, but I would no longer suffer at his disappointments.

Four more. Callard approaches his half-century.

I've never known the sensation of being the one in control, the boss, the one who decides who plays and who doesn't. But now, in my Owzthat world, I'm not the duffer. I'm the one giving the orders. I'm Michael Lowe. These players of my imagination can exist only if I allow them to; they owe their existence to me and me alone, and I sense they're profoundly grateful to me for giving them life.

This time it's a six.

Thus my entombment most evenings and weekends up here in the attic, playing the inaugural Test series between England and the West Indies for the Simkins Trophy: then a knockout cup, now, on Christmas Eve, the last match of my inaugural County Championship. One hundred and eighteen two-innings matches, with a place for the lucky few on board a jet airliner leaving on Boxing Day as part of the forthcoming MCC tour of Australia.

Another six. '*Splendid batting this, Peter, clean hitting, beautiful to watch but hard on the poor Glamorgan bowlers ...* '

At first the names of the players were taken from the world round me: Callard, Bowser, Hooper, Struve, and the trio of fast bowlers Melchior, Barr and Kydd. But a glance through the Brighton telephone directory has given me hundreds of new names with which to swell the ballooning network of teams, competitions and countries being sucked in with each new day. Alford, Barnes, Cooper, Denton, Egham, Franklin, Garland, Hunter ... more than enough for seventeen counties, eight Test-playing nations, even reserves coaches and second-XI squads.

A single. Then another. Then a two.

I suppose it was inevitable that I'd begin making the sound of ball striking bat with my tongue to accompany each roll, but the entire BBC commentary team moving into my bedroom seems to have happened when my back was turned. One day it was just the clocking noise, then suddenly I was replicating Brian Johnston's plummy vowels and Peter West's fumbling enthusiasm. And here they all are, sitting on the end of my bed, keeping up a running commentary on each ball, each run, each appeal.

'*Have you anything to say to viewers just joining us, Peter, about the session of play just gone?*'

'*My goodness.*'

My own players have slowly, with infinite stealth, started to take hold of me, to the point whereby I no longer know whether I invented them or they invented me. At first they were just names in an exercise book, but they've now become fully rounded, flesh-and-blood creatures who occupy my thoughts and on whose lives, both professional and domestic, I provide a mumbled commentary under my breath day and night.

Take Callard for instance.

What does the name suggest to you? Apart from Creamline Toffees, that is. Callard. Any ideas? I imagine a sandy-haired sort of bloke, tall and strong, probably a fast bowler, a bit like Kenneth More in *Genevieve*. At first that's all he is, just a rough mental image, but by degrees he's acquired a county, Derbyshire, then a small house on the outskirts of Bakewell, then a wife and a couple of children, a Morris Oxford on loan from his county's local vehicle sponsors, and now, with the New Year fast approaching, he loves cooking and gardening. By this time next year he could be divorced with a new girlfriend in Rio de Janeiro. I can no longer dictate to him.

Or the Glamorgan captain, Trebor. Any thoughts? I reckon a tall, flinty-looking bloke with receding hair. He's scored three centuries so far with a top score of 187 not out against Leicestershire at Ashby-de-la-Zouch. Unpopular with teammates but remarkably single-minded and follows a strict fitness regime. Lives in the Mumbles. Speaks fluent Welsh. Vegetarian.

If nothing else it's a whole lot better than Shaggerarder bowling to Rommel.

That's why I'm up here on Christmas Eve. Because I begin a tour of Australia as soon as Christmas is over and we have to finish this match tonight. Their flights have been booked, tickets have been sold at all the grounds and they fly out on Boxing Day. So I have to finish this series before midnight, at all costs. There won't be a chance tomorrow what with presents and meals, yet by 11am on 26 December MCC are due to play the opening match against an Australian Presidents XI at Canberra. This championship has to be decided tonight. At all costs. I can't leave them. They won't go back in their tin.

'*No, it's an unfortunate scenario, Peter, and one that the games administrators may have to take a long hard look at in future scheduling.*'

I retrieve the roller from below the bedhead, clean the carpet fluff and old toenails off it and roll it again. LBW. Thank God. With any luck this match will be over and I can get downstairs in time for supper and the Christmas carols sing-a-long with Auntie Lena on her ukulele. I really wouldn't want to miss that. Who's in next?

There's a knock on the door.

It's Mum. What on earth is she doing up here? She should be downstairs, enjoying herself with her family.

Mind you, so should I.

'Are you all right, Mikey?'

'Yes, Mum.'

'What are you doing in there?'

'Nothing.'

I know what's going on in Mum's mind. She fears the worst. All the symptoms are there, the sudden unexplained withdrawal to my bedroom at every opportunity, the weight loss, the sound of me talking to myself at all hours of the day and night. Mum thinks something terrible has happened, that I've suffered some trauma or fallen into the clutches of malevolent forces. And now this, the final straw, my barricading myself in the attic on the most wonderful night of the year.

'We all want you to come down, Michael. Please come down. We're all going to have a game. We're about to play Twister.'

I know for a fact Mum hasn't been on all fours since the Blitz.

'I'm fine. I won't be long.'

'But it's Christmas Eve. You never miss Christmas Eve.'

'I won't be long, Mum, just leave me alone.'

'What are you doing?'

'I told you, nothing. Leave me alone.'

There's a pause. I can almost taste her unhappiness. But it's no good. I can't do it. I just can't. The fact is, I can't leave my boys up here by themselves. My mates, Callard, Bowser and the rest, they've earned their Christmas too. If I go down now I'll forget about them, and then they won't exist. And what sort of a buddy would do that to his mates? What sort of Christmas is that for them?

'I'm fine. Just leave me alone. I'll be down in a minute.'

A few seconds later I hear Mum lumbering back down the stairs. She's given it her best shot by coming up here and pleading and I still won't come down. She'll be worried sick. It'll ruin her own evening. In fact, her entire Christmas.

And for a moment I feel ashamed.

'*What do you make of it, Brian?*'

'*You have to feel some sympathy at the present situation. But it's a tough game, Peter.*'

Shot

The great Albert Trott of Middlesex once hit a cricket ball over the roof of the pavilion at Lord's. The sensation of hitting a perfectly timed cricket stroke with a piece of sprung willow ruined him for ever, as he spent the rest of his life trying, and failing, to repeat the shot and relive the exquisite sensation. His game went to pieces, and he finally blew his brains out with a service revolver in lodging houses in north London.

It's 3 February 1967, the eve of my eleventh birthday. Tomorrow morning I'm receiving my first genuine cricket bat. By 'genuine' I mean it will be made from willow, will have a V-shaped splice at the top of the blade, will be properly sprung so that it doesn't feel like you're playing with a coffin lid when you hit the ball, and will have a proper rubber handle with dimples to provide consistent grip during the long hours at the crease.

And there's something else. Above all, it'll have a label full of instructions for proper care stuck on the back. No more 'Do not put bat in mouth' warnings, but mysterious rituals involving linseed, lint cloth, brown-paper covers and fine high-grade glass paper, and procedures of which all cricketers speak but which are rarely witnessed in public. Sanding. Oiling. Knocking in.

Dad hasn't mentioned it, of course. He's tried to put me off the scent by talking about Action Men and Scalextric. But I know. I *know*. No more kiddie bats from Taiwan, items purchased from toy shops and packaged in cheap plastic mesh, shaped from compressed sawdust with childish logos emblazoned on the face, props for beach cricketers. This will be the real thing. I even know which one I'm going to get. They're all hanging up in the window of our local sporting goods emporium, Kilroy Sports and Games in Grand Parade.

Mr Kilroy is a typical Irishman, garrulous, charming, ever ready with a saucy compliment for Mum or a friendly tweak of my ear. He's also rumoured to be in terrible financial difficulties after weeks of backing donkeys at the bookies. That old nag doddering past the post three hours after the others is the direct reason for my imminent delivery of a top-of-the-line willow wand from his shop window display. I used to hate horseracing almost as much as speedway, but I've got a lot to thank it for now.

One of the problems you face if you run a newsagent's is the number of customers who are behind with their bills. Dad tries to play the tough guy, but the fact is he's just too soft. A few weasel words from his creditors about cash-flow problems or personal difficulties and he'll soon cave in, allowing them to do what they always do and settle the bills by offering him some item from their own stock in lieu of payment.

Eva's Continental Delicatessen in Sydney Street recently settled up for six months' worth of unpaid-for motorcycle magazines by persuading him to accept a crate of baby pears in Calvados from Uruguay. The Home Brewing Centre in Gloucester Road gave him three yards of rubber tubing and some demijohns, while the Kensington Wool Shop offered 250 wire coat hangers in recompense for six weeks' worth of unpaid *Daily Express*es. We've had sets of chimney-sweeping brushes, a stuffed moose head, and a full-size xylophone that collapsed at 3am, persuading Mum that a jazz combo was trying to break into the shop.

And now Liam Kilroy of Kilroy Sports and Games is apparently on the verge of bankruptcy and eight months behind with payments for the *Racing Post*, *Sporting Life* and the *Angling Times*. And Dad wants me to have a cricket bat.

Five different bats. Five different dreams. I've spent weeks gazing in at them as they hang there in his window: pristine rectangles of biscuit-coloured willow, each with the signature of some cricketing hero burnt across the top of the blade in skimming black lines. The Ken Barrington, for instance: his name massive, impregnable, safe as the Bank of England; or the Gray Nicholls Ted Dexter Autograph, with the batsman's name slashed carelessly across the splice as if he'd been in a hurry to catch a private jet to some fashionable party in Cannes. Or what about the one next to it, the Tom Graveney County Pro? Or the Lillywhite's Colin Cowdrey Truespot? Or even the Gary Sobers Crusader short handle at the end? With that I'll be driving on the up past point or lofting sixes against the spin, the sort of strokes to send crusty old brigadiers spluttering into their coaching manuals.

It proves a difficult night. My dreams are crammed with jumbled cricket visions juxtaposed absurdly with unlikely characters from my domestic environment and the world of popular entertainment. In one troubled scenario, Mrs Brooks, one of our regular customers, a woman in her sixties with no teeth and a penchant for stuffing handfuls of Victory V lozenges into her holdall when our backs are turned, is helping me to erect a cricket net in our upstairs toilet with my invented Pakistani Owzthat star Abdul Hashish-Orandi.

In real life I've never seen Mrs Brooks display the slightest sign of interest in anything, apart from once making the startling observation that most of the residents of central Brighton are 'only on earth to make up the numbers'. But at 3am she's issuing imperious orders to one of the most dashing batsmen ever seen on the subcontinent as to how twenty-two yards of netting and scaffolding might be successfully erected in a first-floor lavatory by wedging the poles down inside the toilet bowl.

By the time I've clambered free they've been joined by Michael Miles, genial host and Quiz Inquisitor of ITV's popular game show *Take Your Pick*, and I now find myself a contestant in a nightmare version of the celebrated Yes–No Interlude. Except that he and Mum seem to be coalescing into the same person. The prize for successfully answering his barrage of quick-fire questions without using those two dreaded words is a cricket bat from Kilroy Sports and Games.

'So you like cricket, do you?'

'I do like cricket, Michael—'

'You didn't nod your head then, did you?'

'I did not nod my head, Michael.'

'Are you looking forward to your doings in the morning?'

'I am looking forward to my doings, Michael.'

'So which bat would you prefer: the Tom Graveney, the Gary Sobers? I suppose Dexter is your favourite, isn't it?'

'I don't have a preference, Michael.'

'No preference?'

'That's right, Michael.'

'So who's your favourite cricketer, do you wear a box, have you ever been to Lord's?'

'My favourite cricketer is Colin Milburn, I do not wear a box, no, I've not been to Lord's—'

BONG!!!

I wake with a start. My ordeal is over. I swing out of bed, ferret for my slippers and pull on my dressing gown. Outside it's still dark, the only illumination the pallid yellow sodium glow of a street light. And it's raining. As I reach the ground floor a voice on BBC Radio Brighton is already issuing a severe weather warning for all the county's roads. Dad is lugging the morning papers in from the porch, while from the basement kitchen the aroma of Mum's attempts at a special birthday breakfast pervades the house, burning bacon and stewing plum tomatoes.

Dad too has obviously had a bad night. He's dressed in an acrylic zip-up cardigan over a flannelette pyjama top and an old pair of tuxedo trousers. A strand of crinkled Sellotape clinging to his knuckles suggests an early and presumably bad-tempered encounter with wrapping paper. Somebody has urinated on the morning papers while they've been sitting in the porch so he's now got to dry out a hundredweight of assorted newsprint in front of our Magicoal flame-effect fire and then persuade his customers to part with good money for them.

The presents have been heaped hastily in the corner of the rear parlour, a pile of oddly shaped packages and parcels, the biggest and most impressive an object resembling a full-size short-handle cricket bat. Dad would normally like to be there while I unwrap my presents but already the rush hour is building up, so I'm left by myself. I'm happy with that. At least I won't have go through the charade of pretending to be interested in reading the messages in all the cards.

And my campaign of heavy hints has hit the bulls-eye. Our assistant Vi Hacker has bought me a proper junior pro cricket box, made of tough pre-moulded plastic, shaped like a tiny bicycle saddle and in the same garish pink as the candy shrimps we sell in the shop. Fred and Ida Wackett have bought me a proper cricket ball, Uncle Jim and Auntie Joyce have sent me a set of stumps, and Uncle Percy has given me a pair of batting gloves with green rubber spikes attached to the fingers.

Brother Geoff has bought me a magnificent maroon cricket cap with a prodigious peak and an adjustable headband, while Pete, who's obviously earning good money, has left me a set of magnificent buckskin pads with proper leather straps and buckles. Even Auntie Gladys has tried her best. Hers may only be a copy of Palgrave's *Treasury of Inspirational Verse For Children*, but even she has had the decency to insert a little note inside pointing the way to page 24, a poem with a cricketing theme called 'Vitae Lampada' by Sir Henry Newbolt …

> *There's a breathless hush in the Close tonight –*
> *Ten to make and the match to win …*

Auntie Lena has bought me a jigsaw.

I can't wait any longer. Turning to the star prize I tear greedily at the paper. I wonder how they see me? Will it be with the dashing hauteur of Dexter, the graceful elegance of Graveney, or the dazzling informality of Sobers? The brown dimpled handle is even now poking through. Any moment now I'll be both taking the money and opening the box …

* * *

Eric Russell was born in Dumbarton, Scotland, on 3 July 1936. Joining Middlesex at the end of the Second World War, he became a solid if unremarkable opening blocker for his adopted county. With the features and manner of a funeral director dressing a corpse, the mere sight of his lugubrious hangdog features and balding forehead trudging down the pavilion steps is enough to drive most spectators to the sanctuary of their *Daily Telegraph* crossword. If Gary Sobers is a swashbuckling pirate and Ted Dexter a test pilot, Eric Russell is the cricketing equivalent of a quantity surveyor.

But of course it all makes sense. The chimney-sweeping brushes, the baby pears in Calvados, the disintegrating xylophones … If Liam Kilroy is to get out of his financial difficulties, he's not going to start parting with things he can still get good money for on the open market. He's going to be rootling round in the deepest recesses of his stockroom for items he can no longer give away, like that stash of bats over there underneath the stairs for instance, those ones with the signature of a batsman of whom big things were once expected but who is now no more than a footnote in my *Playfair Cricket Annual.*

Dad pops his head round the doorframe and asks if I'm pleased with my presents. I manage to stutter a few words of gratitude before my face crumples into an expression of the deepest misery and dismay. He looks utterly shocked. But the shop doorbell is ringing again, announcing the arrival of another customer, leaving me alone with Eric Russell and a pile of piss-covered *Daily Sketch*es steaming in the centre of the carpet.

I don't know who to be most sorry for. The management of this failing sports goods business, the cricketer himself, or my gullible father, now standing in dismay and bewilderment at the memory of my crumpled face and quivering lip.

Square Leg

The village of Lancing is an anonymous straggle of 1930s bungalows along the coast between Brighton and Worthing. It boasts a seafront of dilapidated and vandalised beach huts interspersed with clumps of tussocky grass and the odd grubby café, beyond which an uninviting shingle beach looks out onto a sea the colour of old raincoats. For much of its length it is covered in something called bladderwrack, a form of particularly greasy seaweed resembling bubble wrap that festoons the pebbles and provides an aromatic home for millions of tiny sand flies, which swarm up in dense clouds the moment you sit down on it.

It's also the unprepossessing setting for my first proper outing with the Eric Russell Special.

It's the third week of March. Winter has finally given way grudgingly to spring, and Dad has assured me that once we've had our picnic on the beach he'll take me across the main road to a large area of parkland known as Brooklands and spend an hour or so bowling to me so I can feel the thrill of leather on willow for the first time.

It's been a long wait for this, my first ever outdoor session with a proper bat and a hard ball. Forty-three days in fact, from 4 February until this chilly Sunday, and every day of it padded up in full cricket gear from morning till night. Driving rain and fog has foiled each attempt. The only thing I've put to any use is Auntie Glad's Palgrave's *Treasury of Inspirational Verse For Children*, which I've read three times from cover to cover.

There's a breathless hush in the Close tonight –
Ten to make and the match to win ...

Even now a full day's play is far from guaranteed: a bracing wind
whipping along the coast has kept all but a few other hardy souls
off the beach, and apart from a couple of other wind-lashed families picnicking nearby and a solitary fisherman digging for
lugworms down by the shoreline we've got the place to ourselves.

As Mum hands out our dessert, a bowl of baby pears in
Calvados with Walls ice cream, a watery sun breaks briefly
through the scudding grey clouds and suddenly it all feels a bit
more promising. From the main road the tinny jingle of the first
ice-cream van of the season, trundling past on the main road
towards Sompting, carries in the wind. A bee drones past,
searching for spring flowers.

At 3.15pm Dad announces he wants to go for a swim. He
sits down on the rug, covering his midriff with a beach towel,
and lays a pair of dark green woollen bathing trunks on the
pebbles beside him. A fresh cloud of midges billows up into the
air. Mum sits happily behind him reading a copy of *Reveille* and
finishing a Cadbury's Creme Egg. Changing into trunks in a
sitting position on a carpet of wet seaweed is not easy, but after
several minutes of discreet wriggling he finally manoeuvres his
trousers down below the bottom of his beach towel, followed
shortly by a large pair of baggy Y-fronts. He leans gingerly across
the pebbles to retrieve the trunks and delicately manoeuvres
them up over his ankles and under the towel.

There are any number of reasons why my first ever innings,
against Dad at Brooklands on Sunday 19 March 1967 might be
aborted. We might have rain, or Brooklands might be closed for
essential maintenance, or our car might get a flat tyre, or Dad
lose his ignition keys, or Mum get a chicken bone stuck in her
throat. I've waited so long, so long, that I'm prepared for
anything. Almost anything.

The bee has landed on Dad's swimming trunks. In those

precious few seconds between him laying them down on the seaweed and pulling them on over his legs, the bee, presumably attracted by the dark foliage-like green colour of the material and the eye-catching Aertex gusset, has crawled into the inner lining and settled there for a nap. When suddenly and violently disturbed it makes a furious and panic-stricken attempt to extricate itself using the only weapon that bees have at their disposal.

Dad is stung on his right testicle.

The first any of us are aware of the incident is a bellow of pain, followed by a shout of 'Jesus Christ!' Dad staggers to his feet completely naked, his thighs imprinted with the pattern of hundreds of pebbles and his flaccid penis waving like a Walls sausage in the direction of a family of nearby picnickers.

Mum tries to rise from her picnic chair, but an hour's inactivity has sent the legs beneath her sinking slowly into the pebbles, and by now she's only a matter of inches from the ground. With Dad sliding round like an elephant seal harpooned on the floes of Newfoundland, the adjacent picnickers and the lugworm digger are already frantically gathering up their possessions and moving away. I too try to struggle upright, but clambering to your feet from a sitting position on seaweed in full cricket gear is no easy matter either. In any case, what can I do? Hold his hand? Massage the affected part? We'd be arrested within minutes.

'Hand him his bloody doings,' roars Mum from her chair.

I slither across and throw Dad the means to re-establish his modesty. He continues hobbling round for several more minutes in frenzied agony while Mum asks him about forty times in succession what the hell's happened. Eventually Dad is able to splutter that he's been stung by something, and when Mum asks where, he shouts back where-do-you-bloody-think-you-silly-bitch and the whole afternoon threatens to turn nasty.

By the time I've returned with a cup of sugared tea from Brooklands café across the road, Dad is standing still naked but with his towel held out from round his waist and Mum peering in through the gap and trying to conduct some sort of forensic investigation of the crime scene. The beach is now deserted. An investigation of the lining of his trunks confirms the culprit, now twitching his final death throes in the Aertex crotch.

Two hours later the swelling has gone down. Dad can now stand and even walk as long as keeps his thighs well apart. We've finally made it across to Brooklands park but Dad's warned me he won't be able to run and I should try to hit the ball straight back at him unless I want to spend the remainder of the afternoon fetching it myself. He says it'll encourage me to play down the line. We drag a handy litter bin into position behind the stumps to act as wicketkeeper, lay it on its side, and prepare to begin.

But there's no need to run. I can't hit the ball in the first place. Each delivery is the same dispiriting procession of swinging and missing. Playing for pretend in a tiny parlour is one thing, but now that I'm playing for real the bat feels like a ton weight in my hands. Dad bowls a series of slow donkey drops and looping lobs, each one more luscious than the last, but after twenty minutes I've hardly made contact.

He tries everything. On the rare occasions when he bowls it faster, I'm too late. When he slows it down, I've played four shots before it even arrives, only to watch it limply bounce between my swishes and hit middle stump halfway up. When the ball misses the stumps the death rattle of it striking the mesh of the litter bin is like some funeral knell, each noise a testimony to my continuing ineptitude.

'Hang on a minute. Let's try it a bit closer.' Dad gingerly picks up his cardigan, which acts as bowling mark, and plops it onto the grass ten yards nearer my end. As he rolls up his shirt-sleeve and spins the ball from hand to hand, Mum looks up from her copy of *Reveille*. 'Go on,' she shouts cheerily. 'You can do it. Just slosh it.'

I crouch over the bat again. Apart from barely having enough strength left now to lift it, I'm aware I'm making a complete prat of myself in front of the other families dotted round us on the grass. By now I'm puce with shame and misspent effort. If it goes on like this any longer, I'm going to ask if we can abandon the whole idea and play war instead.

Dad shuffles in a couple of gentle paces and his arm performs a laborious arc in the sky. The ball floats down towards me. I step back and close my eyes. Just slosh it, she said …

A split second later my hands experience a new, delicious and slightly scary sensation. Instead of a hollow thud, the ball cannons off the blade as if set off by a small explosion. Travelling like a ground-to-air missile straight back down the wicket about eighteen inches off the ground, it ricochets off Dad's right kneecap before he can react.

Dad goes down like a felled ox.

Within seconds his prone figure is surrounded by a knot of onlookers trying to offer assistance. For the second time in two hours my father finds himself having to remove his trousers in front of strangers, this time revealing a swelling the size of a Tunnocks Snowball erupting just below his kneecap. He can't drive home. He doesn't think he'll be able to press the pedals.

Luckily the cafeteria has a phone. Half an hour later Uncle Percy arrives in his Humber Hawk to drive us all back to the sweetshop, with his wife Elsie following behind in our own car.

'I think it's time you got some proper coaching,' says Dad as he eases himself into the passenger seat. But I'm hardly listening. I haven't heard a word of anything that's happened since the accident. At any age the sight of one of your parents prostrate and helpless on the ground is a worrying one, but my mind is elsewhere, in some beautiful private place I've not known until now. I've finally hit a cricket ball as it was meant to be hit, and suddenly the prospect of doing anything else with my spare time, even if it saves Dad from having to have his leg amputated, seems impossible.

The great Albert Trott of Middlesex once hit a cricket ball over the roof of the pavilion at Lord's. Today, at Brooklands recreation ground and ornamental boating lake, I understood how he must have felt.

Long Leg

If it's true that you never forget your first pair of long trousers, it's equally true that you never forget your first pair of cricket flannels. And if I'm going to have some proper coaching during the Easter holidays I'm going to need some – and quickly. Mum hopes to get ones that will last me several seasons. Mum wants ones with an elasticated waistband.

I don't want an elasticated waistband. Elasticated waistbands are for old ladies with paunches and rover trolleys, those women who crowd our shopfront on Saturday mornings with requests for pear drops and copies of *The People's Friend*. I want a pair of proper whites, thick flannel ones the colour of Cornish ice cream, yellow and buttery. I want tiny adjustable fastenings round each side that you can let out or in according to how many Peppermint Creams you've eaten. I want a proper fly button which you have to wrestle open for minutes on end to get your willy through, I want creases down the legs you could use to open letters with, I want huge turn-ups. Above all, I want astronomical dry-cleaning bills every time I get grass stains on them. That's what constitutes a pair of cricket trousers. Elasticated ones are for old dodderers playing bowls.

Dad readily agrees to my request for proper flannels and I'm immediately suspicious. Because I know Dad. I know the way he thinks, and I know the way his mind works. He obviously has a scheme for trying to sort it out on the cheap. But where? And then I realise. There's one place and one place only that sells proper cricket flannels at a price Dad would regard as competitive.

I begin to plead with him. I'll have man-made fibres with an elasticated waist after all. I don't mind. Really. In fact, I'd prefer it. But he's adamant. Handing me some instructions he's written on a piece of scrap paper with his moustache pencil, he tells me to pop down to see Mr Dranse. 'He'll sort you out,' he assures me.

No.

'I've already spoken to him about it.'

No, no.

'I told him you'd pop in this morning. Off you go.'

Dranse's second-hand clothes emporium is a couple of hundred yards further down the road from our shop. From the street you'd think it simply specialised in surplus army equipment as the entire ground floor is given over to discarded supplies from around the world: tunics and battledress, tickly shirts and camouflage gear, berets and balaclavas, plus items it's difficult to imagine being in demand from anyone: Turkish fezzes, pairs of cracked white gaiters and portable cooking stoves last used by the Algerian military reserve in 1955.

Mr Dranse himself adds to the general air of Victorian decay. A figure with greasy white locks kept in place by years of Brylcreem and huge matted hairs protruding from his nostrils, he has a deathly pallor from decades spent in the gloomy interior wandering among these dusty shelves. But it's the prospect of visiting the shop itself that is making me so uneasy. Our paperboy Denis is one of the few lads of my age who has been in there and survived, but he has terrified me with talk of what he's seen and heard.

He says he's heard things scrabbling above him on the first floor. He's told me that he knows for a fact that Mr Dranse buys clothes from the local mortuary and sells them without dry-cleaning them first. He says his brother has assured him on the Bible that Mr Dranse has recently been called across to Eastbourne by John Bodkin Adams, the infamous doctor once accused of poisoning a number of his patients, in order to purchase an entire wardrobe of the doctor's unwanted clothes. Dr Adams was acquitted of the crimes but our paperboy's brother says everyone knows he did it, possibly in the very suits now languishing somewhere in Dranse's shop.

What is beyond dispute is that when not tending the shop, Mr Dranse trawls the nursing homes and hospices in a sixty-mile arc from Hastings to Bognor Regis. He's proud of the service he offers: he claims that it relieves the nursing staff from the onerous task of disposing of piles of unwanted clothes, as well as providing them with a few extra shillings to be used to buy custard creams for those still remaining.

I turn up soon after 10am with Dad's message grasped in my fist. The shop is empty. I hand Mr Dranse my letter of introduction and he studies it for several moments before breaking into a wide grin, revealing a set of enormously long, yellowing teeth. 'Cricket whites eh?' he says. 'Let's see what we can find, shall we?' He beckons me in past a row of shelves groaning under the weight of Greek ceremonial slippers towards the dark interior of the shop.

The first room we pass through is full from floor to ceiling with piles of pinstripe trousers. They lie in great mouldering heaps on every available surface, thousands and thousands of them, all of which once graced the carriages of early morning commuter trains from the south coast to the city of London, but whose owners have since been consigned to nursing homes or the flames of the local crematorium.

'This way if you please, young man.' He beckons me with a scaly finger. The air is thick with flakes of dead skin and the sharp sweet smell of dried sweat. I want to put my hand over my nose. We push onwards through a small channel in the middle and towards a back room.

Dranse pushes heavily at a half-open door, behind which is a huge pile of battered homburgs and dented bowlers that have toppled over. He kicks them out of the way and nods me through. The space beyond the bowlers is dedicated to waistcoats and dinner jackets, mostly double-breasted with huge lapels and the telltale sheen of threadbare material. Some have military flashes or Masonic insignia still pinned to their breast pockets. In the far corner a long pole is wedged between the walls of an alcove, from which hang hundreds of forlorn dress shirts, some with collars half attached, one or two even with dried blood spatters on them from ancient shaving accidents.

'This way if you will,' says Dranse, opening a door leading up a rickety flight of steps to the next floor. It's lit by a bare twenty-watt bulb swinging from the ceiling. But there's no going back. I follow him up the steps, trying not to put my hands on the treads to steady myself.

'Sportswear,' says Dranse, pushing at another warped doorway.

We enter the room. Again, it's filled from floor to ceiling: seven-foot-high stacks of white pleated tennis skirts, mounds of grubby ballet pumps and sports blazers, and, bursting out of a series of wicker baskets in the centre of the floor space, hundreds of old vests. But Dranse is already heaving them out of the way, pressing forward like an explorer in some vast textile jungle. He has his eye fixed on a huge cardboard box with thick rope handles lying beside the far skylight.

'Here we are,' he says. He opens the box to reveal thirty or forty pairs of cricket flannels, ranging from brilliant white to darkest oatmeal, and begins holding each pair up for inspection. The smell from the trousers mingles with the disrupted vests and rotting sports blazers.

'What waist do you require?' When I answer that I have no idea, Dranse looks pleased. He fumbles in his trousers and pulls out a tightly rolled length of linen tape measure.

'Let's take a few measurements, shall we?' he says.

Before I can stop him he's knelt down in front of me and lassoed my waist with the tape measure round the snake belt of my shorts. He pulls me nearer to his head and squints at the number.

'Thirty-six inches.' He grins. 'A boy who likes his dinner, eh?' He takes the end of the measure and pushes it into the soft flesh where the top of my leg meets my underpants. 'Hold this, young man,' he says, taking my clenched fingers and kneading them into my groin before pulling the other end of the tape down until it is level with my ankle socks. The top of his head reveals a few flecks of ginger still evident among the greasy white strands of hair, and a pungent aroma of snuff and Brycreem wafts into my nostrils.

Mr Dranse is confident he's got exactly what I need. A recent consignment has come in and he's sure he spotted some flannels just my size. He stands stiffly back up and rummages deeper into the box. Eventually he pulls out a pair and holds them against me. There's no hiding place here, no cubicle to retire to, away from prying eyes scrutinising each chubby thigh, every stain. Nothing. Just me, bare floorboards, skid marks, no changing facilities, and Mr Dranse.

I gingerly unhitch my shorts and pull them down. Mr Dranse studies me for a moment before handing me the trousers. I've seen a photograph of John Bodkin Adams in the local paper and he must be just about my size and shape, a short, squat toad of a man with a huge waistline and short legs.

'What do you think?' asks Dranse thoughtfully when I've pulled them on. He leans across to a shabby wardrobe in the corner and wrenches the door open, spilling dozens of frayed boaters onto the floor. On the inside of the door a fractured piece of mirror is attached. Dranse repositions it until I can see myself.

The trousers come up nearly to my breastbone. If I pull them down to the waist the trouser bottoms cascade over my sandals, obliterating all but the patterned toe ends. Charlie Cairoli at the Blackpool Tower Circus stares back. For some seconds the only sound is Mr Dranse's laboured breathing and an anonymous rustling from somewhere underneath a nearby pile of gym shoes.

'Do you want me to wrap them?' says Dranse.

'No thanks,' I reply before he's even completed his sentence. The prospect of shuffling back up the road in a large cream marquee is still marginally more palatable than removing them again in front of his prurient gaze, and by thrusting my hands deep into the pockets I can hold them up until I reach home. I'm about to follow him back into the Aertex forest when my right hand touches something deep in the front trouser pocket. Something round and smooth. Like a pill.

My imagination might come in handy in an Owzthat county championship, but now it can only lead to the fatal prescription. Bodkin Adams, having been called from the crease where he was batting for Polegate against Pevensey and Camber, has rewarded the old trout for interrupting him by administering a fatal dose. That'll teach her to call him out on his one day off. In the twilight darkness of her bedroom he empties the contents of the pill bottle into her drooping mouth. Any minute now she'll be stone cold, but it'll be many hours more before she's discovered, by which time he'll be back at the wicket having resumed his innings and rattled up a half-century. When at length he is called upon to pronounce, an explanation of natural causes will be accepted without question.

He closes her eyes with his chubby fingers and prepares to leave her room. It was a bore that she called him out mid-innings to attend to her, but still, the provision she's made for him in her will should more than compensate for those few lost overs. In the end she didn't even require the full bottle; in fact, the final tablet is still on the bedside table next to her dentures. He'd better not leave it lying around, just in case. Mustn't get sloppy. Tell you what, he'll pop it into his cricket flannels and dispose of it later.

But he never makes his fifty. Because the Sussex Constabulary are on to him.

'Found something?' says Mr Dranse.

I withdraw my hand and hold it up to the skylight for closer inspection. I'm clutching an ancient and half-sucked wine gum.

Backward Point

Sir Arthur Conan Doyle has written one of the most famous stories about cricket.

'Spedegue's Dropper' tells of an asthmatic schoolteacher who spends his spare time lobbing a cricket ball over a cord slung between two fifty-foot trees in a dark corner of the New Forest. His life is turned upside down when an England cricket selector stumbles upon him practising this unlikely craft while out on a woodland ramble. Plucked from obscurity and rushed up to London in the selector's shooting brake, the diffident Spedegue sends the visiting Australians plummeting to defeat in the deciding game of the Ashes by bowling hundred-foot-high lobs which land perfectly on top of the batsman's stumps. He becomes a national celebrity overnight.

The story, which I read in a copy of *Reader's Digest* on the shop counter, comes back to me now. As I prepare to bowl.

It's the Friday after Easter and I'm on my last afternoon of a three-day junior cricket coaching course out at the county ground. Each afternoon has been spent practising with actual Sussex first-team players, one afternoon batting with Alan Oakman, then fielding with Don Bates, and now, on the third afternoon, a bowling masterclass in the indoor practice school. And Les Lenham is shaking me warmly by the throat.

'You see?' he says, as he swivels my head back and forth between his fingers. 'Bowling is a side-on action. Without that you'll never become any good at it. You have to look at the batsman over your left shoulder at all times. Left arm high, left eye behind left arm, left shoulder pointing at the sight screen behind you … if you get chest on, you're finished, so keep it like I'm showing, with …'

'Michael.'

'With Michael here.' He grips my Adam's apple with renewed vigour and tilts my jaw back. We're standing in a long wooden hut festooned with cricket netting. The same wooden hut, in fact, in which I sat last summer eating fruit pies and listening to the Gloucestershire captain talking about the 4.30 at Wincanton. But now the café has been transformed into what is described with some optimism as the 'Indoor Practice Facility'. Skirting the netting on all sides are vast piles of catering equipment: ancient fridges, tea urns, crates of shandy, industrial-size jars of salad cream, heated glass-display cases with 'Thank goodness for Ginsters' printed along the top, battered cash registers and rows of neatly stacked trestle tables. The air is heady with the savoury aroma of Marmite and stale lager.

'So, to summarise, clear follow through, and a nice easy swing of the arm. These are the basics of good away swing bowling, but in fact you won't bowl anything decent without it, not unless you're a freak, Chandrasekhar or someone of that sort. And you're not a freak, are you, Michael? No fear of you wasting away is there – is there?' he adds, thumping my stomach with his free hand.

He jerks my head backwards and forwards again as his audience of young boys in cricket whites gaze on in awe. 'Here is no good, here is good, here is no good, here is good. It's that simple.' He releases his grip and I meld back into the gaggle of eager onlookers, rubbing my jaw.

We've already spent some minutes standing in a line practising bowling actions, myself and the ten or twelve other boys who form my particular group, whirling our arms round and round while Lenham walks up and down the line like some cricketing drill sergeant. 'Now it's time for some action,' says Lenham. 'Let's see how much you remember. I want to see a straight run up, big delivery stride, high side-on action like we've just been doing. Let's see if you can get me out. Give me a chance to see what you're like, then we'll do some fine-tuning.'

He wanders down to the far end of our net where a bat and a pair of batting gloves are resting in front of a set of spring-loaded cricket stumps. 'Try to pitch it about a foot in front of where I'm standing, what we call a good length.' He indicates a spot in front of him.

The conditions aren't ideal. The room is lit by a set of some-what indifferent fluorescent lights, the bowler's run-up is badly scuffed by the marks of a free-standing chip-fryer which customarily occupies the space for six months of the year, and the netting itself is old and saggy and no longer able to reliably stop the ball. A bit like Les Lenham, in fact. According to my *Playfair Cricket Annual* his career bowling average stands at six wickets in ten years for 306 runs at an average of 51 apiece.

Nonetheless there's been a special thrill to find myself prac-tising with professional cricketers. I've seen Les Lenham bat on several occasions for Sussex, and although he rarely scored any runs he certainly gets out very elegantly. Wavy-haired with a pert nose like one of those small dogs you see on adverts for Pedigree Chum, on the field of play he's the epitome of the seen-it-all-before elder pro: laid-back, unhurried, and expert at finding a new excuse every time he's out. Someone moved behind the bowler's arm, he got an unlucky snick, the sun was glinting off a car windscreen; his ability to use minute bodily gestures to express an entire unspoken scenario of misfortune and cosmic injustice as he walks back to the pavilion would rival the abilities of Marcel Marceau. This is rumoured to be his final season with the club before taking up a coaching position, and he already has the slightly jowly look of a sportsman who's got his sights firmly aimed at an office chair.

He taps the crease as we each take a ball from a cardboard box and form a neat queue at the bowling end of the net by a huge gas oven begrimed with cooking fat.

This will be the first ball I've ever bowled in front of my peers.

I'm last in the queue. Ahead of me a lithe young boy of ten or eleven runs in and bowls a gentle delivery, which Lenham cannons into a large catering pack of Bird's Coffee. 'Well done. Nice try,' he says. 'Hold the ball so the seam is pointing towards the slips; it'll help your natural action.' The boy smiles happily and returns to the back of the queue. Lenham takes his guard again.

'Next.'

Another boy runs in and bowls a fast ball which Lenham thrashes into a stack of folded trestle tables. 'Don't let it drift down the leg,' he shouts. 'Aim at middle and off and allow it to swing … '

As I await my turn I find myself thinking over the last three days. It's been a steep learning curve. Most of the other boys in the event are from minor public schools in the Sussex Weald. And they can all bat or bowl a bit. Like the boy next to me, who comes from Lower Dicker. Or the blond kid next to him from Ditchling, who has personalised name tags sewn carefully into every item of his kit, and who on our first afternoon of batting even played one or two drives through mid-on off the back foot which had Alan Oakman purring with pleasure.

I, by contrast, not only couldn't manage the drive through mid-on off the back foot, I couldn't even manage the back foot. I'm not sure I even managed the foot. All I was able to offer was my trademark slosh. In fact, Oakman professed himself profoundly unnerved by my ability to hit any ball, of whatever length, loop, flight or speed, in the same direction, a direction which is officially known as midwicket but which I still think of as between ladies' tights and the Suchard milk and plain assortment.

When Oakman attempted to spend a few minutes teaching me the rudiments of a forward and backward defensive, I was bowled eleven consecutive times, as well as getting hit in my own lower dicker.

Another boy ambles past me. He slips slightly, recovers in his delivery stride and offers up a high looping ball that hits the far end exactly where Lenham had suggested. Lenham pulls it lazily round the corner, where it goes through one of the rents in the netting and strikes the sign saying 'Gents' on the loo door. He then walks up the pitch and holds the boy's outstretched palm in his gloved hand. 'Grip the ball slightly deeper in the palm, that'll hold it up a shade which will help deceive the batsman in the flight. But good stuff.' With a pat on the boy's head, Lenham goes back to resume his innings.

Two more to go.

Let's hope whatever happens that this is going to be more successful than Don Bates's fielding masterclass.

I suppose there are some people whose idea of fun is to spend their leisure time smashing cricket balls hundreds of feet into the air and then watching while hapless juveniles are forced to stand underneath and try to catch them. Luckily for the security of the nation, most of these sick individuals are safely detained at Rampton and Broadmoor. Unfortunately all-rounder Don Bates must have escaped in order to complete his contract with Sussex.

It didn't help that on my nominated catches Bates kept calling my name out as Simmonds, although at least I could initially claim the reason for not attempting to get underneath it was because I thought he meant somebody else, rather than because I was scared stiff. But after the second time the excuse was already wearing thin. And with the sky covered by a canopy of high white cloud I couldn't even go for the old 'Sorry, lads, the sun was in my eyes' trick I'd seen so expertly employed by a series of Sussex players in recent matches.

It was the waiting that was the worst part. I can remember every microsecond. Bates saying from somewhere beyond my eyeline, 'Now watch it into the hands. Don't take your eyes off it, just relax, keep your hands soft.' And then the ball descending at what seems to be an unfeasible speed. And Bates's honeyed advice, 'Nicely balanced now, just imagine your palms are a huge pouch.'

And at last the ball landing on my finger ends with a sickening crack. Just like it did last time. And the time before that. As on each previous occasion the crowning humiliation of inadvertently sitting down on my backside on the wet ground like a baby with the ball plopping gently off my finger ends onto the grass between my legs. The barely disguised snigger from one kid, and the entirely insincere 'Bad luck' from an eleven-year-old who seems to know all the adult players by their Christian names.

And Bates's dreaded final words. 'Have another go.'

Still, that was yesterday. Another boy canters past me to try his luck bowling at Lenham. Any moment now I'll have the chance to put everything right. If Spedegue can be discovered bowling lobs in a forest clearing, it should be possible for me here in the home of south-coast cricket in front of a seasoned pro. The boy delivers the ball from the back of his hand, and although it bounces barely halfway down the strip, round about where the cash tills are normally kept, it spins and climbs and Lenham has to rock back before thrashing it past backward point.

'Lovely ball. You bowl leg spin, do you, Moby?'

'I try to, sir.'

'You're well on the way. Try and develop a top spinner, release the ball slightly flatter – you'll get a lot of LBWs that way. Good boy.'

One more and then it's me.

A straw-haired angel who specialises in bowling off breaks passes me and unfurls a gently spinning delivery that sends Lenham back onto his stumps. At the last moment he unfurls a withering hook that rockets into the roof of the net, hitting one of the fluorescent light strips in the process and breaking the cathode ray.

'Good stuff, Sebastian,' he shouts. 'Left arm a little higher and try bowling round the wicket – it'll help the spin … '

It's nearly my turn. I wasn't expecting to have to rely on my bowling skills to catch the eye of the professionals, but now that I'm here perhaps this will be my first step. But there's a nagging doubt in the back of my mind.

The reason I've taken the name of Spedegue so much to heart is that, like him, I've reason to believe my own bowling action is unique. That was the very word used by Dad when I first tried to bowl in our back yard earlier in the week. He said he couldn't see how it was humanly possible to bowl a ball while throwing my head violently down and simultaneously wind-milling both shoulder blades. But the fact is I find it impossible to propel it in the suggested direction with a straight arm unless I employ an action like that of a rotary clothes drier.

It's just one of those things. I look like someone trying to headbutt his own kneecap while attempting to scare off a swarm of bees. But it's my natural action. Nearly two hours in the back yard and I don't seem to be able to bowl any other way. Hopefully Lenham will have some suggestions as to how I can improve and refine it. After all, I'd like to be an all-rounder one day.

Lenham settles down again at the far end. I lumber in, both arms instinctively start to rise as if I've been held up in a robbery, and my last glimpse of Les Lenham is of him tapping his bat on the rubber matting. Then he's lost from view in favour of a patch of trouser material halfway up my right calf. A twirl of arms, a headbutt and a swarm of bees, a violent jerk of my head back up to the horizontal, and somewhere in the middle of this chaotic process I feel my hand release the ball.

When I look up a pace or two later I'm greeted by a curious sight. Lenham is staring open-mouthed at me like a cartoon character. He doesn't seem to have played a shot. The ball is lying in the netting behind the stumps.

'Did you trip?'

'No, sir,' I reply, with a smile, offering him a glimpse of a half-chewed Fruit Salad.

'You didn't trip?'

'No, sir.'

He puts down his bat and walks up the pitch.

'What's your name?'

'Michael. Michael Simkins, sir.'

'Do that again, Michael.' He starts walking back. Then he momentarily checks his pace.

'Can you do that again?'

'Yes, sir. No trouble.'

He walks back down and picks up his bat. One of the others throws me a spare ball and I amble in again. Headbutt, bees, twirl, my right calf, a step or two more, I look up. Identical sight. Ball lying some way off in the rear netting. Lenham still standing open-mouthed, not having moved any other part of his body. I seem to have completely bamboozled him.

'Um … '

A pause.

'Erm … '

'Yes, sir?'

'Ehhmm … '

He seems lost for words. Perhaps this is the moment when I turn things round. Like Spedegue. Behind me the others are looking on in awe. I'm the only one who's been asked to bowl three consecutive deliveries. This is just how Conan Doyle describes the discovery of Spedegue, followed by a bevy of open-mouthed selectors literally lost for words as the quiet, unassuming, asthmatic schoolmaster waits patiently for their verdict.

'One more please, Michael.'

I run in, much faster. This time it's just a blur, head down, butt the kneecap, swarm of bees, follow through. Look up. Again, Lenham open mouth. Ball at back of net.

Lenham puts his bat down and walks up the pitch again. He puts his arm on my shoulder and takes me to one side by a cardboard container full of roller towels.

My head is spinning. Is it possible that I'm some sporting prodigy? It has been known. I've read about them in Mum's magazines – brilliant children who can play the violin, complete

complex mathematical equations or become world chess champions. Such things do happen. Think of Spedegue.

And suddenly I see it all. The letter to my headmaster from
the club secretary, requesting special dispensation for me to be
released from lessons so I can be selected to play for the county
in their first match against Yorkshire at Headingley in three
weeks' time. The trip up with a chaperone, the hotel room, the
anxious wait for my first over, the nod from Sussex captain Jim
Parks, and then the first ball, the headbutt, the bees, the ripple
of derisory laughter from ten thousand hard-boiled Yorkshire
supporters, and then the look up, to see the great Geoff Boycott
himself standing twenty-two yards away, open-mouthed in awe
and confusion, and behind him the scattered stumps, and the
joyous shouts from wicketkeeper and slip cordon.

Lenham squeezes me gently on my shoulder and looks at me
with infinite kindness. I never noticed before, he has glittering
blue eyes.

'Michael?' he says.

'Yes, Mr Lenham?'

'Michael, I'm sorry. I can't do anything with that. I'm sorry.
We'll refund today's part of the coaching fee.' He smiles gently.
'Go home … '

Off Drive

A few weeks later Dad announces he's taking me in the car to the nearby village of Keymer to pay a visit to his brother Percy. Percy has a bungalow with a hundred-foot back garden including a beautifully manicured lawn, and the trip promises the possibility of some early season practice.

Or so I think.

'There's something I want to talk to you about,' says Dad as we pull away from the kerb. His voice is heavy with concern.

He's certainly picked the right place to talk about it. If you want a long conversation with my father, just climb into his car and ask him to drive you somewhere. God knows why he's so slow. He's got a Rover with four gears, automatic transmission and plenty of pep under the bonnet, yet he seems determined to hold the official title of Grand UK Sunday-afternoon Pootling Champion. I suppose everyone's parents have some embarrassing trait that singles them out and makes introducing them to your mates a toe-curling experience. The particular cross that it's my lot to bear manifests itself once Dad gets behind the wheel of a car.

'It's about your school work,' he explains as we grind up past the station towards Seven Dials. Already a bread delivery van behind us is flashing its lights in annoyance. 'Are you being bullied?'

'No, Dad.'

'So what is it then? You realise how important this summer is, don't you?' I sigh heavily and turn to look out of the window.

He's about to trot out the speech about the importance of passing exams again but by avoiding his gaze I may be able stop him before he gets going. That sweetshop over there is selling chocolate misshapes at 2s. 6d. a large bag. That's a competitive price.

'Did you hear me? I asked you what's important about this summer.'

'It's the eleven-plus,' I mumble.

'That's right. It's the eleven-plus.' He slows down to allow the van to scream past. 'Mrs Turnbull says that on current indications you're not expected to pass it. And you know what will happen if you don't pass the eleven-plus, don't you?'

Yes, Dad. I know. The eleven-plus is the exam I'm about to take in about three months' time, one that will determine the rest of my life. Both my older brothers passed it without difficulty when they were my age, but somehow I seem to be considered a dead cert for failure. It's not that I don't want to work hard, it's just that with my Owzthat county championship taking up most of my free time, plus a punishing schedule of touring and one-day contests, there just doesn't seem much time for schoolwork. In any case, I'm going to be a professional cricketer, so what does it matter? Geoff Boycott's hardly Malcolm Muggeridge, is he? And I'd like to see Bernard Levin taking on Wes Hall in failing light at the pavilion end. Genius has no need of schooling.

Nonetheless, the exam is only a matter of weeks away and I can sense it steadily approaching, week by week, silently, inexorably, the awful obstacle which must be surmounted or refused. Beechers Brook in the Grand National. Scramble over it successfully without breaking your neck and miles of lush pasture stretched away into the distance, followed by cheering crowds and silver trophies and slaps on your rump from thousands of men in trilbies and car coats. Failure means a set of screens and a man in a white coat and gumboots approaching your stricken carcass with a revolver.

Dad has already laid out the importance of getting a good

mark. Many times. Success means a good school. It means science labs, conjugations, mortar boards and school songs; it means an open door to a decent red-brick university, a career as a solicitor or working in Shell or BP, a house up in Woodingdean by the time I'm forty, regular holidays, a car with a retractable soft-top and election to the local Rotary Club.

Failure means something very different. It means four troubled years at a secondary modern such as Dorothy Stringer, where the teachers wear balding corduroy trousers and only venture out in pairs. It means classes in metalwork and car maintenance and a criminal record by the age of twelve. It means leaving at sixteen to go and work nightshifts at the Sunblest bakery in Whitehawk. It means a drink problem by the age of twenty-three and a heart attack at fifty after an entire adult life eating fry-ups in the staff canteen.

We've stopped at the road junction. An impressive red-brick building lies straight ahead at the apex, with nicely tended lawns in front of a grand portico, the whole majestic edifice framed by a pair of impressive wrought-iron gates painted in jet-black gloss.

'See that?' He nods towards the gates.

I nod.

'See those dolphins?'

Above the handles of the gates, entwined round each other and through the railings, are three large, metal sea-creatures, brightly painted in blues and reds. Their heads are a ghoulish mixture of pop eyes and fleshly lips, with huge gills and fins. They look like those aquatic creatures that chase round after Troy Tempest in *Stingray*.

'Can you read what it says above them?' he asks.

Over the gates is an inscription in yellow lacquer.

'That's Latin,' he continues. 'That says, "Absque Labore Nihil." Do you know what that means?' He leans over and fishes a bag of sweets out of the glove compartment. '*Labore* means Work. *Nihil* means Nothing. "Nothing Without Work." You're looking at Brighton Grammar School. Best in the area. You could end up there if you'd work harder. That's what I've brought you to see today.' He hands me a Murray Mint.

The lights turn to green. Dad indicates left, checks the mirror and pulls away. 'You see that room up there. That's the art room. And that set of windows just below? Those are chemistry labs. That annexe you can just spot through the trees, that contains the language block and the pottery kilns, and on top of them are the biology labs.' He describes each new building with something approaching reverence, detailing new facilities and planned extensions with loving care.

It all certainly looks very good, but cutting up frogs and sitting round in scarves with cups of coffee listening to Joni Mitchell is not really my bag. I want to be a cricketer. But then, just as we reach the end of the complex, I see something that makes me sit bolt upright as if jolted by a cattle prod.

It's a playing field, bordering the roadside beyond the end of the buildings. Telltale lengths of rope suspended by tall metal poles can only mean that there's a proper cricket square there somewhere. There's another one. And there's a third. On the far side of the field stands a brick pavilion with a large clock fixed on the outside wall. Next to it is a small but serviceable scoreboard, and a pitch roller lying against the lee of the pavilion wall.

'Dad, can you slow down a bit?' A sentence I never thought I'd hear myself say.

A slip cradle lies in the grass by the railings. Nearby are some boundary markers, and over there in the distance stands a huge white sight screen on wheels, the canvas rippling gently in the breeze like a giant sail.

And then I see them. Thirty or forty boys in various shades of cricket white, practising in a series of nets, in their midst a clean-cut man in a purple tracksuit and gym shoes, obviously a master, barking instructions and demonstrating the rudiments of playing a handsome on drive.

A lorry swings past us nearly taking off Dad's side-view mirror. A bloke with bushy eyebrows and an expression of pure hatred leans across and shouts something at us before roaring off in a haze of exhaust fumes. Dad plunges his foot onto the accelerator, sending a half-sucked Murray Mint slithering down the back of my throat. I break into helpless coughing, and by the time I've hoicked the offending item back up my gullet and onto my pullover, the school is gone. All around us are prosaic rows of semi-detached villas.

'You all right?'

Oh yes, Dad. I'm all right. In fact, I'm very all right. Like a refugee from a Bounty ad, I'd come in search of paradise and found it.

We drive on in silence. Dad switches the radio on and we sit with our thoughts as Jimmy Young tells Raymondo how to make a savoury meat flan with apricots. I see now what Dad is talking about. He was right. I have to get through the eleven-plus. I have to get to that school with the dolphins on the front. Not for the chemistry labs or language annexes. No, I have to get onto those pristine squares, those nets, that slip cradle, that coach polishing my on drive. I want to push that sight screen round the boundary edge more than I've ever wanted anything.

Nothing Without Work. That's what the inscription said. And now I've seen it, I've suddenly got the impetus to do something about it.

I only hope I haven't left it too late.

Twelfth Man

Before I know it, it's nearly a year to the day since I first saw Colin Milburn hit 94 at Trent Bridge. But now I have other concerns on my mind. A year on and life is not so simple. Today is the day when my eleven-plus results are due to arrive.

I've spent the morning watching the Test match on the box: England are playing India in a laborious and one-sided affair, and with Milburn out yesterday evening (*c* Kunderan, *b* Chandrasekhar), there isn't much to see except the slow procession of Indian wickets at regular intervals. In any case, I'm too nervous to concentrate properly. I've other things on my mind. Like the arrival of the fatal envelope.

In the weeks since glimpsing those Ambrosian playing fields up on Dyke Road, the necessity of getting into the grammar school has been all-consuming. If effort counts for anything I may just have made up for lost time, sacrificing everything to prepare for the exam. My Owzthat tin has remained virtually unopened. Even my calorie intake has plummeted. Now all I can do is wait.

But it may be some time. The local sorting office is on a go-slow, and by midday we still haven't received our post. I can't just sit here slowly chewing the sleeve of my T-shirt with anxiety, so I decide to go down to the seafront and pay a visit to Louis Tussauds Waxworks. I'm not allowed in the Chamber of Horrors in the basement, not unless accompanied by an adult, but at least I can have a look at the main exhibition. One of our customers, who's a Cub Scout master, thinks he saw a wax effigy of Milburn in the gallery of sporting greats at the end of the exhibition when he visited it earlier in the week, and says I should have a look.

He can't be sure because at the time one of the Cubs had become separated from the troop, and he admits the final couple of displays passed in a blur as he searched desperately for the missing child. Happily it all ended well enough, with the infant being discovered safe and sound beside James Hanratty, the A6 murderer. But he's pretty sure he glimpsed Milburn in the last gallery before the exit. 'Big bloke, wearing cricket whites, looks a bit like Fatty Arbuckle? You can't miss him, he's just by Bobby Charlton. When you get to Yuri Gagarin you're nearly there.'

The visit proves a bitter disappointment. Either Louis Tussauds have only about five different head moulds or they are trying to make a pointed comment about the dangers of inbreeding. Former leader of the Labour Party Hugh Gaitskell looks like Leslie Crowther, Clement Attlee looks like Mahatma Gandhi, Dwight Eisenhower and Harry Truman look like Laurel and Hardy, while Dusty Springfield is in an even more parlous state: she stares reproachfully back at me with that famous beehive hairdo and those giant panda eyes, and with one arm lying on the floor at her feet having fallen down through the sleeve of her dress.

Even Milburn disappoints: a large figure clad in a nylon shirt, white jeans with children's pads loosely dangling from the knees, a pair of green-flash tennis shoes without any laces on his feet. And his head seems to be made from the same mould as Nikita Khrushchev in the gallery of international statesmen. Suddenly I feel profoundly miserable. What am I doing, running away from my fate like this, hiding in here among a load of glassy-eyed dummies? The sooner I get back home the sooner I'll be put out of my misery, one way or another.

When I walk back into the shop I can see instantly from Mum's expression that it's arrived. 'It's on the mantelpiece,' she says simply.

I weave along the back of the sweet trays and open the door. There's Dad, sitting just as he always does at this time, by the table with *The Rise and Fall of the Third Reich* splayed out in front of him. The telly shows India are now four down. We should wrap this up by teatime.

'Letter for you, Mikey.' He nods towards the mantelpiece.

There it is. Between the clock and the hand bell in the shape of a dairymaid, from East Sussex Education Authority.

'Are you going to open it?' says Mum from the open doorway. I take the envelope down and hand it to her. She flicks a glance at Dad and begins ripping the seal. A single piece of A4 paper is inside with the county logo embossed on the top. She scans the page up and down before her gaze fastens on the final paragraph. She says nothing for several moments.

A yell from Jim Parks signifies another wicket has fallen. Borde has been bowled by Illingworth for ten.

'Well?' says Dad. 'What's the verdict?'

Mum looks up at me. 'You've doingsed,' she says.

'My goodness,' says Peter West.

Overthrow

On 24 May 1969, the BBC carry a story in their early evening bulletin about Colin Milburn. He's been injured in a car crash. Details are scant, but it's obvious that it's been a bad one, and for the next few days the papers are full of details of his recovery and the prospects of him returning to pursue his career.

Some days later he appears at the doors of the hospital for a press call and an interview with *Grandstand*. Bare-footed and holding a cricket bat, his normal garb of cricket whites replaced by pyjamas and a paisley dressing gown, all the usual Milburn traits are there as he poses for flash cameras: the mop of tousled hair, the cheeky yet slightly shy grin, the familiar thumbs-up sign. But there are other things that are not familiar. Ugly gashes across his forehead, stitches like the seams of cricket balls criss-crossing his cheek, and worse, much worse, there's a piratical patch over the eye, the eye that had to be surgically removed in the hours after the accident due to the amount of glass from the shattered windscreen buried deep within it.

His left eye.

I'd been praying it would be his right eye. The less important eye. The one that a right-handed batsman can still do without. But now he's on telly I can see it's the leading eye. The eye that any right-handed batsman uses predominantly to judge the line and length of the ball.

I tell myself he may be all right. Look at the Nawab of Pataudi. He played for Sussex and India with huge success despite damaging an eye in a car accident. In fact, he was more prolific after it than he was before. In fact, he's scoring more runs now than—

You prat, Simkins. You pick up a bat and try hitting a cricket ball with your left eye closed. You haven't a hope and you know it. And the terrible thing is, despite the thumbs-up, the lopsided grin, the saucy asides to the nurses gathered round his bedside and the talk of recovering in time for the forthcoming Ashes tour this winter, so does Colin.

As his cricketing ambitions fade towards the gentle oblivion of coaching holidaymakers at Butlins, mine are following a parallel trajectory. By the time Milburn has come to terms with the end of his career, I've all but forgotten my own hopes of playing for England. That simple sheet of A4 from the education authority put paid to that.

Not that I don't make it to Brighton Grammar. On the contrary, eight weeks after the arrival of the letter I'm already learning the words to the school song, my first Latin prepositions and how to light a Bunsen burner. The reason for my non-appearance in school cricket is that I'm nowhere near good enough to be considered.

At least at Middle Street there was only one Michael Lowe to deal with. But virtually every kid with an aptitude for cricket seems to have ended up in my year at the grammar: dashing batsmen, wily bowlers, sizzling slip fielders and gazelle-like cover points. Paul Herring, Julian Bennett, Paul Grimshaw, Mike Donald: young, fit teenagers with shocks of blond hair, supple bodies and hand–eye coordination that could only be the gift of some unseen divinity. William L. Shirer would have been happy with this lot leading the parades at Nuremberg. With so much natural talent ahead of me, my chances were sunk before I'd even undone my satchel.

The Owzthat continues, of course, servicing and giving life to enough fictional beings to populate an entire series of *The Prisoner*. Kent win my first ever full championship, Somerset my Gillette Cup, and Eric Smith leads a successful defence of the

Ashes in Australia with Wally Sanderson of Worcestershire scoring consecutive hundreds at Adelaide.

I still make regular pilgrimages to Hove, enjoying the quasi-religious thrill of suffering for my pleasure as Sussex continue to fail in a whole variety of cups and competitions. I even attend all three days of their fixture with the touring New Zealanders without missing a single ball. When the club secretary makes a public-address announcement demanding that juniors desist from infiltrating the members' pavilion in search of autographs, the tourists' leading batsman Bevan Congdon responds by sitting out in the popular seats as a gesture of support for the next generation of fans. I support his stand against pettifogging authority by joining the queue of ecstatic kids now waiting for his signature. Until now my idea of rebelling against my elders has been confined to leaving my greens uneaten on the side of the dinner plate. Congdon provides my first frisson of political activism.

A year or two later the visiting Indians come to Hove for a similar fixture. As usual the match attracts a crowd of young autograph hunters, including myself, but this particular fixture proves a nightmare for the juniors crowding round the back of the pavilion in pursuit of the Indian team. The club office has managed to produce a scorecard in which the name of every single Indian player is misspelt.

Their fast bowler Abid Ali has progressed from Abbas to Aludali by the afternoon reprint, but the opening batsman Jayantilal remains stubbornly Jayeriti, and Govindraj, Govourday. Even their legendary spin bowler, the mighty Bishan Singh Bedi, is down throughout the match simply as 'Bissan'. I spend the entire afternoon attempting to track down the Indian wicketkeeper, described as Mouird, only to be told the individual in question hasn't even been selected for the tour. Brenda, the woman selling the offending scorecards, admits it's the worst day of her professional life. But I'm secretly pleased: suddenly the names of my Owzthat Indian squad, including the exotically named Abdul Hashish-Orandi, don't seem as far-fetched as I once thought.

Meanwhile, I settle into life at the grammar school. I learn about Henry VII, how to make a coil pot and why railway lines expand in the heat. My weight starts to decrease in tandem with my sweet tooth until by the age of fifteen I'm looking less like Donut from *The Double Deckers* and more like Raymond Burr's teenage son. But whether pushing rollers or waiting for signatures, my cricketing activities are now largely those of the interested spectator.

But then fate intervenes. Towards the end of my fifth year at the grammar school, the petroleum giant Esso reignites my dream to play for England again, like a Colibri Monogas table lighter in a chemistry lab.

Strutt

It's eight o'clock on a summer's morning in 1972. And the head of games at Westbourne Preparatory School, the imperiously named Rayleigh G. Strutt, is already screaming at me.

'YOU ARE KEEN,' he bellows. 'YOU WOULD NOT BE READING THIS UNLESS YOU WERE, AND I WANT YOU TO *REMAIN* KEEN ON THIS MOST GLORIOUS GAME, AND IN ORDER TO REMAIN KEEN YOU MUST HAVE SOME SUCCESS!!!'

I drop the book on my lap and stare out of the window. How long did they say this journey was? I might get car sick if I read while travelling, but I can't blame it on Rayleigh Strutt. Fact is, I'm shitting myself and we aren't even past Bognor.

I'd only brought along *Schoolboy Cricket: A Boys' and Masters' Guide* in order to remind myself of the basics of the game before this, the most important day of my cricketing life, but I'm in no mood for being shouted at. There'll be enough of that later today if I make a complete twat of myself.

I wonder if there's anything in Rayleigh Strutt about maintaining a positive attitude?

We accelerate out along the dual carriageway towards Worthing. Alf, our driver for the journey, switches on Radio 1, and the voice of Tony Blackburn blends indistinctly with the roar of the engine. Through the windows the ribbon of bungalows and small businesses bordering the coast road flashes by as we pick up speed. Pedestrians are moving with that careful grace of people who are aware they've got to spend the entire working day in the same shirt. It's going to be a hot one.

The Southdown motor coach hired to transport the Brighton Grammar School Under-Sixteens cricket team to Winchester College and our date with destiny is already beginning to feel stuffy. Someone is eating a sandwich and the smell of peanut butter mingles with petrol fumes and dusty upholstery.

Whatever else he is, Rayleigh G. Strutt is no William L. Shirer. His guide, a modest hundred-page textbook on how schoolboys can improve their game, is already more than twenty years old and long out of print. From the inscription on the inside front page it was originally the proud possession of Lionel, with the hope that he'd have a very happy Christmas with much love from cousin Ruby, Huddersfield, 1952.

I imagine Lionel to have looked a bit like the gangling twit depicted playing a joyless forward defensive push on the front cover. You know who I mean: he or somebody like him appears on the front of my Merit chemistry set, my Magic Robot, and a hundred other children's toys and hobbies produced over the last twenty years. A freckly milksop wearing a woollen tie, with creases in the sleeves of his shirt, the one throwing his hands up in glee because he's just rolled a six or the Magic Robot has just spun round three times and indicated that Charlie Drake is the capital of Venezuela.

This variant is a spindly-legged child in a cricket sweater and gym shoes. His features are concealed behind a classically bent left arm as he lurches forward. I imagine Rayleigh Strutt is just out of picture ready to chastise the youth with birch twigs if he does anything silly, like look as if he's enjoying himself.

His baleful prod is superimposed on a scene of other little milksops in the distance playing a match in some Arcadian landscape, surrounded by trees and ancient college buildings. A public school, undoubtedly. Perhaps even Winchester College, the venue for the match we're playing in today, against Willden School from Basingstoke.

If you had asked me five years ago whether I would want to be in this coach, with these people, going on this journey, I would have laughed with scorn at the imbecility of the question. But in the ensuing years since I stepped through the gates of Brighton Hove & Sussex Grammar School with the notion of using their pristine cricket squares as the natural stepping stone to a career as the middle-order mainstay for England, there has never been anything to suggest it was even remotely likely to happen. Even a few weeks ago I would have thought my place, twelve rows back over a wheel arch, was as unlikely as the milksop becoming the next Milk Tray Man. And now that my dream is within touching distance, I'm not sure I want it.

My reverie is broken by the kid in the row in front popping his head over the top of the seat. It's Brian Coverdale, the opening batsman in today's encounter. A cheerful, breezy sort of kid, who seems to have modelled himself on the Artful Dodger, 'Covvey' gets through life by pretending that everything's a bit of a larf. Even today, with the likelihood of him having to go out to face the infamous Alan Anderson, the Willden School wunderkind and reputedly the fastest under-sixteen bowler in the south of England, he seems entirely untroubled.

'Orright, Simmo?'

'Yes, thanks, Covvey. Fab.'

My attempt at breezy insouciance fails to convince.

'No worries, mate, you'll be great. It'll be a doddle. Just give it a bloody good biff. Stuff it up Anderson's arse!'

He makes a gesture suggestive of how such an intricate surgical procedure might be achieved, and disappears. Moments later I can hear the crackle of a crisp packet being ripped open. Smoky bacon, by the smell of it. I trace the words 'Stuff it up Anderson's arse' with my finger in the dust clinging to the inside of the window, completing the message with an exclamation mark and a large enclosing circle.

I'm just putting the dot at the bottom when I spot our games master, Dave Bunker, shouldering his way up the aisle of the coach. The very same Dave Bunker I saw wearing the purple tracksuit in the nets all those years ago while out driving with Dad. The last thing I need now is a stilted conversation with my new buddy on the teaching staff. Rayleigh G. Strutt may have been a martinet in his own way, but I imagine you knew what you were getting when he approached you: rollneck sweater, smouldering pipe in one hand and swishy cane in the other, crisply pressed, grey serge trousers breaking onto gleaming brogues. Dave Bunker on the other hand is a wolf in Adidas clothing.

Don't be fooled by the jaunty jogging bottoms, the well-worn trainers, the use of boys' nicknames to address them, the perpetual smile courtesy of a permanently overshot lower jaw. Dave Bunker has all the latent menace of a character in a Pinter play. This is the biggest day of his teaching career: rumour has it he's applied to join the staff of Loughborough College, the country's principal university specialising in sport, and victory today in the semi-final of the Esso National Under-Sixteen Colts knockout trophy would do wonders for his credentials. He may be Mr Nice Guy now but he has all the smiling bonhomie of an alligator. Failure today is not an option, not if he's going to get to Loughborough.

He stops at my seat. Me, the newest recruit to the campaign, the one who's had to be drafted in at the last moment, the one who's relying on an aged textbook to get him through the day.

'Ah, Simpo. Feeling confident today, are we?'

'Yes, sir.'

'No need to call me sir. You're looking a bit flushed, Simpo. You feeling OK?'

'Yes thanks, sir, Dave, sir.'

'Do you want the air con on?'

'Yes please, Dave, sir. That is, no thanks, sir. Only if you want it.'

'Yes? No? Maybe? I hope you won't call for a run like that today, Simpo. Don't want to run anyone out, do you?' His smile widens, denoting he's made a humorous aside, and he moves off.

But he's right. The idea of running out one of the gilded

angels in today's team doesn't bear thinking about. These kids were playing competitive colts cricket and bowling left-arm chinamen when I was still running round in my tasselled cowboy hat. Until this summer I hadn't faced a single ball in a proper organised match on a proper square. Oh no. You had to be one of God's children to qualify for that. For kids like me there was no room at the innings. And yet how odd life is. To think that at the very moment I'd decided to turn my back, it should be handed to me on a silver platter. To think—

My daydream is again shattered by blaring music. Our vice-captain and principal off-break bowler, Julian Bennett, has persuaded Alf the coach driver to turn up the morning chart show to full volume, for which Alf is rewarded with Bennett's trademark greeting, a blow to the back of the head with a rolled-up newspaper. This despite the notices everywhere commanding passengers that on no account should they speak to the driver while the vehicle is in motion. In Rayleigh Strutt's day that sort of behaviour would have been rewarded with six of the best, but Alf seems genuinely delighted to have a freckled, ginger-haired gobby teenager whacking him with a *Daily Mirror*.

See what I mean? Bennett is simply one of nature's aristo-crats. Academically brilliant, athletically gifted and able to recollect entire sections from *Monty Python's Flying Circus* the following morning, he seems to slouch through everything from end-of-term exams to chatting up girls to bowling lethal off breaks and playing dazzling lower-order knocks with a sort of edgy cheek. He also has an effortless social touch with contemporaries and adults alike.

He barrels back up the coach and begins to lead the entire team in an impromptu chorus of 'I'm A Lumberjack And I'm OK', thwacking his team-mates on either side in time to the music. Everyone joins in, even Dave Bunker. Even Alf the driver. All you need to know about my isolation on this bus is that I'm the only person who doesn't know the lyrics of 'I'm A Lumberjack'. That just about sums up the chasm between us.

The fact is I haven't been able to keep up. I'm still listening to Acker Bilk and laughing at *On the Buses* while they've moved on to Brian Ferry and 'The Upper Class Twit of The Year'. It's a world I don't understand, and kids like Bennett scare me because I don't know what they're on about.

I brace myself for the ritual thwack over the head, grateful to be included in his ceremony and yet desperate to be left alone. There's no arguing with Bennett. He's decided we're going to win and get to the final, and because he's decided, we believe him.

I mumble an approximation of pressing wild flowers and hanging round in bars and sink further down in my seat. To think that it was only when I gave up hope completely and resigned myself to organising my own lunchtime games with the halt and the lame, the bullied, the dispossessed and the psychologically damaged, that I started to make a mark. It may only have been on a piece of daggy grass with an old ball and a pile of blazers as wickets, but once I began arranging my own games I started to find my feet, even though the only bowling attack throughout this time consisted of the two biggest nerds in the year, 'Nancy' Phipps and 'Mongey' Freeman, who could both only bowl underarm and had nowhere else to go during the lunch-hour.

Nancy and Mongey and a pile of coats. Hardly Hall and Griffiths at Sabina Park, but at least they were prepared to play with me, to turn up lunchtime after lunchtime, to suffer my temper tantrums, my constant wrangling about whether a trailing coat sleeve could be construed a part of the wicket or not, my insistence on continuing to run even though the ball had gone through the railings onto the recently electrified main London to Hove railway line. They weren't such bad sorts after all.

I drift off into a fitful sleep, lulled by the sounds of 'Me And You And A Dog Named Boo' and the rhythmic juddering of the rear offside wheel beneath me. My mind flits back to those long dinner breaks, with Nancy offering up donkey drops and feeble full tosses, and Mongey forever acting as both keeper and all nine other fielders. I was very happy with Nancy and Mongey. It may only have been a knockabout, but they never complained, never let me down and never did better than me. What is that expression? 'In the kingdom of the blind the one-eyed man is king'? That was me, nudging and nurdling those long summer lunchtimes for ones and twos, building endless innings of sixty and seventy, often over entire weeks at a time.

And then that terrible moment of being summoned to meet Dave Bunker in the gym. His claim of having watched me through the window of his office, and how the school second XI was unusually short of players that Saturday, and the dread announcement that I would be required to play for them in their annual fixture against a large secondary modern school on the outskirts of Brighton.

Secondary modern, secondary modern, secondary modern, the phrase thumps away in my head to the throbbing of the engines. Not just any secondary modern, but a particularly infamous one on a sink estate on the fringes of the town, whose charges are notorious throughout the county for arson and attempting to steal the hubs of wheels off cars, often while they're still moving, and whose sporting excellence is confined to synchronised head-butting. To think that of all the sides I could have played against for my debut knock, it should be a team so inept that even Nancy and Mongey would have walked into their first eleven. How many times did they drop me in that innings? Was it seven or eight? Whatever, I scored an improbable forty runs before flattening my own wicket when the bat slipped out of my hands while attempting yet another heave to leg.

I'm woken by another blow to the head. The time for daydreaming is over. We're pulling into Winchester College. Bennett begins a lusty chorus of 'Spam Spam Spam Spam'. Within seconds the entire coach is joining in with him. As the bus glides towards an empty space in the corner of the car park, I take a last, longing look at Rayleigh G. Strutt. Chapter 7: 'How

To Approach Away Matches'. At last. Something relevant to my needs. Perhaps this contains the nugget of inspiration I've been searching for.

'What enormous fun away matches are! How important one feels as one marches out of the classroom with apparent unconcern, but smugly noting, all the same, the gaze of the less fortunate ones still sitting at their desks ... '

Who is this tosser? The less fortunate ones? Does he mean all the boys back in Brighton who haven't travelled nearly a hundred miles to have most of their upper teeth splintered by a fast bowler who took 6 for 14 in the previous round and who was described in this month's edition of the *Cricketer* as an exciting prospect, lightning quick and almost certain to become a professional by the time he's eighteen?

A noise of escaping air indicates the doors to the bus have opened. The rest of my team-mates are filing out of the coach and onto the baking tarmac. Our captain, the diminutive Paul Herring, who already seems destined for a career in the highest echelons of the diplomatic service, is heaving his huge vinyl bag, embossed with logos of past cricket festivals, in the direction of a sunlit cricket pitch, glimpsed in the far distance. Behind him Paul Grimshaw is twirling an old practice ball in the air as he waits for his kit from the boot, while Cornwell and Selsby are into a complex physical routine which, if I had any, would be designed to stretch my hamstrings.

And then I see them. Fifty yards away, gathered round the gaping boot of their own gleaming coach in their purple and custard blazers, Hampshire's version of our bronzed and gilded angels, the Willden School under-sixteens. I scan the line anxiously in the hope of finding my doppelgänger, the reserve who, like me, only finds himself in the team by a giddy conflation of circumstances, injuries to a whole string of senior players and about fifteen dropped catches, someone whose body language resembles mine. Somebody with the sweat stains underneath his armpits and a dog-eared coaching manual in his back pocket.

Nobody.

But I recognise one of them instantly. The photo in the *Cricketer* didn't lie. There, in the centre of the throng, casually popping a piece of chewing gum into his mouth in a manner which could only be construed as combative, is Alan Anderson, angel of death: tall, broad-backed, a mop of curly fair hair, the Willden wunderkind.

What did it say about his exploits in the preceding round? 'Various counties will be keeping a keen eye on this young prospect.' Is it my imagination, or is he looking straight back at me? Can he smell my fear too? If not, why is it that as our eyes meet through the glass his features break into a pitiless smile?

It's only then I notice. Between me and my nemesis is a carefully worded message. I'd forgotten about it till this moment, the phrase I'd traced in dust on the windowpane somewhere around Littlehampton.

'Stuff it up Anderson's arse!'

Brace

'You in next?'

I try to ignore him.

'You in next?'

'That's right.'

A pause.

'That bowler's my elder brother.'

I turn to look at the boy sitting a few yards away on the grass. He's obviously one of them. More than that, he's obviously the younger brother of the one who now thinks I'm going to stuff it up his arse. Same mop of curly hair, same bumptious smirk. Probably about eleven or twelve.

'Is that so?'

'Yeah.' He takes a tube of Fruit Polos out of his breast pocket and pops one in his mouth.

'He's fast.'

'Is he now?'

'Yeah.' Sound of sucking. I wish he'd leave me alone. I'm in next, in what to date is far and away the most important innings of my life. In fact I'd come here, on the grass by the boundary rope, a few yards from the pavilion, in order to try and get some peace and quiet, to focus my thoughts away from the clamour and mindless babble of my team-mates in the pavilion – what's the total, how are we doing, when's lunch, what's your favourite *Monty Python* sketch, how many overs has their best bowler still got left, who's in next, what would be a good score at the break – the endless din of overexcited testosterone-fuelled teenage boys with immortality beckoning over the horizon and no other way of dealing with it.

In any case I don't know why they're all asking such footling questions. They already know the answers. Sixty-nine, three, in quarter of an hour, dead parrot, too many, I am, and any score as long as I don't have to go out there and bat in the next fifteen minutes ...

It was Dave Bunker who suggested that the school be put forward for the inaugural Esso National Under-Sixteen Colts knockout trophy. For the lucky few who progressed through to the latter stages of the competition, trips like today's would be required to play the regional winners from other parts of the country. And for the teams who got through to the final, the reward was an appearance at the Oval. Kennington Oval in London, the one with the gasometer, the ground on which the first ever Test match between England and Australia was played, the one where my dad was taken as a child to watch the immortal Jack Hobbs break W.G. Grace's record of centuries, the ground on which Colin Milburn played his last Test match in England. That's the sort of thing that can happen when you suddenly get a multinational petroleum corporation bankrolling things.

The winners are due to receive a handsome silver trophy in the shape of a man's hand holding a cricket ball rampant, and with all competitors on both sides receiving a brand new Stuart Surridge Jumbo cricket bat, value over £100, to be presented individually on the famous old players' balcony at the conclusion of the game by cricketing legend, Surrey and England off-spinner Jim Laker.

A loud appeal echoes from the middle. The elder brother of the kid who's sitting next to me has just whipped a straight one into Paul Herring's pads. Eleven ecstatic teenagers from Basingstoke leap like salmon into the air, all pleading as one with the umpire, who happens at that particular end to be our very own Dave Bunker.

The bottom drops out of my stomach. I want to defecate noisily and at great length, but I can't because I'm in next and in any case I'm wearing pads, a jockstrap, a box, and something new to me, a thigh pad, a large thigh-shaped wedge of plastic draped round the top of my leg and fastened with straps which took me nearly twenty minutes and an instruction manual to work out how to put on.

Dave Bunker's right fingers twitch behind his back. He brings his hand round but it's merely to throw another coin into the air to mark the delivery. Not out. Herring marks his guard again. My heart rate begins to slow to the merely manic.

The one who thinks I'm going to shove it up his arse, puts his head in his hands and trudges back to his mark. Thank God Herring is out there to steer us through till lunch.

Of course, there was no possibility of me being involved in the competition. A couple of innings against sink estate schools on the fringes of the town while my superiors were attending county trials was hardly going to propel me into contention. It would take a maniac with a shotgun or a strain of food poisoning even more virulent than that regularly encountered in our school canteen to bring me within touching distance of making an appearance.

'He's very fast.'

'Is that so, sonny?' I'm hoping that this cool sarcasm and the use of the word 'sonny' despite the fact that he can't be more than a couple of years younger than me might do the trick and shut him up. When I look over he's got the end of his tongue through the hole in the middle of the Fruit Polo and is waggling it at me.

'He put a kid in hospital last week.'

'Did he now?' This is getting on my nerves.

It wasn't until the team emerged triumphant from its third-round match against Chiswick Grammar School that the rest of the school started to sit up and take notice. And when a couple of weeks later the team prevailed in a close fourth-round clash at Ipswich (Bennett 46, Price 25 not out, Grimshaw executing a crucial run-out with only one stump to aim at), there was a feature on it in the *Brighton Evening Argus* and things began to get serious.

So when the headmaster announced in assembly that if we reached the final at the Oval the whole school would be given the day off and a special train would be chartered from British Rail to take all 600 boys and staff up to watch the match and cheer the team on, things really took off. The prospect of a whole day off school aroused even the thugs who spent their time smoking behind the biology labs, the ones who would ask vulnerable female student teachers on their first day of teaching experience if they could have a mass debate. Even they became anxious for team news and weather prospects. They may have no interest in sport, but the whole planet likes a freebie.

'Broke his glasses.'

'Look, I'm trying to concentrate. Can you shut up, please?'

The kid gazes out across the grass. 'Just thought you'd want to know,' he says innocently.

'NOHBALL!!' Dave Bunker steps to one side and signals to the two second-formers operating the scoreboard that it was an illegal delivery. A raucous cheer goes up from my team-mates, but the last thing I need at this stage is an extra ball. In fact, the sooner he completes his over the happier I'll be.

The idea of going to the Oval was entirely academic from my perspective. I was glad that the team was doing well, of course I was, but even with a following wind I was still six or seven places off being selected, and in any case the team was already a winning combo. The batsmen were scoring runs, the bowlers taking wickets, and, most important of all (and this is where I fully acknowledge that my credentials are at their weakest), the fielders could actually run after the ball, rather than looking like Scott Tracey walking across the lounge to the cocktail cabinet in *Thunderbirds*.

But then fate intervened. Team regular Trevor Burton twists his ankle running for a bus. Nick Maddock puts his shoulder out during fielding practice, Adie Hewetson has to take compassion-ate leave because his mum in France has been diagnosed with a serious illness. Ian Nunn gets hit in the eye while wicket-keeping in an inter-house match, Mike White gets caught bunking off school to visit his girlfriend and is suspended, and Andrew Hall goes down with flu.

And so I'm sitting in the canteen one afternoon when Dave Bunker ambles in, wanders over to my table, puts his arm round me, pushes the plate of chocolate pudding I'm about to demol-ish away from me across the table and announces that Andy King, middle-order batsman and regular first slip, has put his back out while practising one-handed pick-up-and-throws in the outfield and will be on crutches till the end of term, so he'd appreciate it if I'd go easy on Mrs Garman's desserts for the next week or two.

'Just in case, Simpo, old boy.'

Herring lets the next one go safely past with all the aplomb of a cabinet minister side-stepping a nasty question on *Panorama*. Twelve minutes till lunch.

Simpo. Suddenly from nowhere, out of the blue, the seas have parted and Simpo is one innings away from playing at the Oval, from having his photograph in the *Cricketer*, from receiv-ing a new Stuart Surridge Jumbo bat and from meeting Jim Laker. No more playing with Nancy and Mongey. The new bulwark of the team is joining in the official practice sessions in the school nets, with Dave Bunker throwing down yorkers from ten yards and talking about long barriers and line and length.

Nancy and Mongey seemed to know. Hence their parting gift to me yesterday evening: Rayleigh Strutt's *Schoolboy Cricket: A Boys' and Masters' Guide*, purchased specially as a good-luck gift and presented to me by them both in a touching ceremony at the end of school.

So everything depends on me doing well today. Even if we win, which at the moment looks unlikely, at least two of the regulars will be fit again by the time the final comes around. If

I'm to be on the team sheet for the Oval I have to impress today. Everything depends on this one innings.

'My brother was in the *Cricketer* last month,' says the kid.

His brother charges in again, the last ball of the over. He approaches the wicket and hurtles past the clenched jaw of Dave Bunker, who now bears that curious look you only ever see on the faces of football managers when their team is locked in a relegation battle and holding on to a 0–0 draw with ten minutes to go.

'He had a trial for Hampshire last week.'

'Look, can you just fuck off—'

The sound of stumps shattering. I turn back, aghast. That's what happens when you take your eye off the ball. Herring has had his middle stump knocked clean out of the ground. Dave Bunker turns away, impassive, impenetrable, but the sinews are standing out on his neck. 'That's the end of the over,' he says quietly. The plums and custards rush to embrace the new trialist for Hampshire. If they can only slip another wicket before the lunch-break, they'll be as good as there.

Herring looks despairingly back at the carnage of what was until just now his wicket and begins walking back to the silent pavilion with that curious bobbing gait of his that is surely destined to be lampooned by a thousand political cartoonists and Commons sketch-writers in years to come. His path back takes him past the ramrod figure of his games master. They pass within feet of each other without exchanging a word.

'Looks like you're in then,' says the kid.

Lever

Law 19 states: An incoming batsman shall be Timed Out if he wilfully takes more than two minutes to come in – the two minutes being timed from the moment a wicket falls.

When I try to stand up I realise that I've lost all feeling in my left leg. In my anxiety about the lunch-break and the futile wrangling with this oik next to me, I've been kneeling on it for nearly twenty minutes. The blood supply must have been restricted. It's dead. When I try to put any weight on it, it collapses as though I'm standing on a giant kebab.

'Go on, Simmo.' My team-mates are calling to me from the pavilion. What a bloody fool. Why didn't I do some exercises, wander round a bit, jog up and down like they do on television? You wouldn't catch Geoff Boycott before the innings of his life kneeling with his full weight on one knee trading insults with a twelve-year-old.

Too late now. I lean down, pick up my bat and begin lurching out towards the middle. Every second step I jack-knife forward as if I've just been shot in the hip. It's an ignominious entrance for my big moment.

Paul Herring is nothing if not the genuine article. Disappointment and fury are etched on his forehead, but as captain he still has an overview of the game to consider. The expression on his face is one I've only seen once before, when Harold Wilson was on the *Nine O'Clock News* during the sterling crisis. As he catches sight of what appears to be Quasimodo lurching towards him, his face creases further into a sharp frown.

'Have you pulled something?'

'No, I—'

'What's wrong? Have you shat yourself?'

'I'll be all right … ' I splutter. 'It's just … ' Just what? Just a coronary thrombosis? Gangrene? How long does it take for diseased tissue to atrophy? But Herring is waving his bat back towards the square where the opposition are already taking up their positions again. 'OK, eight minutes to go till lunch, nothing silly, just stay out there. Understand?'

I've got to play the most important innings of my life with a left leg that's lacking any sensation and a jumble of sanitary equipment rapidly unravelling somewhere within a pair of trousers once worn by an infamous poisoner. It's difficult to see how any sportsman could flourish under such conditions.

'Now listen. The kiddie from the far end moves it away a bit off the seam, but watch your crease because the kiddie keeping wicket is standing up for him, and the kiddie who just got me out is quick but straight up and down. You got that?' he says, touching me on the shoulder.

I attempt to speak but merely summon up an indeterminate rasp. My mouth feels like the inside of Tom Graveney's jockstrap. What I'd give now for that wine gum I so recklessly tossed away all those years ago. I can hardly ask for a drinks break: I haven't even reached the middle.

'I said, have you got that?'

I nod miserably. In the distance Dave Bunker is already staring at his watch and the fielders are back in position. Who was it I had to watch out for? Something about a kiddie? The cricketers I'm shambling towards now are not kiddies, they're virtually fully grown men.

The following minutes pass in a blur. I stand glued to the spot at the non-striker's end as Brian Coverdale plays the next torturous six balls. A couple of times he plays and misses but he negotiates the bowling without calamity. More importantly, he doesn't attempt a run. At the end of the over he strides breezily up the pitch, a wide smile on his face.

'Orright, Sim?' he says, patting at a rogue blade of grass. 'No worries, mate. You'll be fine. Just hang on in there. Only six balls to get through. Watch out for a bit of rabbit.'

This is it. I mustn't look intimidated. Don Bradman said 90 per cent of the game is won or lost in the mind. But how to look cool in conditions like these? Various celebs on telly recently have taken to wearing their shirt collar turned up to denote detached nonchalance. Perhaps I'll try it. It certainly works for Jason King.

The Willden captain, a short stocky boy with piercing blue eyes, is ordering his fielders to various new positions round the bat. I can hear and see every detail: the pattern of silly mid-off's cricket whites picked out in the violent green of fresh grass stains, the rapid ticking of short leg's Quartz watch, the creak of the new pair of silly mid-on's cricket boots. I catch a faint but distinct whiff of his breath. He's obviously had a Caramac bar in the last three hours. I didn't know Mackintosh's were still selling them in the south-east. They must be doing well.

Dave Bunker has a long look round the field and lowers his hand to allow the final over to commence. He stares thunderously down the pitch at me. If I should get out now, the consequences don't bear thinking about. Silence descends. For about three seconds.

'OK, Al. Let's have the fat geezer.'

From somewhere in the far distance, the trialist for Hampshire runs in to bowl …

* * *

What is it about poetry that humanity often reaches for it in times of crisis?

Perfectly sane individuals, who wouldn't normally allow a line of verse within three feet of them unless it was something along the lines of 'There Was A Young Lady From Slough', start going all dewy-eyed and reaching for the muse as soon as their lives hit the buffers. Regular straight-up-and-down blokes who wouldn't know Rudyard Kipling from Mr Kipling start going on about how much 'If' inspired them to acquire a deeper understanding of life in all its myriad complexity. Why is it? Is it something about the ability of the poetry to transcend and crystallise the human condition?

Ever since the moment when my name was pinned up on the team sheet six days ago I've been swimming through each day in a thick soup of paralysing fear. Endless fantasies involving worry, humiliation, misery, degradation, failure and ignominy. Dropping the vital catch, tripping down the steps of the team coach, running out our best batsman. Or something infinitely more subtle and searing, perhaps splitting my trousers in front of the opposition while running round the boundary, getting locked in the pavilion toilet, or trapping my foreskin in the zip of my cricket whites and spending the morning at Basingstoke Royal Infirmary.

Now that nightmare has become a reality. The plane that runs out of fuel halfway across the Atlantic; the endless corridor of identical doors behind which you can hear a loved one calling desperately for your help. It's here. My worst nightmare made manifest. And now the only piece of poetry I've ever committed to memory, the one from my Auntie Glad's *Treasury of Inspirational Verse*, is percolating up through my nervous system and running round in my head as I await probable decapitation.

There's a breathless hush in the Close tonight –
Ten to make and the match to win –
A bumping pitch and a blinding light,
An hour to play and the last man in.

Is it a bumpy pitch and a blinding light? Or a bumping pitch and a blindy light? Is it ten to make? Or twelve? It doesn't really matter. The point is, those lines of verse given to me all those birthdays ago by my misguided aunt are flooding back into my head as if someone has turned on a tap.

Because it's beautiful out here. It's more than beautiful, it's stunning. Dreamlike. Ethereal. I've never walked onto a ground like this before. Until now my cricket has always been played on blustery school fields surrounded by sombre post-war semi-detached houses, with arterial roads bordering the pitch choked with cars full of idiots thinking that shouting 'Owzthat!' from the passenger windows is the funniest thing in the entire history of the world.

> *And it's not for the sake of a ribboned coat*
> *Or the selfish hope of a season's fame –*

It's as if the boss of Universal Pictures has decided to make a multimillion-pound movie about cricket and said to the set designers, 'GIVE ME YE OLDE ENGLANDE FOR CHRIS-SAKES.' In every direction the vista is a visual cliché. Beautiful honey-coloured Victorian school buildings stretch out in the distance. Slate roofs, ivy-clad walls and parapets, dreaming spires and towers framed by a perpetually moving garland of swifts twisting and plunging in dizzying patterns.

In a distant archway two schoolmasters in gowns and mortarboards are silhouetted against a blue sky dotted with the sort of fluffy white clouds that only a child of six would draw. From a window in some far-off cloistered chapel the sound of a madrigal choir singing a mellifluous version of 'Now Is The Month Of Maying' drifts gently down on the breeze, mingling with the rustling of tree branches. Out here in the middle the air is sweet enough to spread on toast. Tantalising scents of wild herbs mingle with the more insistent aromas from the canteen, smells of shepherd's pie and jam roly-poly.

For all I know the poor sod in the poem having to go in to bat in the gloom with only six balls left and ten more runs needed is labouring under difficulties not unlike the ones I'm facing now. Stiff with nerves, sweating like a bastard, surrounded on all sides by gobby fielders making allusions to the uncertainty of his parentage.

But his captain's hand on his shoulder smote –
'Play up! play up! and play the game!'

One man, with the entire team's destiny resting on his shoulders. Paul Herring smote me on the shoulder for God's sake. He may not have quoted the poem but you could argue that his exact words constitute a modern translation. Lacking Sir Henry Newbolt's poetic flights of fancy maybe, but the same sentiments more urgently expressed.

He's relying on me. Dave Bunker is relying on me. Come to think of it, the whole school is relying on me. I've got to get through to lunch. And even though I may end up with an extensive dental bill I'm going to do it. And with style. Not just hanging grimly on awaiting certain decapitation. If I'm going down I'm going down with all guns blazing. I may perish in the attempt, but it's time to step up to the crease and show them what I'm made of.

From somewhere far away, twelve stone of muscle and bone steams towards me.

It's time to play up, play up, and play the game.

Block

Five balls later. Five of the most dramatic balls of my life.

I've hit the quickest under-sixteen bowler in the south of England for a luxuriant cover drive, an imperious square cut, a withering pull, a murderous on drive and finally a huge lofted hoick back over his head towards the topmost boughs of that distant grove of trees. Extraordinary. I never had any idea that such shots existed within me. They seem to have been unleashed by some unseen celestial hand. Even Dave Bunker is staring open-mouthed at what he's just witnessed.

The only snag is that I haven't actually managed to hit the ball.

Each of the five shots I've played has failed, in some cases by a considerable distance, to connect. All five deliveries have ended up in the wicketkeeper's gloves, each to a chorus of oohs and aaahs that would do justice to a children's fireworks display. I would have been run out by a mile off the fifth had the wicket-keeper's shy at my stumps been a direct hit, but fortunately he was still gobsmacked along with the rest of his team-mates.

Brian Coverdale walks down the pitch towards me. Even he seems to have lost his perpetual grin.

'Sim, Dave's told me to tell you he wants you to play a bit more cautiously for the last ball. He isn't sure yours is the best way to play out till lunch.'

'Is that what he said?'

'Not exactly.'

'What did he say?'

Covey looks down at a loose blade of grass between his feet

and prods it with his bat. 'He said, "Tell that bloody tosser to get a grip."'

He ambles back. In the distance the bowler is already pawing at the end of his run. One ball left. Perhaps Dave was right after all. I'll go a bit easier from now on. I don't want the kid to get discouraged; he may ask to be taken off.

It comes at me like a tracer bullet. I offer a strangled prod that would have Rayleigh G. Strutt purring in his grave. There's a faint snick.

A faint but perceptible snick. Even before it's landed, short leg issues an instinctive whispered 'Yesss'. He's heard the gentle, fatal, Judas kiss of leather glancing willow on its way through. And my heart shatters into a thousand pieces. The ball thuds into the gloves of the kiddie keeping wicket. Eleven pumped-up teenagers leap skyward, rending the quiet Hampshire air with a collective cry of primeval tribal jubilation.

I open my eyes and look up. It may still be a bucolic paradise to everyone else but it looks like Lewisham on a wet Sunday afternoon to me. I've nicked the bloody ball through to the keeper off the last ball before lunch. The kid who once thought I was intending to stuff it up his arse now realises I was in fact merely intending to play his first five balls as if I'm Magnus Pyke attempting to morris dance, and then meekly snick his last through to the wicketkeeper. He's now charging down the pitch towards me like the Wild Man of Borneo trying to get out of his cage at the Essoldo Sports Hall.

But not in order to get at me. From the moment the ball edged my bat I was already yesterday's news. He thunders past me without a second look, on and into the arms of his team-mates. Their glorious future is opening up with each ball.

My own future is similarly mapped out. But it is very different. It's a long walk back to the pavilion under the Medusa stare of Dave Bunker, the lack of eye contact as I remove my pads in a lonely corner of the changing room, the long, silent lunch-break blankly shovelling forkfuls of rapidly congealing shepherd's pie round my plate, and then the opposition's innings, with me trembling with anxiety every time the ball comes to me lest I cock things up even more and compound my own misery.

And then the interminable drive back to Brighton, the empty seat next to mine, the disappointed faces of Mum and Dad when I tell them I missed the first five and snicked the sixth, and even worse their stolid bumbling words of comfort, 'Never mind, I'm sure you did your best,' and 'You can't do well all the time.' And then the announcement of the result in assembly tomorrow, the long collective groan of six hundred boys now denied a day's loafing in south London, and the subsequent search in the corridors and playgrounds for a suitable scapegoat.

And so on. Elevation to the stature of public enemy number one, the dropping out of school, and the inevitable shipwreck of ending up at the age of seventeen working nightshifts, having driven Mum and Dad to an early grave through parental worry and stress. And on to the final degradation, death by cirrhosis of the liver in a shabby flat by the age of forty, surrounded by half-eaten meals and porno mags. Three attend my funeral.

'Not out,' says Dave Bunker.

The fielders seem frozen in mid-air.

'Not out,' says Dave Bunker. 'That's lunch.' He calmly removes the bails and begins walking purposefully off towards the pavilion, followed by his opposite number at the square leg position.

'Come on, Simmo,' says Covvey. 'Din-dins ... '

Hoist

The ball that brings me my hundred at the Oval a fortnight later is surprisingly feeble, almost anticlimactic. Just a regulation short one, sitting up meekly outside the off stump, almost too wide for me to hit. And yet I've noticed that the bowler has been showing signs of tiring for some minutes now, worn inexorably down I imagine by what has been one of my most withering displays.

I've been waiting for this moment for a long, long time. Indeed, sometimes it feels as though my whole life has been building to this one climax. There have been moments recently when I thought it would never happen. Now it's here. And it's time to finish the job. After all I'm seeing it as big as a football. I rock back, and a split second later it hurtles away through extra cover for another four. I've scored a century. I can hear the sound of cheering rolling on like a distant clap of thunder.

I've done it. This one's for you, Colin.

I allow myself the merest nod of the head in the direction of the bowler whom I've just carted for three successive boundaries. But something's up. He's standing halfway down the wicket, bent double, holding his side.

'You all right, Nancy?'

'No, I'm not,' he replies, wincing. 'I think I've got a stitch. Mum told me this would happen if I did any exercise after eating my sandwiches. Anyway we'll have to pack up now; the ball's gone under that car over there.'

On the far side of the Oval car park, Mongey is already on all fours peering anxiously under a maroon Volvo parked by the entrance to the club shop. It's one of a number of sleek up-market automobiles fringing our playing arena, each one embossed on the side with the name of a Surrey pro. Virtually the entire first eleven seem to be parked here this afternoon, their courtesy cars jostling for space with those owned by the senior management of Esso UK.

Mongey takes my bat and begins prodding gingerly under the rear wheels. Nancy looks anxiously about him. 'You'd better be careful,' he says. 'This car is owned by Pat Pocock.'

'I've had enough anyway,' mutters Mongey from beneath the chassis. 'If I stay under here it'll bring on my asthma.'

A collective groan of dismay erupts from the stands. The fall of another wicket, by the sound of it. For some time now our efforts to overhaul the total set earlier in the day by King Edward VII School Morpeth, a tricky 115, have been foundering, after a solid start. By my reckoning we'll be down to our last pair. Perhaps I should abandon my innings and see how the boys are doing, just to show solidarity.

I leave Mongey rummaging under Pat Pocock's exhaust and wander across the tarmac to a gap between the pavilion and the Bedser stand. Out on the vast green outfield the solitary figure of Grimshaw trudges disconsolately back from the middle, trailing his bat behind him. He's been bowled for nought, having a huge yahoo in an effort to achieve the sixteen more runs needed from the final over. Morpeth are only one wicket away from triumph. Our last man, Cornwell, is clattering down the steps and marching out into the middle. The situation is hopeless. Even Rayleigh G. Strutt would be hard-pressed to keep his chin up.

My brief dream of Oval glory died in circumstances closely resembling a farce about an hour after my phantom dismissal at Winchester. Over lunch Dave Bunker reminded me that if he'd wanted a clown in the side he'd have picked Charlie Cairoli. He'd also reminded me my job was to hold an end up while Coverdale did the biz, and that I wasn't to be intimidated by all those fake appeals from the opposition when I hadn't touched it.

Except, of course, I had.

He didn't know it. But I did. Not that it made much difference. My innings ended seven overs after lunch, when attempting a quick single my thigh pad again slipped down my leg, resulting in me being run out by about ten yards. Herring's comment on my return to the pavilion – 'What happened? Did the kick-start fail on your Zimmer frame?' – summed up the entire miserable episode. A curiously bittersweet feeling of relief flooded through me. At least this empty charade was now over.

Fortunately it didn't matter. Willden were a one-man band. Chasing 104 they collapsed to 50 all out soon after tea and we were through. The return journey in Alf's coach was like the party to which I hadn't been invited: a haze of dancing and endless choruses of Gary Glitter's current anthem, 'Come on, come on ...' Except of course I wasn't coming on. I was going off. Back to oblivion. Even though my name was still on the invitation list, in reality I was already sitting outside on the pavement with a bottle of lemonade and a straw.

* * *

The sun is dropping over the Oval and in the distance milky-white clouds are bubbling up over Big Ben. Cornwell marks his guard, while up on the players' balcony, like some cricketing Napoleon contemplating imminent retreat from Moscow, sits Herring, his feet up on the railings, a towel draped over his diminutive shoulders. He allows himself a taut smile when Cornwell thrashes his first ball back over the bowler's head for a boundary, but he knows the game is up, and when another mighty swipe misses and Cornwell is clean bowled to provide Morpeth the trophy by twelve runs, he barely allows himself a twitch of disappointment. That man's a politician to his boots.

Seconds later a thousand-plus boys are gleefully clambering over the boundary boards and gathering in front of the pavilion. I wander in among them, feeling the exquisite bright green turf underneath my feet. It's like walking on a sprung dance floor.

Delicious. At least I can still say I've stood on the famous Oval playing surface.

After a couple more minutes, England bowling hero Jim Laker ambles out onto the balcony. In twos and threes the winning and losing teams spill out from the darkness of their changing rooms and form an informal line at opposite ends of the balcony. Overhead Concorde wheels a lazy parabola in the sky as it roars away to the west and on to the Atlantic. One by one the players inch their way along to the middle for a medallion, a certificate, a handshake and a Stuart Surridge Jumbo cricket bat. Huge great things with thick handles, beautiful straw-coloured blades and sweet spots the size of a dinner plate: the sort of bat you could mishit a ball with and still reach the next county.

Each player in turn raises his prize aloft before briefly posing for photographs for tomorrow's newspapers and cricket periodicals. Herring, Bennett, Donald – the ones who only a fortnight ago were my new comrades-in-arms. Now they seem as far off from me as Concorde up there in the heavens. Covvey waves down at the throng and momentarily catches my eye. I smile back at him, hoping to elicit a private acknowledgement of our shared history. But none is forthcoming. I'm no longer part of his crowd, I'm just one of the cheering masses below.

The last one to be called up is our twelfth man, Adie Hewetson. It was the sudden illness of his mum in France that opened the way for me but now he's back where he belongs, drinks carrier and team mascot. He holds aloft his commemorative bat – my commemorative bat – and kisses the blade before following the others as they disappear into the darkness of the pavilion.

What now? What of my former team-mates, up there in the changing room, throwing ice cubes at one another, shaking up cans of Pepsi and making jokes about wanking. Some will go on to play decent club cricket, perhaps even county standard, and for one or two, our pace bowler Mike Donald or Julian Bennett perhaps, even an England Test cap. Herring will try to play, of course, when Cabinet duties allow, but he'll be too busy dealing with international relief efforts in Botswana or journeying – probably on that very Concorde up there – to further East–West arms agreements at the UN.

As for me? I've come about as far as I can. I've scored several fifties in the front of our shop, I've made Les Lenham laugh with my bowling action and I suppose I've done my duty to Colin Milburn, even if it is only in the car park. Enough is enough. Quit while you're behind. Already the players are leaving the balcony. Our train home doesn't leave Vauxhall station for another hour and a half. Some kids are sitting in the early evening sunshine doing their homework or playing cards. One of the sixth-formers has produced a guitar and is strumming a gentle tune in the outfield.

A hand taps me on the shoulder. It's Nancy.

'Mongey's found the ball. It wasn't under Pat Pocock's car at all. It was wedged in the exhaust of Graham Roope's Ford Escort.'

'So?'

'Well, we've got to hang around another hour yet. Your luck has to run out sooner or later.'

A couple of minutes later we're back in the car park by the Hobbs Gates. Wasn't it Boycott who used to take a fresh guard on reaching his century in preparation for the second? I reckon I've got about twenty minutes to make the 97 more needed for this special landmark. Another juicy long hop loops through the air towards me and seconds later it's rocketing through a huge vacant area around midwicket, threaded with supreme precision between John Edrich's wing mirror and the radio aerial on Robin Jackman's Vauxhall Vectra.

And my tongue instinctively slides up to the roof of my mouth …

Tackle

That four off Nancy proves to be virtually the last time I pick up a bat in anger for the next fifteen years. With O levels and A levels to be got through it becomes steadily more difficult to keep up at sport, and after one or two more desultory appearances for the school second XI, my career peters out a couple of summers later when a boy called Tim Tremlett splatters my stumps for a third-ball duck at a school in Southampton. Tremlett goes on to play county cricket for Hampshire. I don't. 'It's not really working out, is it, Simmo?' is the phrase with which Dave Bunker finally severs my fragile hopes. At least he gets my name right.

I'm becoming preoccupied with other things anyway. Like girls. With my weight still falling off at the rate of at least half a stone a year, I eventually secure my first date, with a girl called Emma from the nearby Hove County Girls School. A sunny outdoor type with huge thighs and rosy cheeks, she agrees to go out with me for an evening stroll to Patcham Place, an area of parkland on the outskirts of the town well known as a meeting spot for young lovers.

When we arrive an evening match is taking place on the cricket pitch by the main road. We sit for a hour or so on a bench in fading light as I press my worldly credentials by explaining to her the various developments and tactics out on the field.

Describing the advantages of posting a fly slip for the left-hander may not rank among the best chat-up lines in the world, but it obviously does the trick, because she allows me to put my arm round her. By the time I've got round to explaining the difference between a leg break and a googly, I've got my free hand up the back of her pullover, and seconds later my fingers fasten for the first time in my life on crisp elastic and the chill metal of hook and eye. As our lips meet and with my own fly slip threatening to assert itself, I bunch the clasp and elastic together with my fingers and in a trice have undone it. All those years spent secretly unwrapping Opal Fruits under my school desk with one hand while writing with the other have paid off in spectacular fashion.

* * *

Emma moves to Greece to be the nanny to the offspring of a composer of radio jingles, and I never see her again. But at least I've broken my duck. I've now got a career to forge. It's time to turn to my other great passion, acting. After three years at drama school I begin the long slog round regional theatres picking up a play here and a pantomime there: Canterbury, Scarborough, Bristol. And who knows? If I succeed on the stage I may yet fulfil my dream of facing the world's greatest bowlers, even if it's only as part of the Lord's Taverners team with Lance Percival as my batting partner and Parky as captain.

The game remains my constant companion during these long seasons in rented digs. I spend my nights dressing up as vicars and policemen and my days watching, playing or thinking about cricket. At Scarborough I attend the first ever floodlit match to be held in England, a night-time event staged in October at the local football club between Scarborough CC and the Rest of the World, in which Dennis Lillee bowls to a terrified Scarborough CC opening batsman while a couple of hundred bemused locals shivering in overcoats look on from the terraces. While playing in a charity match for the Harrogate Theatre team I give the artistic director out LBW first ball while doing a stint as umpire and am rewarded by being cast in the following play as the non-speaking corpse rather than the detective who solves the crime.

At Bristol I witness a seventy-ball century from Desmond Haynes, and while at Chesterfield I see Geoff Boycott compile another in just under an entire day. During his innings a nearby spectator offers to help one of the players move the sight screen and succeeds in wheeling it over his own foot. It proves to be the first, second, third, fourth, fifth, sixth and seventh time I hear the word 'wanker' uttered on an English cricket ground.

* * *

In 1982 I help to bury Dad. Two days after Argentinian forces invade the Falklands, he has a stroke from which he never recovers. Even at the end, several weeks later, when he's unrecognisable, cursing and dribbling in a pair of pyjamas now several sizes too big for him, it never occurs to me that he may not pull through. But as I'm leaving his hospital bed on a baking-hot Sunday afternoon after my latest visit, a woman in a blue nylon overall and rubber gloves draws me to one side and tells me that my brothers and I must prepare Mum for the fact that her husband is going to die in the next few days.

For some moments my brain refuses to process the information. I feel sure that I've been accosted by some mad cleaner with delusions of grandeur, one of those oddballs who infiltrate important institutions and then act out their private fantasies. Yet even as I'm scanning the corridor for a handy security guard to come and escort her off the premises, it dawns on me that this is what ward sisters are dressed like nowadays. The days of Hattie Jacques in a starched pinny have long gone. Anyone who has to wear uniform as part of their public duties now seems to resemble a Kwik-Fit fitter: railway staff, traffic wardens, even cricketers. This woman is not only bona fide but is gently telling me that Dad's innings is nearly over.

The notion of going straight back and informing Mum of the news is too hard to bear. I can't go home. Not yet, at three in the afternoon in bright sunshine. And I can't stay here, blundering about aimlessly in the car park of Brighton General

Hospital. I need to go somewhere isolated, somewhere private, and process this quietly terrifying news before attempting to tell her. A place where I won't be disturbed, somewhere deserted and forgotten where I'll be left alone to shed the tears I can already sense welling up massively inside me without fear of embarrassment or interruption.

Sussex County Cricket Ground.

I catch the bus out to Hove and sit all afternoon in the furthermost corner, while below me Sussex and Essex act out the comforting ritual of a John Player Sunday League match. If ever I needed an environment in which to experience at a deep level the pulse of life, of ebb and flow, of birth and death, decay and regeneration, it's watching Sussex trying to bat on a dodgy wicket against John Lever and Stuart Turner.

Since my last visit a large new seating area has been built at the sea end named the Arthur Gilligan stand, although with biting winds forever whistling round its top tier it's known to all as the Gulag Arthurgilligan. I mount the staircase to the top and sink into a battered deckchair, where the sounds of seagulls and cricket shots and genteel applause both assist and camouflage the huge, keening yelps that erupt from somewhere deep inside me at thirty-second intervals.

It's difficult to contemplate that he's actually going. The man who spent endless evenings in the shop bowling countless balls to me and seeing nothing for his efforts except the gradual yet relentless destruction of his premises and stock is ending his days in a hospital ward trying to keep his end up as one by one his vital organs collapse like Bangladesh facing Malcolm Marshall. The man who taught me everything from a forward defensive through to the best way to eat a Cadbury's Creme Egg has been given out without the benefit of a third umpire.

At the end of play I walk home along the seafront, confident that I can now face Mum and break the news to her gently and tenderly without going under myself. But it's a false dawn. The moment I see her I burst into fresh floods of unstoppable tears. She lumbers over and gives me a hug and asks me what's wrong.

I eventually manage to stutter the bad news: that Dad's not going to get better and has at best only a matter of weeks.

'Bless you, dear, I know that,' she says.

* * *

By 1985 I've graduated from small repertory companies and have finally picked up a year's contract at the National Theatre. But with the call from the Lord's Taverners still several BBC sitcoms away, I'm going to have to think of other ways to combine my love of cricket and a passion of hearing the sound of my own voice in public. How?

The answer has been staring me in the face. My transistor radio is tuned as a matter of course throughout the summer months to BBC Radio 3 and the live commentaries of the *Test Match Special* team. It's become an indispensable part of my daily existence, and, like most avid listeners, I can even do a passable impersonation of the entire team: the soft burr of John Arlott and the braying jollity of Brian Johnston. I'd even used my approximation of Fred Trueman's complaining Yorkshire drone for a play in which I'd recently appeared, set in a pub on the outskirts of Sheffield.

Arlott, Johnston and resident toff Henry Blofeld all seem to have stumbled into cricket commentary by dint of good fortune, enthusiasm and an ability to convey live action by the use of words alone. Why shouldn't I? After all, I'm an actor, which surely is a second cousin to broadcasting. And in any case Johnston was an old wartime mate of my dad's. If I could get to meet him in person, who knows where the camaraderie of the Royal Army Service Corps dance band might lead?

The problem is, how to get to him. The *TMS* commentary box is always located inside the secure cloisters of pavilion or press box, environments impossible for the casual spectator to infiltrate. I could write to him, of course, or to the producer

Peter Baxter, but how many letters must they get from listeners wanting to apply for a job for which there are no vacancies? No, my only chance is to engineer a meeting in person. But this isn't going to be easy. Even if I could get into a Test match ground, it would be impossible to get near enough to introduce myself.

Then, in September 1986, Sussex get to a one-day final at Lord's. And a mate who belongs to the MCC offers me the surreptitious use of his membership pass. Suddenly I'm inside the citadel and within striking distance. For one day only.

Morning, Johnners. Morning, Blowers.

Morning, everyone.

A VIEW FROM THE BOUNDARY

Quiet Studio

Saturday, 6 September 1986. Sussex are playing the mighty Lancashire in the NatWest Trophy final at Lord's, the concluding event in the cricketing calendar before stumps are drawn for the last time and we break open the Ready Brek. Instead of having to spend the day squashed in with inebriated fans throwing cherry tomatoes at each other in the cheap seats, I can watch the game from the greatest vantage point in the world, the top tier of the famous old pavilion, a building sacrosanct in international cricket. More importantly, I should now be able to get close enough to the *TMS* commentary box and Johnston himself to press my case. It's my first and possibly last chance. I can't afford to blow it.

My mate has really stuck his neck out for me on this one. The rules and regulations governing behaviour and conduct while in the building are terrifying. The dress code alone runs to several pages of closely typed small print – dandruff-flecked blue blazer, pensioners'-check Tootal shirt, pair of stained cavalry twill trousers, faded panama hat and balding suede Hush Puppies. As for impersonating a member, both for the perpetrator and the member himself, the penalties don't bear thinking about.

It's only as I'm waiting outside my flat in north London for the number 16 bus on the morning of the match that I realise I've forgotten a vital component. I may be sporting a suitably crumpled jacket and slacks, but now I recall that regulations also demand members wear a tie at all times. I'm not even sure I've got one to hand, and by the time I've searched the flat I'll be late for the start and the best seats will be gone. Luckily my local branch of Oxfam is just opening for business across the road. Within seconds I've grabbed one from the rack and am sitting on the top deck, trundling down the Kilburn High Road towards St John's Wood.

When I arrive at the ground shortly after 9.30 there's already a long queue of middle-aged men waiting to be allowed in. What was it my mate warned? Although I shouldn't have any trouble getting into the ground itself, the pavilion would be another matter. The goons guarding the doors here are notorious throughout the cricketing world for being surly, suspicious and curt in equal measure, and there are numerous accounts of famous players from Fred Trueman to Sunil Gavaskar being turned away because they aren't carrying the correct accreditation or are recklessly wearing an open-necked shirt. As for a membership pass being illegally transferred to a non-member ... It doesn't bear thinking about. If I'm to impersonate my mate successfully, I'm going to have to keep my wits about me.

At 9.45 sharp the gates swing open and a line of M&S easy-care fabrics begins shuffling forwards. As predicted, a flash of the pass is all that's required to get me into the ground. Ahead of me stands the mighty red-brick pavilion built by Thomas Verity in 1889, at the rear of which is the set of anonymous, white, double-fronted glass doors through which I must pass if I'm to find Brian Johnston. It's the only entrance and the only exit.

It seems entirely appropriate that I should be on a mission to locate a man with whom Dad passed the last year of the war. This whole scenario, with me attempting to avoid detection and arrest in an alien environment by using false papers, feels like something out of *The Colditz Story* or *The Great Escape*. Ahead of me a pair of baleful-looking stewards in green blazers stand on either side of the doorway. One is a stout individual with a shock of thinning, baby-blond hair, who bears a startling resemblance to Hermann Goering. His colleague is a smaller, shrewish man with a pencil moustache, cold, slitty eyes, and one of those haircuts that only Nazis in British war films seem to favour.

Already a crush of impatient members is building up as their membership cards are scrutinised. It's only as I catch sight of my reflection in the windscreen of a nearby van that I realise I should have chosen my tie more carefully. From a distance it might pass for the familiar MCC colours of egg and tomato stripes, but in close up it's a bright yellow offering with a motif of what appear to be the Smurfs in pink and red pixie hats, interspersed with the crudely stitched features of a smiling Father Abraham.

Too late. It will have to do. I'm almost at the entrance doors. It's now or never.

Goering studies me with a look of mild suspicion. 'Membership card, please, sir?'

My friend's pass has fallen through a tear in my jacket and precious seconds evaporate while my hand chases it round the inner lining. Stupid, stupid mistake. You couldn't imagine Richard Attenborough or John Mills leaving such details to chance. Already my forehead is moistening with sweat. Goering is looking with disgust at the Smurfs – why didn't I take a bit more time?

At last my fingers locate it. Thank God. Goering looks at it for what seems an eternity.

'Unusual names those, Crichton McKinnon?'

Crichton McKinnon? Obviously my mate's middle names. What a hoot!! I'll have some fun with that next time we meet up. But Goering is already handing me back the card and moving to one side.

'You know where to go, do you, sir?'

I nod. Don't be caught out, not now you're nearly past the checkpoint. Keep your mouth shut unless absolutely necessary, that was my friend's advice.

'Thank you, sir. Enjoy your day.'

It's worked. He's already turned his attention to the next in line. Seconds later I'm trotting up the polished staircase towards the first landing. Before me lies the inner sanctum, the legendary Long Room, the Valhalla of cricket, where spectators can mingle with their sporting gods as they progress back and forth from changing room to pitch. Any moment now and I can be standing among them, gazing at cricket bats used by Jack Hobbs and blazers worn by Don Bradman. Perhaps I'll even get a look at Rachael Heyhoe-Flint's bust.

Hang on. Mustn't be greedy. Remember what my mate said. Get to the top turret, select your seat, don't look too keen. Remember, this is supposed to be my second home. I wander into the bar, down a refreshing pint of Theakston's and start climbing the famous old staircase.

* * *

The way I look at it, there can only be one result, a huge and humiliating defeat for my team at the hands of a side who have systematically crushed us under their heel for over a decade. Particularly as Lancashire have playing for them today Clive Lloyd, a player whose murderous hitting has been described by no less than the great John Arlott, doyen of commentators, as 'like a man knocking a thistle top with a walking stick'.

If only I could come up with stuff like that.

But when the umpire's finger goes up to send the world's most destructive batsman loping back towards the pavilion for a big fat duck to give Sussex their third wicket in as many overs, I break my own golden rule to keep my mouth shut and nearly blow my cover. Leaping to one's feet and bellowing like a circus elephant running amok in a shopping arcade is obviously among the permitted code of conduct. But surely the day can't get any better than this?

In fact, it's hardly begun.

It's after I take a wrong turning on my way back from the gents' that I see it. Slap bang in the centre of the balcony, a tiny white-painted hut a few yards along with three simple letters painted on the door. *TMS*. The combination of a permanently open bar and the warm autumnal sunshine had all but driven the purpose of today's quest from my mind. But now I've stumbled upon it by accident. The small side door opens to the hut and Peter Baxter, *TMS* producer, steps out. Behind him, crammed together with his colleagues like an oversized gnome in a potting shed, I snatch a glimpse of Johnners' proboscis-like nose. The door swings shut again. Baxter loosens his tie, takes a few lung-fuls of fresh air and perches on the handrail to watch the remaining balls of the over.

This is the moment. If I don't seize my chance I may not get another one. I've had four pints of Theakston's, and, after all, Dad wouldn't have lied to me about his friendship. Would he? Not for all those years?

'Excuse me. Would it possible to speak to Brian Johnston?'

Baxter turns his head and smiles amiably back. After all, I'm a member. There's no need to panic. I'm not going to pull out a machete or ask him if he knows God loves him.

'Is he expecting you?'

'Um … not exactly. I'm the son of an old friend of his.'

Baxter checks his watch. 'He's just finishing his stint on mike, but I'll go in and ask if you like. Who shall I say it is?'

'My name's Michael. Michael Simkins. My dad was Benny Simkins. They were in the war together … '

'Just a mo. I'll push a note under his nose.' He smiles pleasantly once more, quietly opens the door to the commentary box and disappears inside, offering another tantalising glimpse of the mighty Johnston unclamping a set of headphones from his monstrous ears.

What have I done? My mate made me promise not to open my mouth, and yet here I am trying to strong-arm my way into the *TMS* box on the basis of a completely dubious story probably invented by Dad to keep his youngest son amused in the long afternoons on Lancing seafront. I've staked my entire day on a piece of improbable fiction from a man anxious to press his cricketing credentials on a son who palpably worshipped him. Of course my dad would try to suggest he was best buddies with one of the voices of cricket. Wonderful in its way.

I'm just about to retreat in panic when the door to the hut opens and the huge figure of Brian Johnston fills the tiny doorway. He wears a cream suit, an MCC tie and his trademark correspondent's shoes. He shoots out a huge mottled hand, flecks of cake crumbs and marmalade still clinging to the finger ends.

'Benny Simkins!! Good God, I haven't heard from old Benny for years. Wonderful musician, and told the filthiest jokes in the whole British army. And his lovely wife, Peggy. It must be over thirty years ago now. And you're his son! Lovely to meet you, Michael – come in and meet the others.' Before I can speak he ushers me up the steps and into the commentary box.

The following forty minutes pass in a dream. *TMS* is everything you could ever hope for, except with more cake. The tiny cubicle is full to bursting with excited middle-aged men, not only the commentary team but various friends, celebrities and hangers-on who, like me, have managed to blag their way in for a few precious minutes in this cricketing Shangri-la.

One by one Johnston introduces me in gleeful hushed whispers, each one accompanied by, 'He's the son of the filthiest joke-teller in the British army.' Christopher Martin-Jenkins says how nice it is to meet me, David Lloyd says, 'Good on yer, son,' former Sussex captain John Barclay assures me it's his absolute pleasure, and Henry Blofeld even calls me his dear old thing. Bill Frindall also behaves exactly to type, complaining that I'm standing in his light and not to open the door without looking first as the wind disrupts his papers.

Moments later I'm handed a glass of champagne followed by a large slice of fruitcake covered with marzipan and frosted with icing. The cake emerged from a white cardboard box and was apparently a gift from Doreen in Shrewsbury. And there I sit, eating cake and drinking Veuve Clicquot, while far below Sussex add 137 for the second wicket.

It must be nearly an hour later when the four pints of Theakston's start to make their presence felt. In any case, I don't want to overstay my welcome. I had planned to delicately bring up the purpose of my visit, but with live commentary taking place it would plainly be inappropriate to ask for extensive career advice. Now I've made contact I can drop Brian a line asking for some help and take it from there. I lean across to indicate that I'm going now and rise from my stool. But he signals for me to linger a moment longer.

With that he pulls from his coat pocket a tiny set of clockwork plastic feet, silently winds the key on the ankle, and just as David Lloyd is about to do his end-of-over summary, Johnston leans across and sets them trundling across the desk in front of him. My last memory is of seven middle-aged men spluttering with barely suppressed glee while the eighth sits frowning at me as I open the door to leave.

I stumble uncertainly down the steps again and stand with my hand gripping the guardrail. My head is spinning. That's what I want to do. I want to be a cricket commentator. To spend my days opening cakes from Doreen and playing practical jokes on my chums and watching cricket over a glass of bubbly.

* * *

By 8pm the ground is deserted. The only sounds are tons of bottles and beer cans being swept between the rows of benches. I've stayed in my seat long after the match, long after the glorious moment when Paul Parker lifted the trophy on the balcony below, long after the players have packed up and made off for a knees-up at a West End nightclub, long after the bar has closed and the last of the members have staggered off to their homes. I've just sat here nursing a final pint, watching the lights come on in the surrounding flats, enjoying the first faint twinkling of stars in the night sky and savouring my last few moments as

Crichton McKinnon on the summit of the most famous building in the game of cricket.

It's time to go. I drain the dregs, stub out my celebratory panatella on the ironwork of the railing, and rise, albeit a little uncertainly, to my feet. The famous old Father Time weather vane on the grandstand is now almost shrouded in darkness, and as I begin a slow and careful progress down the old central staircase towards the exit doors the wall lights are burning brightly.

I thought I was about the only person left in the building, but as I descend to the final landing I find myself stumbling down the staircase alongside an old man. Elderly, grey-haired, the familiar garb of blue blazer and slacks, though I notice with one arm slightly shorter than the other. Our eyes meet as we grip either side of the balcony, and he flashes the bluest of blue-eyed smiles.

I'm looking at Len Hutton. Sir Leonard Hutton, captain of England 1952 to 1954, the nation's greatest batsman since Jack Hobbs, scorer of the highest number of runs in a calendar month, Test selector, and most recently adjudicator of the Man Of The Match award on the pavilion balcony a little over two hours ago on this very ground.

And I think. What the hell. I've had five pints. Why not? What's the worst that can happen?

'Great match, Sir Len.'

'Yes, I enjoyed it.'

We totter down another set of treads in silence.

'Hope you don't mind me saying this, Sir Len. But I thought it was wonderful that you gave the Man Of The Match award to Dermot Reeve … '

Sir Len stops mid-tread. His face breaks into what can only be described as a relieved grin. 'Oh, did you think so? I was so worried because I know he's not the most fashionable player, and his spell was relatively early in the day, wasn't it? But I thought his contribution really was the difference between the two teams. Didn't you?'

'I did, Sir Len.'

'I'm so pleased. Thank you.'

'Not at all. It's been a really lovely day.'

'It was a real scorcher, wasn't it? Mist early on as well.'

'So did I, Sir Len – fast asleep I'm afraid … '

With a final wave he hobbles off down the last few steps and after a cheery goodnight to the two stewards he steps through the rear doors and is lost from sight.

Above, below and all around me portraits of the great and the good stare back in warmth and affection, every cricketer who has ever trod these stairs seems to be smiling on my efforts. And now I've trodden these stairs too, and had a tête-à-tête with a cricketing Zeus.

I sway gently down to where my new friends Hermann and Heinrich are still virtually bent double in supplication at Hutton's departing figure. In the glow of the lamps even they look like blokes I'd be happy to go on holiday with.

'Marvellous to see Sir Leonard again,' says Hermann.

'Fantastic,' I agree.

'One of nature's gentlemen,' says Heinrich.

'Absolutely.'

'Had a nice day, sir?' asks Hermann.

'Bloody marvellous.'

'Always a lovely occasion, the NatWest,' says Heinrich.

'It's one I won't forget, if I never come here again,' I reply. 'Wonderful place you've got in here.'

'Why, is this your first visit, sir?' Himmler's eyes narrow and he flicks a glance at his now-scowling colleague.

And suddenly I recall Gordon Jackson in the final moments of *The Great Escape*. Having absconded from the prison camp and successfully survived outside for several hours by answering any enquiries from suspicious civilians in fluent German, he blows his cover by answering 'Thanks' to a casually tossed 'Good luck' from a Nazi official just as he's about to board the bus to freedom.

Himmler mutters something in Goering's ear. He nods curtly and fixes me with a stony stare. I can already hear the sound of approaching jackboots on the cobbles over by the Grace Gates.

'Could we see your membership card, please?'

Tape Running

'Wanted. Commentators for new 0898 telephone service. Vacancies in all seventeen professional counties. Successful candidates will be expected to have a thorough knowledge of the game and its history, and to be able to talk fluently about it in a live situation. Applicants should record a five-minute cassette demo tape of their voice, preferably talking extempore on some element of the game, and send it together with their name and address to ... '

Applicants are invited to send their demo tape to an address in what Sir Arthur Conan Doyle would have described as an unfashionable part of London.

It's nearly six months since my visit to Lord's, and although I've done nothing to pursue my dream in the intervening period, I now see that fate has decided to deliver it to me personally and on a silver platter. Looking at this advertisement in the classified pages of today's *Guardian*, I suddenly sense what Conan Doyle's Spedegue must have felt when the Test selector came across him in that forest clearing. All those so-called wasted years, in his case lobbing a ball over a rope, in mine muttering whispered commentaries to myself as I pushed those rollers back and forth across the lino, are going to pay off. This is the moment when life makes sense. The moment when I finally get to become a cricket commentator.

It's only through complete coincidence that I'm even reading today's *Guardian*. I rarely read a newspaper at all and when I do it's only the sports sections and theatre reviews, and I haven't even managed that recently. For the last month and a half I've been walled up inside the great Soviet monstrosity of the National Theatre building on London's South Bank, rehearsing a revival of Arthur Miller's classic play *A View from the Bridge*. And what with learning lines, taking accent classes and hanging about in the bar gossiping with usherettes, I haven't picked up a paper at all.

But with the show having opened to rave reviews, I've begun reclaiming my days again. Which is why I'm sitting here on a cold February morning in a house in Hendon, waiting for my friend Gilly to make me a coffee and passing the time by reading the newspaper lying on her draining board.

The advert itself reads a bit like the start of a Sherlock Holmes mystery. The world's most famous detective is always being called upon to sort out poor unfortunate individuals who've answered advertisements like this one: classifieds in the back of daily newspapers requesting people with red hair and the surname Garideb to sit in an attic room in Hoxton and read the *Encyclopaedia Britannica* for eight hours a day. Even the name of the person to whom it should be addressed seems faintly Holmesian. Sebastian Short. 'Ah, my dear Watson, have you not heard of Sebastian Short? The third most dangerous man in London ... '

Gilly returns with a tin of Marvel and tells me to be careful. She listens to *You and Yours* on Radio 4 and only the other day they were warning listeners about exactly this sort of thing. One moment you're answering intriguing ads offering opportunities of a lifetime and the next thing you know all your life savings have been spirited away to a bank account in Lagos.

What would Holmes say to this? 'When you have eliminated the impossible, the remainder, however improbable, must be the solution.' At the bottom of the ad is something I hadn't noticed on my first two readings. A vital clue, as crucial as discarded ash on the veranda outside the window or a boot imprint across a muddy lawn. It's a tiny logo, consisting of a pair of crossed cricket bats rampant over a ringing Bakelite telephone. The company is apparently named, with a reassuring lack of imagination, Everyball.

It's got to be bona fide. Only somebody versed in the administration of the professional game could come up with something so ineffably dreary.

And it stands to reason. Most leading football clubs already have their own dedicated premium-rate call-up service, and if you try to use a public phone box nowadays you can hardly find the receiver for adverts trumpeting special 0898 services. Admittedly most of what's on offer for your pound-a-minute is somewhat more exotic than finding out how Glamorgan are doing at Colwyn Bay, but obviously somebody has decided there's money to be made by making a continual commentary available for die-hard enthusiasts with a handy office phone and nobody to monitor their calls.

I've missed a vital component, however. I'm not looking at today's newspaper at all. The copy I've been reading is already ten days old. Gilly only had it laid out on the table because she's been using the media and communications pullout section to mop up a glass of fresh orange juice her son Jack had upset over her new carpet at breakfast. The deadline for applications is in fact tomorrow night. If I don't move now I'm sunk.

The first problem is how to record a decent demo tape. Gilly immediately offers assistance. She has an old portable cassette recorder upstairs that she uses to help her son Jack learn his tables in school. He records his own voice practising them and if he gets through each set without a retake she gives him extra pocket money. Consequently it's a well-used piece of equipment: the Record button is missing and the facility only functions if a thick pencil in wedged into the hole, and the motor speed has never been constant since Jack dripped Marmite into the workings.

She runs upstairs and fishes the machine out, throwing in a couple of spare tapes for me to record over for good measure.

Both recorder and tapes are heavily festooned with Mutant Ninja Turtle stickers, but no matter. It'll do the job.

But there's a second problem. Where do I find some cricket to describe? It's February and the entire northern hemisphere is shrouded in mist and rain. The only live cricket anywhere in the world is England's current tour of Pakistan, but that's only on Sky and I don't have a satellite dish. I could watch it in a shop window in the Kilburn High Road, but if standing outside my local branch of Dixons talking into a kiddie's cassette recorder doesn't get me arrested, trying to reproduce the snatches of conversation between Mike Gatting and Pakistan umpire Shakoor Rana almost certainly will.

So what about a brief snippet of something from my Owzthat league perhaps? But Gilly thinks this would do my chances no good at all. Describing metal rollers tumbling across linoleum would hardly persuade the third most dangerous man in London that I'm the next John Arlott.

Then I have a brainwave. I'll catch the next train down to Hove and do a live descriptive piece on a county ground in winter, describing the long burnt-out summer days lying like spent cartridge cases on the frosty ground, weaving in a bit about the ghosts of Ranjitsinhji and Maurice Tate to stress my background knowledge, and then on to a brief description of Sussex's chances in the coming season and why it's impossible to get a decent sandwich in the Wilbury stand.

It's already 10am. My tape must be in the post by 6pm. In any case I've got another performance of the Arthur Miller play back at the National at 7.30. I gather up the cassette recorder, Jack's spare tables tapes and a pencil with which to trigger the recording mechanism, stuff them into a holdall and set off for Hendon Thameslink. I must catch the next Pullman service down to Brighton via Gatwick Airport and Three Bridges if my plan is to succeed.

My cape and meerschaum, please, Watson. The game's afoot.

* * *

Two hours later I'm standing outside the Tate Gates on Eton Road. Bill Frindall himself couldn't have come better prepared. As well as the recorder, tapes and pencil I've bought some new batteries, a notebook and even a tea towel to put over my head to act as a windbreak while I'm recording. I've thought of everything.

Nearly everything. The gates are locked. The ground is completely shut up for winter.

It never occurred to me I might not get in. I assumed that, like Lord's, there would be someone there day and night, summer and winter. Lord's has a steady stream of humanity flowing back and forth; it even has special off-season guided tours of the ground. But Sussex wouldn't be open for anything like that. There's nothing to see at Hove. The only old relics here are to be found drinking tea in the committee room.

Just as I'm giving up hope an elderly man totters out of the chalet wheeling a bicycle and holding a brace of bin bags. The very same chalet that witnessed my debacle with Les Lenham nearly twenty years earlier. In fact, the old place looks exactly the same as I left it, except that someone has stuck a colourful sign over the main doors advertising 'fresh hot food and cooking just like home'. He deposits the rubbish bags by the front door and is just preparing to ride off when he spots me frantically signalling to him through the gates.

'Are you from Rentokil?' he asks.

'Er – that's right. Rentokil.'

'I thought you were coming after lunch?'

'They've asked me to put in a preliminary report.'

He looks unconvinced.

'Hence the cassette recorder.' I offer up my notebook, pencil and battered machine. I should have removed the Mutant Ninja Turtles sticker from the top; Holmes wouldn't have let such a detail go unaddressed. But the old man leans down stiffly, draws a pair of massive bolts from the ground and begins swinging open the giant gates.

'How long will it take?' he asks. 'Only we've got pre-season nets starting in three weeks and if the club cricketers start finding vermin in the cricket bags they'll be asking for their money back. They're cunning devils, aren't they?'

'Difficult to say. The sooner I make my report the sooner we can get someone round. I'll only need fifteen minutes so if you don't mind … ' Ahead of me lies my goal, the bare ground and surrounding stands from which I intend to paint my vivid word picture.

'Don't you want to see the chalet?'

'I'll start with an overview, if you don't mind. Need to see where the little things are coming from, don't we?'

'Fair enough. Let me know if you need anything.'

Minutes later I'm sitting by the boundary on a bench with the tea towel over my head, gazing out at the square. The sound of Jack practising his eight times table from the cassette recorder confirms that everything is in order. All I have to do is to remove this tape and replace it with the spare one so thoughtfully provided by Inspector Lestrade.

I try a couple of dummy runs, experimenting with different vocal tones and how best to wedge the pencil into the hole, until eventually I'm happy with the shape of the piece. Perhaps this wasn't such a good idea after all. The pitch and surrounding stands are completely deserted. Nothing seems to be moving at all. I could have stayed at a home with a photograph and saved myself the train fare.

Then fortune strikes. From between a gap in the fence a huge Alsatian dog, which I recognise as the pet of the head groundsman, leaps across the boundary boards and gallops onto the pitch. Moments later the groundsman himself appears with a grubby basketball. With a gigantic kick he boots it high into the air. With a yelp of delight the Alsatian races after it towards the far end of the ground.

Perfect. I clear my throat, stuff the pencil top in the gap where the button once was, and press Record.

'I'm sitting here by the main scoreboard at Hove in the depths of winter, a ground on which I've spent much of my life watching county cricket but which now seems in suspended animation, waiting for the returning sun to bring warmth and light and usher in another season. A season in which Sussex will once more attempt to win their first ever county championship … '

With each sentence I gain more confidence. The grounds-man's Alsatian reaches the ball and begins pushing it back towards his master with the end of his nose, giving me a perfect live action vignette to describe. Within moments I've shimmied seamlessly onto the state of the pitch itself and its reputation for suiting fast medium-swing bowlers able to use the sea fret that rolls up from the nearby promenade most evenings at about 5pm.

'And finally, in the distance, the Tate Gates, dedicated to the great Maurice Tate, doyen of swing bowlers and darling of the side between the wars. We can be sure that he'll be looking down from above and wishing all who watch cricket here next summer a sunny day, a vacant deckchair and a pint of Harveys at close of play … '

That'll do. I'm beginning to sound like Jess Yates off *Stars On Sunday*. In any case it's time I got it in the post and off. I wrench the pencil from the recording hole and rewind the tape.

'I'm sitting here by the main scoreboard at Hove in the depths of winter, a ground on which I've spent much of my life … '

It's OK. True, the speed is a bit inconsistent – or rather, it's consistent but a tad fast. Frankly it makes me sound a bit light on my feet. But why not? Homosexuals need a voice in sport too. And anyway the distant honking of a car horn suggests Rentokil have arrived.

I remove the tape, pop it into my shoulder bag, along with the tea towel, the pencil and the cassette recorder. There's a post office that also sells Jiffy bags on my way back to the station. By tomorrow morning the third most dangerous man in London will be making his judgement on my efforts.

Live Feed Active

London. That great cesspool into which all the loungers and idlers of the Empire are irresistibly drained.

Two of them are currently seated in an anonymous office block in Hoxton. One is hoping the next few minutes will result in him fulfilling his dream of becoming a cricket commentator. The other is hoping his plastic fork won't break while he's eating his M&S prawn salad.

Sebastian Short certainly doesn't look like the third most anything. A squat, sturdy man in his late thirties with closely curled hair and a round face intersected by a pair of designer spectacles, he looks the epitome of the well-heeled city type. He sports a beautifully tailored suit, highly polished black shoes and one of those blue shirts with contrasting white collars that are so favoured by stockbrokers and antique dealers, the waist of which is starting to strain beneath the assault of several years of business lunches. His features are set in a permanently repressed smile, as if he'd like to tickle me under the chin with a feather duster but has been told it isn't good business practice.

In between mouthfuls of prawn he's giving me an introductory talk about the aims and ambitions of what he assures me will be a major new innovation in the way the summer game is perceived. No more hanging about for the pages of Ceefax to unravel or listening for desultory half-hour bulletins on *Sports Report*. From April all lovers of cricket will be able to gain access to live ball-by-ball coverage of every county championship down a domestic phone line, plus Sunday League and knockout matches, and all for only a pound a minute.

He takes another mouthful of prawns. Already his eyes are wandering towards an individual jelly trifle that sits on his desk awaiting its doom.

He resumes his narrative, but it's becoming difficult to concentrate. The fact is, I'm beginning to feel distinctly nervous here. Perhaps I've been reading too much Conan Doyle, but the surroundings are distinctly at odds with his claims for the media and telecommunications giant he apparently represents. This office block, for instance. It appears to be entirely unoccupied. Even the room in which we're sitting looks as if it had been furnished only moments before I stepped through the door by a team of inexperienced theatrical-set dressers.

The Adventure of the Empty House.

Everything about this interview suggests a scam. The floor is covered in those interlocking squares of industrial-strength carpet that give you third-degree burns if you sit on them, while the only other items of furniture are the metal desk, two aluminium chairs and an aspidistra on a dusty window ledge. The Venetian blind above it is broken, one end drunkenly concertinaed with the other still tightly shut. The view from the window offers no escape either, merely a concrete stairwell from which a dead pigeon impaled on some razor wire stares back with a single unblinking eyeball.

Even the plastic telephone and ghetto blaster on his desktop look as if they are props. What would happen if I were to lean forward and lift the receiver, only to hear silence? Perhaps I'm about to be set upon by men in hoods and marched off to the nearest cashpoint.

This is exactly the sort of scenario you read about, the kind of encounter that starts with a prawn salad and ends with body parts being scraped out of a drain in Muswell Hill. And not a soul on earth even knows I'm here. I deliberately didn't tell anyone about my interview today in case the gods punished me for my hubris and I was disappointed by the outcome. The only evidence to suggest that Everyball is a legitimate concern are the three million cassette tapes piled up around us on all sides of the room.

Short dabs the sides of his mouth with a white handkerchief from his breast pocket. He takes a swig of tepid coffee from a polystyrene beaker, wipes the fork clean with a tissue and begins peeling open the protective film on his trifle.

'Sorry to have to eat while talking,' he explains in cultured Home Counties tones. 'I'm here by myself today with only a coffee machine for company. Now, where were we?' He scoops out a forkful of custard.

What would Holmes make of it all? Five minutes in his company and the master detective would have garnered virtually every detail about his past, present and future. What was it he said in *The Adventure of the Creeping Man*? 'Always look at the hands first, Watson. Then cuffs, trouser knees and boots.'

Very well. His hands. Plump, honey-coloured skin but beautifully manicured. Obviously a man who spends a lot of time in the open air, but not in manual labour. A sportsman perhaps? Or a journalist? Those shoes he's wearing don't come cheap. And those cufflinks are bespoke: perhaps a gift from some grateful member of the underworld.

And what of his choice of food? Pre-packed items suggest someone on the move, but it's M&S, which can only mean a private income. A prawn salad indicates someone worried about his weight, but the jelly and cream dessert? Undoubtedly someone irresistibly drawn back to the comforting embrace of his schooldays.

As Holmes himself said in *The Man with the Twisted Lip*: 'One can learn a great deal from the observation of trifles.'

His voice drones on and on. A fly lies on its back on the desktop, sizzling with fear and waving its legs furiously in the air. I nod my head and offer up an occasional 'Mmm-mm?'

'So now you know all about us.' He takes a last forkful of raspberry jelly and tosses the carton into a nearby waste bin with deadly accuracy. 'That's our story in a nutshell. Now, let's turn to you. Your application.' He reaches underneath the desk and pulls out a yellow ring binder stuffed with forms and scrawled with a huge S in black felt-tip on the cover.

'Salter, Sexton, Sillwood.' He licks his stubby finger and sifts through an assortment of letters, ranging from officially typed foolscap to tiny lavender-scented notelets and sheets with *HMP Broadmoor* embossed along the top.

'From what I recall you say in your letter that you believe you have considerable potential as a live cricket commentator, and that you'd like the chance to put it to the test; also, you have a good practical knowledge of technical equipment, an ability to learn quickly and get along well in a group environment.'

'I hope so.'

He locates my letter, lines of desperate self-advertisement in garish red biro filled in on Gilly's kitchen table. 'Let's see. Ah yes, here we are.' He prods his glasses up the bridge of nose and studies the page closely.

'"All of which" – and I quote – "will hopefully be shown in my short demonstration tape enclosed with the letter."'

He puts the letter back in the folder and snaps it shut. 'It was this last claim that I found so intriguing, Michael. Which is why, quite frankly, I thought it would be interesting to meet up with you.'

He slides open another smaller drawer and produces the cassette tape from my freezing sojourn at Hove, the one with the word 'KOWABUNGA' emblazoned in transfers on the top, and slides it into his ghetto blaster. 'Have you actually heard this?' he asks.

'Not since I made it, but if it sounds a bit like Dick Emery—'

He stops me with a raised palm.

'Let's listen to it, shall we? I'd be interested in your thoughts. What was it you asked me to look out for? Considerable potential in live description, good technical skills and a particular knowledge of Sussex cricket.'

He presses Play and leans back in his chair, pressing his finger ends together. The machine emits a couple of muffled clunks followed by the familiar hiss of worn tape going through miniature spools. And then a voice speaks. The voice of an eight-year-old child in a bedroom in Hendon.

> *One eight is eight,*
> *Two eights are sixteen,*
> *Three eights are twenty-four,*
> *Four eights are thirty-two,*
> *Five eights are ... um ...*

'Forty.' That's the voice of Gilly. The child's voice pipes up again.

> *Forty. Six eights are forty-eight,*
> *Seven eights are fifty-six,*
> *Eight eights are ...*

'Sixty-four.' Gilly again.

> *Sixty-four,*
> *Nine eights are seventy-two,*
> *Ten eights are eighty,*
> *Eleven eights are eighty-eight,*
> *Twelve eights are ... er ...*

'Sixty-four.' This time it's the third most dangerous man in London. He leans forward with the inscrutable smile of an assassin and presses Stop.

'If it's any consolation it isn't the worst demonstration tape of all the many I've received.' He indicates the teetering mounds of cassettes. 'When I first heard it I wondered whether you were auditioning to be the scorer. But I have to say that although it shows an admirable grasp of statistics, it hardly convinces me that the person whose voice that is would be able to manage seven hours of live county cricket. In fact, I'm not sure he'd be allowed to stay up late enough for twenty overs in the last hour.'

It's a catastrophe. I obviously drew the wrong cassette out of my bag in the melee at the post office, one of the spares I never got to use, and stuffed that in the post by mistake. They all looked the same with those bloody turtles all over them. A schoolboy error. How could I have been so stupid?

I launch into a desperate apology, starting with the discovery of the ten-day-old *Guardian* and the Five Orange Pips, going on to the Solitary Cyclist and the Giant Rat of Sumatra, and ending with the Hound of the Basketballs. Finally I depict the chaotic scrum that was the queue at the Queens Road Post Office in central Brighton on pension day.

'I already had an inkling that it must have been a day of some travails for you. However … ' He reaches forward and traps the still-rotating bluebottle with his thumb. 'I'm afraid I may have to disappoint you. The position of regular Sussex commentator is already filled. A young man who played to a good standard in Zimbabwe and is currently training to be a lawyer. Knows his stuff, based in Hove and would be glad of the contract over the summer months.'

The buzzing slows to a futile hum. He brushes the quivering body up in his hands and deposits it gently in the dregs of the coffee, where it flails feebly in the murky liquid. And my dreams with it, tumbling down the Reichenbach Falls while above us Moriarty and Sir Sebastian Short stand watching with detached amusement. The bluebottle gives a last lurch, and sinks below the surface.

'Well, thanks anyway.' I rise heavily to my feet. His Last Bow.

'Just a moment.' He glances at the yellow ring binder again. 'You state on your form that you're an actor.'

'Yes, that's right.'

He reaches into his breast pocket and pulls out an MCC diary. 'And you mentioned, if I recall, that you're currently appearing in Arthur Miller's *A View from the Bridge* at the National Theatre.'

'Yes.'

'Which I believe stars the wonderful Michael Gambon.'

'That's right.'

'A magnificent actor. My father's favourite, in fact. I understand it's an unmissable production.'

'I think so.'

'So do the critics. The *Observer* called it one of the seminal productions of the last fifty years. The *Sunday Times* advised that one would kill to get a ticket. And the *Telegraph* called it a profoundly moving experience, confirming Arthur Miller as one of the giants of twentieth-century drama and Gambon as one of its greatest actors.'

'Indeed.'

'Which is why, I imagine, the show is entirely sold out for the entire run.'

'Is it?'

'Not a seat to be had, according to the box office to whom I applied for seats the other day.'

'We do seem to be full. We're in the Cottesloe Theatre, you see. It's by far the smallest of the auditoriums. Auditoria.'

'What a pity. My father celebrates his birthday next Saturday and had his heart set on seeing the production. He adores the theatre, always has done. Miller too is one of his favourites – he saw the original London production with Anthony Quayle in 1956.'

He leans forward. 'There are a couple of positions available for roving commentators still up for grabs. Individuals who could fill in on an occasional basis in case of illness or indisposition. The odd match at the Oval perhaps, or Lord's. Even Hove I expect.' He taps the side of the cassette on the desktop as if he were Professor Moriarty toying with a packet of Abdullah cigarettes. 'Ideal for someone with your parallel career, I should imagine – £80 a day and your evenings free.'

What was it Holmes said in *A Study in Scarlet*? In solving a problem, the grand thing is to be able to reason backwards.

'How many tickets were you hoping for?'

'It's his eightieth, you see. I have relatives coming from all points of the compass. Cocktails beforehand, dinner at Sheekeys afterwards in a private room.'

'How many were you hoping for?'

'It's going to be a substantial gathering of the clans. Some of the more obscure cousins I haven't seen myself for several years. There's a relative from Canada for instance—'

'How many were you hoping for?'

'We'd pay the going rate of course. I wasn't expecting any concessions.'

'How many were you hoping for?'

'Would sixteen be out of the question?'

Sixteen???? The man's deranged. Berserk. On a Saturday evening? It's impossible. I would be hard-pressed to find sixteen for the entire run of the play. Even Moriarty himself wouldn't display such a cruel sense of humour. There's no point in even trying. The company manager would have a heart attack.

But then I imagine me, in the *Test Match Special* commentary box at Lord's with a pair of headphones, surrounded by heroes of the game, my mouth stuffed with Dundee cake, winding up a pair of clockwork feet and setting them tramping across Brian Johnston's bald head. On £80 a day ...

What was it Holmes said? There is nothing so stimulating as the case in which everything seems to go against you.

'Leave it with me, Sebastian.'

He extends a manicured hand. 'You've just made my father's year, Michael. First game will be at Lord's on April twenty-sixth. Benson & Hedges Cup zonal round between Middlesex and Combined Universities. Welcome on board. You're familiar with the laws of the game, I take it? No balls, wides, the LBW rule. What about umpire's signals?'

I demonstrate the sign of four.

'Perfect. We'll be in touch.'

That's A Wrap

In his seminal book on the connection between cricket and suicide, *By His Own Hand*, David Frith catalogues with elegance and sensitivity the massive and profound pressures the game exerts upon the individual during long hours at the crease or wandering for days on end round the boundary rope with nothing to do but chew over his last and most desperate failure.

I reckon there might be a second volume to be written on the subject. This time he could concentrate on the connection between suicide and sitting in a leaking caravan on the boundary at Chelmsford cricket ground trying to find ways of describing a pointless end-of-season mid-table clash between two teams who have nothing left to play for, with a fellow commentator who keeps up an incessant prattle in a nasal twang each time I draw breath.

In fact I'd better keep talking. Don't want to give him the chance to butt in before the end of the over.

'So Boiling comes in again, he bowls, and it's chopped to gulley, no run, and the score remains sixty-nine for one after thirty overs, with Waugh on forty and Hardie seventeen, the man out Gooch for six.'

It's two years after my meeting with the Hoxton creeper, two summers in which I've fulfilled my dream to be paid to watch and talk about the game I love.

My colleague today for this end-of-season fixture between Essex and Surrey, Paul Reagan, would be baffled by any talk of causal linkage between cricket and hanging yourself from the nearest tree. He adores it. Every pocket of his shirt and jacket is bulging with folders, charts, *Playfair* annuals, jotter pads, field glasses and Post-it notes. He savours every moment of his job with a pure, unsullied fervour rarely seen outside hospital radio. Even a match like this at the fag end of the season. The moment I draw breath he'll be in like a rat up a drainpipe, giving his views on the over just gone, the over to come, the state of play, what happened in the same match last year, what might happen tomorrow ...

'Boiling in again. Hardie drives, Boiling stops it with his boot, no run, the score remains at sixty-nine for one, with Waugh on forty and Hardie on seventeen.'

Not that I want to criticise my colleague. Paul Reagan is a nice bloke, and an ideal Everyball commentator. He's enthusiastic, knowledgeable, still lives with his mum, is happy to be kitted out by the House of Millets and likes nothing better than a Birds Eye microwaveable meal for one and a railway modelling magazine.

'Boiling in again.'

But I'm learning something during my long stints at the mike this season. Being paid to watch and talk about cricket may be a whole lot better than digging coal down a mine or stripping carcasses in an abattoir, but it's a different thing from watching it of your own volition. If things become insufferable you can always go and do something more useful with your time, like collecting beer mats or seeing how many red estate cars drive past your lounge window in a given period.

'Boiling in again ... '

Once you've sold your soul it's different. You have to watch every ball whether you like it or not. And you must find something to say about it. You can't just doze off or pop to the local charity shops in the high street.

'Boiling in again ... '

And as I sit here now, in this tiny Formica-filled caravan, I've done a lot of thinking. And I've come to realise something. I don't like cricket any more.

It's been a curious couple of summers since I joined the staff of Everyball. Whether at Southampton, Canterbury, Hove or Lord's, the routine has remained the same. I've arrived at 10.30 in the morning, my task to locate the other regular with whom I'm to share the burden of eight hours chit-chat. This isn't difficult because:

a. There are usually only seventeen people in the crowd anyway.
b. The obligatory Everyball tie is a vibrant combo of blue and puce that can be seen across the ground.
c. Being ex-journos or failed players, my colleagues for the day will be installed either in the café or the bar.

Usually we're given our own hut or a corner of the score box to sit in, perched among fertiliser bags and bottles of slug killer. If the match is at one of the more rural grounds it's nothing more than a trestle table and a couple of tip-up seats on the boundary edge, exposed to broiling sun, torrential rain and the murderous shelling of cricket balls from impromptu games on the outfield during the lunch-break.

'Boiling in again ... '

At some grounds the announcement that I'm part of the Everyball commentary team has resulted in a free scorecard, cheery greetings from the girls working behind the bar and a free ham salad lunch in the players' canteen. (This isn't always a blessing – watching Derek Pringle devouring a chicken leg drenched in runny mayonnaise at Horsham remains the most nauseating interlude I have ever been party to at a live sports event.) At others, notably Lord's, we're regarded as spineless loafers who should be despatched immediately to the nearest Jobcentre.

But *TMS* it's not. It's not even close. *TMS* has a posse of commentators to ring the changes so that no individual ever has to be on mike for more than twenty minutes at a time. We have to talk for eight hours a day. They have access to television playbacks and the best view in the ground. We sit in some forgotten corner. The commentators on *TMS* have cakes and bottles of home-made wine with which to get through the day. We have to make do with stale sandwiches and a tube of Werther's.

'Boiling in again … '

And crucially, *TMS* is on the radio. Most of our callers are either obsessives illicitly using the company phone or men who have wrongly dialled up our number hoping to speak to a pre-op transsexual. The length of the average call is under a minute, and it's not easy to indulge in airy badinage about pigeons or red buses going down the Harleyford Road under such strictures. You couldn't even wind up a pair of clockwork feet in that time, let alone set them down on the table.

'Boiling in again … '

Not to say that there haven't been moments. Of course there have. In the tour match at Hove a year ago, Viv Richards hit a straight six through into the commentary booth in which I was stationed, delivering the ball onto my lap and half a plate-glass window down the back of my collar. I even got to keep the ball afterwards. I spent another delightful afternoon with Derbyshire's Kim Barnett sitting at my side as impromptu summariser, dispensing remarkably candid and perspicacious insights into his team-mates. He couldn't have known that earlier in the day I'd summarised his innings of thirty in an entire pre-lunch session as possibly the most turgid display of batting I'd ever witnessed. No matter. If I avoided contact with all the people who've slagged me off on stage I'd never step outside the door.

But then there have been the other times.

The matches when we've been left untended in a shed for days without seeing anyone, two anonymous middle-aged men in ripped office chairs with a telephone console. It's been hard not to feel like a leper at times such as those. At one venue my lunch was pushed under the doorframe of our booth while I was still commentating.

'Boiling in again … '

And there have been the other, still worse, times when the eight-hour stints at the mike have been so grindingly dull, such a relentless water torture, that I've had a terrible urge to say something terrible and stupid and crass, just to see if anyone, a listener, my fellow commentator, even mission-control back in Hoxton, is even listening any more.

'And Boiling runs the full length of the pitch and joins Waugh in a chorus of 'The Birdie Song' and Mother Teresa signals one short and the score stays at Brazil one, England nil, with Sigmund Freud taking strike and Stephen Hawking requiring a runner …'

And that was before the final straw. The incident last week at Hastings that convinced me that today, my final contract of this season, must also be my last.

I'd always liked Andy Babington. A large loose-limbed medium-pace bowler and native of Sussex, I'd seen him come up through the ranks until he'd finally won his county cap and became an integral part of the side. He'd always struck me as the sort of honest enthusiast who'd become a professional through hard work, honest endeavour, a sunny personality and a love for the history and traditions of the great game. So I wasn't surprised when, during the match between Sussex and Gloucestershire last week, he'd stopped behind my commentary table and seemed to be taking a keen interest in the literature which, like all good commentators, I'd brought along with me to flesh out the bones of the encounter.

In this case it was my *Gallery of Famous Edwardian Cricketers*, a huge and glossy compendium of photographs of players from cricket's Golden Age. It was lying open on a study of the great Gilbert Jessop, legend of Gloucestershire cricket, Edwardian hero, and a man who on this very ground in 1907 had hit the fastest century ever then recorded, taking just forty-two minutes. All good background stuff to pad out the drinks breaks and change of innings.

It was a lovely to see a cricketer of today paying homage to a revered predecessor, taking time to honour a giant of the game leaping out from some long-forgotten crease to smite the ball into the middle distance.

And then Andy Babington asked, 'Who's that twat?'

Those few words sealed my decision.

The fact is I've got too close to it all. When you're sitting in the crowd you can project whatever fantasies you like onto the players out on the field. They can remain your heroes. Distantly glimpsed gods to be dressed in the garb of your own imagination; in my case, blokes just like you who love the game and sit up talking along about it long into the night, who have pride and interest in its noble lineage and the heroes who have trod the turf before them.

But of course they're not. Most of them are just great hulks who happen to be very good at hitting a four or bowling an inducker. Most of them couldn't tell Jack Hobbs from Russell Hobbs, and equate having a sense of humour with putting Black Forest gateau in your jockstrap. If you told them you were a great fan of Jessop's they'd probably ask if you could put in their films for processing while you're there.

So it's time for me to go. If I want to get my love of cricket back I've got to step back from it all. Earlier today I even found myself praying for rain so that we could stick on a recorded summary, slope off to the pavilion bar and watch a Western on the telly. When the prospect of watching Audie Murphy seems appetising, you know things are bad.

I have only one regret about it all. In the two years I've been doing the job, I've never come up with a single good quote: the one telling description that would cause my fellow commentator to purr with pleasure or somebody phoning in to think my phrase alone was worth a quid to hear. The sort of thing that made John Arlott the doyen of commentators, the priceless epithet that was his trademark and that still gets reproduced in compendiums of cricket prose or collections of famous quotations year after year.

'So Tuffy Mann of England has bowled George Mann of South Africa. Another case of Mann's inhumanity to Mann ... '

'Asif Masood approaches the wicket like Groucho Marx chasing a pretty waitress ... '

'Funny name Cunis, neither one thing or the other ... '

And his tribute to my dad's hero Sir Jack Hobbs:

The master: records prove the title good.
Yet figures fail you, for they cannot say
How many men whose names you never knew
Are proud to tell their sons they saw you play ...

Dad was one of those men. And I'm one of those sons. No wonder Arlott hung up his headphones and sloughed off to Alderney and a slow delicious death by claret after that little lot. He had nothing left to prove. What I'd give to have come up with something, anything, one-tenth as memorable. But I've not managed it. And after today it'll be too late.

There's a nudge in my ribs.

Did I just nod off? Surely to God? No, but the next worst thing. I've missed a ball, and Reagan is reminding me, as if I needed it, that Boiling's in again. Not only that, but Boiling has got one to rise and it's struck the Essex batsman Mark Waugh on the hand. The batsman has thrown off his glove and is inspecting his little finger, which in the context of today's action is a major incident of thrilling proportions.

'So what did you make of that, Paul?' Always a good standby when you didn't see it yourself.

Paul Reagan's dentist's-drill whine clicks effortlessly into gear. He can't wait. In fact, I could go home now if I wanted and he'd need nothing more than the odd drink of water and a rubdown with some linseed oil to see him through to stumps.

'Well, Michael, it undoubtedly leapt and has caught Waugh on the back of the hand, and the Essex physio is running onto the pitch with the magic sponge and a drink of water so there'll be quite a delay, and the score if you're ringing in is sixty-nine for one …'

He's off. All is well.

And so I've decided this is it. I'm not going to bother next season. I've lost my love of the game, and I want it back. It's been great, it really has. But I've had enough. Something has happened which I never imagined: I'm actually bored with the sound of my own voice …

Reagan on the other hand is nearly out of his chair with excitement.

'The physio attending to Waugh's hand has got something out there to bring the swelling down, and the score is sixty-nine for one … '

He indicates for me to take over while he reaches for his field glasses. I slide into automatic pilot as I regurgitate the scorecard, fall of wickets and latest weather outlook, just as I've done hundreds of times before. I'm going on holiday next week, and by the time I return the season will be over. Rumour has it that next year the entire Everyball enterprise is going to be relocated to the office in Hoxton anyway, with a skeleton staff confined in little booths regurgitating ticker tape updates from Reuters. Apparently take-up hasn't been as great as they'd hoped. There just isn't enough demand for pre-op transsexuals to go around.

Reagan cuts in excitedly. 'Mike, it looks like the physio is wrapping a packet of frozen peas round the swelling on the bats-man's hand, extraordinary really, one would have thought there'd be more high-tech solutions nowadays, but I suppose the old ways are the best … '

I turn to Reagan. Sitting there in his Millets shirt and his cords and bottle-top glasses and thinning hair and fevered expression. And I think to myself, what the hell.

Mann's inhumanity to Mann.

'Interesting incident this, Paul, especially because it's occurred before. I've read a famous book by Tolstoy about it.'

Reagan glances at me and swallows hard. He doesn't like

flights of fancy or comments that divert from the Everyball formula of stats, strokes, overs left, runs needed and career averages. Oblique references to things he can't comprehend make him nervous.

'And with the score at – I'm … er … I'm sorry, Mike, I don't quite understand … A famous book?'

'Well, haven't you ever read *Waugh and Peas?*'

And do you know? At that moment the door to the caravan blows gently open. Maybe it's just a faulty door catch. Or maybe it's the ghost of John Arlott putting a gentle hand on my arm. 'Come on, sonny,' I can hear him saying in that charcoaly Hampshire burr. 'You won't do better than that. *Waugh and Peas.* Come and have a warming glass of something … '

I scrawl 'Fancy an ice cream?' on Reagan's jotting pad. He nods furiously and is off without a glance, cataloguing for any eager listeners the last fifteen occasions on which an Essex batsman has had to receive treatment on an injured figure on the third day of a county championship match at Chelmsford in September.

The air is cool and sweet after the stale farts and staler feet of the Everyball caravan. I think I'll have a lolly. Paul will be all right. He'd prefer it this way. And who knows? Next year I may come back again. Essex versus Surrey at Chelmsford could be a good match. But I'll make sure I've paid to get in and that nothing comes between me and the game I love apart from a boundary rope and a packet of Scampi Nik Naks.

A couple of rosy-cheeked schoolkids are playing a game of cricket with an old bat and a composite ball behind the caravans. One of them lashes a fierce pull in my direction, and without thinking I stick out an arm and bring off a stinging one-handed catch. Probably one of the best I've ever taken. A shiver of half-remembered pleasure ripples through me. God, how long is it since I actually caught a cricket ball?

Actually I wouldn't mind swinging a bat again. Perhaps I gave up on my dream too soon. Not of playing for England, of course. I'm never going to be much good, but it must still be possible for me to enjoy playing for fun, as a way of losing a bit of middle-aged weight, getting some fresh air and widening my circle of friends.

And then there's that visceral thrill of connecting perfectly to send the ball skimming to the boundary. I can still summon up a tiny tingle of pleasure at the memory of it. It's been nearly ten years now, but I'm still only in my early thirties.

I wonder if I could still do it?

Harry

The following spring I answer an ad in the classified section of my local newspaper inviting keen cricketers to join a local team for a Saturday afternoon league. It seems the easiest and most effective way of seeing if I would still enjoy the same camaraderie, the humour, the odd, oblique view it gives practitioners on the foibles of human life. I even purchase some new kit and a Duncan Fearnley bat to show willing.

But Saturday league cricket turns out to be a strange and menacing world. A bit like an episode of *The Avengers*, it may appear normal, but everyone stops speaking when you enter the pub.

For instance, all club cricketers seem to be called Dave. The bloke I have to ring up to get a game in the first place is called Dave. His best mate Dave gives me a lift to the ground on the outskirts of the town, but first we have to make a detour to pick up Dave who has the kit bag.

The other players in the team are Dave Smith, Dave Garrard, Dave Kelly, Dave Finney, Dave Brown, Dave Wyatt, Dave Clarke and Dave Davies. There's also a bloke everyone calls Davey because he's a bit of a wit, in that he likes dropping lighted matches down your cricket shirt and putting dog turds in your cricket boots.

Not that I've got anything against Daves. Some of my best friends are Daves. But Saturday cricket seems to attract a certain sort of bloke, and all of them wash up in either this team or the ones we play against. Before they can play they each seem to have to put on an array of surgical appliances and elasticated supports: knee pads, shin pads, trusses – all supplemented by a variety of aftershaves that could fell Wes Hall at a hundred yards. Their pre-match warm-up involves gathering round the open driver's door of their cars to listen to live football commentary on the radio, or chatting up the divorcee with the enormous knockers who runs the adjoining tearooms.

To my joy and surprise I score a couple of decent twenties and even a thirty-odd, but it's impossible to enjoy my unexpected success as each innings is played in a climate of impending fear lest I do something stupid. Dropped catches or first-ball ducks are mercilessly berated or ridiculed both during and after the match, with the result that each fixture usually ends with a beer-fuelled altercation in the pub. And I'm no aesthete, but conversations about how to fix a faulty starter motor on a Vauxhall Cavalier and whether Tina takes it up the arse have a limited appeal.

After several matches in May and June I stop returning Dave's calls, and my gleaming kit bag is soon gathering dust in the loft. It's odd. I thought I would enjoy the crack but be useless at the game, whereas the opposite has occurred. I've batted far better than I thought possible and have discovered a new poise and confidence at the wicket that I could only have dreamt of as a kid – the trouble is I have nobody to share it with. By the first week of July I've put my own ad in the classified. *Brand new Duncan Fearnley cricket bat, excellent condition, hardly used, a few marks on edges.*

But then I get a contract to appear in a season of plays at the Chichester Festival Theatre, and while there I'm asked if I could cobble together a side to take on the resident stage technicians, who are organising a match to raise money for a local charity. A phone call to a few actors I know who've mentioned a love of the game reveals unexpected enthusiasm for such a project. Ex-actor Barney Kent is now a drama teacher at a luxury school for posh refugees' kids in leafy Surrey and thinks he can corral a couple of members of the staff room, and my best mate Jason

Buckingham, an affable young toff whom I met when we acted together at Bristol and who is 415th in line to the throne, offers to bring along Guy McKenzie, an Aussie actor who bowls lively away swing. With the game being played in West Sussex I'm even able to recruit a few old school mates from the past – not Nancy or Mongey, but a few others whom I dimly recall – Chris Buckle who sat next to me in geography, and Gordon Quill, with whom I occasionally did amateur dramatics.

Then the college professor who owns the flat above mine in London, who lectures on the poetry of William Wordsworth and homoerotic influences in the films of Alfred Hitchcock, announces he's a keen opening batsman. Then an itinerant musician I occasionally have a drink with in my local pub announces he used to play regularly back in Spalding and would like to see if he can still do it. Then a mate of my brother's, an Irishman called Pat Rafferty, informs me he bowls occasional slow left arm. Before I know it I've got a full eleven, all with their own cricket whites.

We lose. But I score thirty-nine going in first including a sumptuous drive through mid-on for a boundary, a shot I've not attempted since my coaching session at Hove with Les Lenham in the chalet. We challenge the technicians to a rematch, which we win, with me top scoring on twenty-seven.

The following summer we advance from two fixtures to ten; we buy a club kit bag, and even some kit to go in it. With each game we acquire more players, almost all of them blokes like me who've tried league cricket and got fed up with being shouted at when they fumble the ball and tired of being asked to compare foreskin length.

And suddenly, without noticing, I've got my wish. I'm captain and prime mover of my own miniature empire. Not merely names attached to metal rollers but real flesh-and-blood human beings who owe their existence on the field to me, and who, like Callard and Bowser, are grateful to me for giving them life and are prepared to do my bidding. At least for the most part. What to call ourselves? As captain and organiser it is my right and privilege to choose the name. The Reprobates? The Luvvies? The UB 40s? The Old Crocks?

And then I see it. Staring back at me one evening from my *Gallery of Famous Cricketers*. Despite Andy Babington's aspersions, the book still continues to fascinate me with its haunting images of long-forgotten heroes from a previous century. And there, on page 189, is an image that encapsulates everything that once made my ten-year-old heart skip a beat back in 1966.

He may not be Colin Milburn, but he must have inspired a previous generation of fatties to believe the game might have room for them in a similar way. A small corpulent man with a tiny faded cap squashed to his head and a burgeoning walrus moustache. Caught by the photographer in the act of hoisting a pair of cumbersome flannels up over his huge girth, Harry Baldwin of Hampshire is one of the most compelling images from the annals of Victorian cricket. He stares back uncertainly at the camera lens, his features a subtle blend of suspicion and friendliness. Here is a perfect icon, if ever there was one, for every overweight, pasty-faced cricketer who has ever hitched his trousers up over his stomach in an effort to discover a waistline. All he needs is an ice lolly in his hand and it could be me.

So the Harry Baldwin Occasionals are born.

For the next fifteen years my life and the fortunes of the Harry Baldwin Occasionals become inextricably linked. Even Owzthat was never as all-consuming as this. Ten fixtures become twelve, then thirteen, and eventually a steady seventeen a season. And the pool of players swells proportionately until the team contact sheet occupies an entire side of A4.

At the helm, and everywhere else, is me, the all-seeing provider, the Big Brother, captain, fixture secretary, locker-up of the pavilion, unblocker of sinks, putter-out of the boundary markers, opening batsman and principal lift-giver for anyone coming from west London. My petrol bills soar, my invitations to weekends away and summer parties decrease and then stop altogether, and my circle of friends reduces and concentrates into the fifteen or so middle-aged cricketers who now form the nucleus of the squad.

I no longer care. In fact, I like it that way. Like the amiable drunk who slips into the hardened alcoholic, the best years of my life are about to become nothing more than a blur. Runs, wickets, statistics, batting orders, road directions and next available public toilet on the M23. I'm content in my oblivion.

I'm doubly lucky in that I'm now going out with a partner who's both understanding and enthusiastic. Julia is an actress from Gainsborough in Lincolnshire with whom I feel an immediate rapport after she reveals her parents owned a sweetshop. After a few conversations in the pub after rehearsals about the merits of Cadbury's Snacks versus Bar Sixes and why it's no longer possible to find a bar of Fry's Five Boys, we begin dating, which in turn leads on to other more profound comparisons. When she announces that she's distantly related to Derbyshire opening batsman John Morris, I can no longer resist.

By the time the Baldwins are up and running, Julia is happily attending each game as a matter of course, helping to put the score up, washing the cups after the tea interval and rallying disappointed players after spectacular failures. The other Baldwins adore her. Even I have to confess that short of going out with Rachael Heyhoe-Flint I couldn't ask for a more suitable partner.

So I meet her parents and we begin looking in estate agents' windows.

For the first couple of seasons I'm able to retain an encyclopaedic knowledge of the Baldwins' week-by-week fortunes. I can tell anyone who's foolish enough to ask how many matches we've won and lost, which batsman is highest in the averages and what happened in the corresponding fixture last time round. But inevitably it eventually melds into an amorphous mass. Any game could be every game. Each weekend may be entirely different but is simultaneously exactly the same. Pick a season, any season:

cut into any part of it, and you'll find the same players, the same events, the same results.

Not that I'm suggesting these years are wasted. As captain and prime mover in the Harry Baldwins I acquire a lot of life skills during my years of addiction. I learn about love, hate, joy, despair, triumph, tragedy, deceit, recrimination, slander, ridicule, indignation, treachery, infatuation, jealousy, bitterness, remorse, disloyalty, revenge, vitriol, cynicism, infidelity, prevarication, bluff, sadism, humiliation, and, above all, anger management. I also learn the location of every Little Chef in the south-east.

And as for the techniques and strategies of cricket? I'm not sure I make much progress on that front. But as the sagging waistband of Harry's trousers suggests in the original photograph, that's the least of my worries.

SECOND
INNINGS

W.G. Gracefullys

A pregnant newlywed wakes her cricketing husband. It's still dark.

'Darling, I need to talk to you, something's happened … '

He sits up sharply.

'Wharrisit?'

'Well, while you were asleep I had to go to the loo again, and then I thought I heard the cat crying to be let out, so I went downstairs, and when I opened the door she bolted out into the back yard … '

'And … ?'

And it was pouring with rain so I tried to catch her and I slipped on the wet grass and fell rather badly. I don't think anything's happened but—'

'Oh Christ—'

'Don't worry, I'm sure it's OK. I just think I need to reassure myself … '

'Jesus, I can't believe it, after all we've gone through.'

'Darling, you're going to have to phone someone—'

'Yes. Yes, of course, I'll do it now.'

'Tell them I broke my fall with my arm. I didn't land on my stomach or anything so it's just to put my mind at rest. Darling?'

But she's already lost him.

'Dave, it's me here. Apparently it's been raining. Ground's absolutely soaked, you can hardly keep your footing. Wifey's just gone arse over tit and she wasn't even running. It's bloody typical, not a drop the last four weekends and now this, just when we've got a match it chucks it down. You'd better see if we can change to the all-weather surface … '

He snaps off the phone and turns back to her. 'Don't look so worried,' he says, squeezing her arm. 'As long as we don't wear studs I'm sure there won't be a problem … '

It's Sunday morning, 6 May 1990. The start of the Baldwins' first full cricket season, and the day I've been looking forward to ever since stumps were drawn in our final match the previous September. Sometimes I've thought it would never come. Yet this is the moment. And I hardly dare look.

But it's great news. A sharp snappy line of brilliant white between curtain fabric and our bedroom window frame sends a surge of pure visceral joy coursing through my veins. Thank God. I lean over and kiss Julia's tousled head, which is just peeking above the duvet. She stirs momentarily.

'Is it sunny?' she murmurs.

I kiss her hair. She must be using a different shampoo. It always used to smell of Silvikrin on Sunday mornings.

'Is it sunny?' she asks again, more anxiously this time.

'I love you, you know that, don't you?' I reply tenderly.

'Thank God,' she mumbles and pulls the duvet high over her head.

I leap out of bed, throw the windows wide open and look down on the dry, sun-kissed street. Elderly cats with wobbling undercarriages are sunning themselves on the hot tarmac. From an open window in an adjoining house the sound of Steve Wright's *Sunday Love Songs* drifts up the street, the warm burnished tones of Lionel Ritchie asking if it's him I'm looking for.

Not today, Lionel. The only thing I'm looking for is a drying breeze, fluffy clouds and a bowling attack of overweight men with large beards.

Our neighbour Sandy is already down there polishing his Range Rover prior to a family day out at Chessington World of Adventures. I suppose that's what people who don't play cricket are forced to do on a Sunday: play with their kids. And look, there right on cue are his two youngsters, little Hamish and Esme, playing soldiers in their front garden. Bless them.

'Hello, Hamish. Hello, Esme. Lovely day!!'

They wave back up at me. Sandy stops polishing the bonnet and looks up. 'Hey, Mike,' he calls up in a syrupy Edinburgh lilt. 'It's surely going to be a hot one for yous all today. Dinna come back until you've got hundred. Think of Alec Stewart!'

I demonstrate a mimed pull shot with my right fist through the open window and give them an elaborate thumbs-up sign. Good old Sandy. He wouldn't know Alec Stewart from Moira Stewart, but he's a good sort. And what a day! What a life! The match is on, the sun is hot and the track is hard.

Come to mention it, it's not the only thing that's hard. It's impossible not to be filled with a feeling of magnanimity for my fellow man. And woman. In fact, piquant sexual desire is welling up inside at the mere sight of Julia's head, still just visible again on the pillow a few feet away.

I know. I'll make her breakfast in bed. It's the least I can do considering she's going to be spending the rest of the morning buttering forty-four tuna and mayonnaise doorsteps and sitting on the M23 for two hours each way.

In any case, it's time I got a move on. There's so much to do: pads to be whitened, boot studs to be tightened, road directions to consult and fellow players to ring up and engage in intense discussions about team tactics. Our extended fixture list means we're kicking off against a team we haven't played before, the W.G. Gracefullys: a side dedicated to W.G. Grace himself, the godfather of the game. Not only do their players sport impressive beards, but their ground on the fringes of the Ashdown forest boasts a pub opposite the pitch and a preserved steam railway at the end of the lane. It should be a great day. Please God we put up a good show.

Within minutes I'm standing in the kitchen with thickly buttered toast and a mug of freshly brewed coffee, glancing fondly as our pet pug dog, little Oona, does the mother of all dumps on the flower bed. Even that looks poetic this morning. Bless her – her bowel movements are almost as reliable as Rex Scudamore's inswinger to the left-hander. Come to think of it, I should give Rex a call, just to discuss tactics. But as if on cue the phone rings.

In fact, it's not Rex but our club treasurer, Chris Buckle. He's calling from Brighton, where he still lives, to say that a strong south-west breeze is predicted over south-east England this afternoon so given that the opposition ground is in the lee of the South Downs would it be an idea to put Barney Kent on from the car-park end as it may assist his gentle outswing.

For the next twenty minutes we launch into an animated discussion of the pros and cons of such a daring strategy. Neither of us have the first clue what we're talking about, and Barney Kent wouldn't know how to bowl an inswinger if his life depended on it, but that's not the point. Discussing tactics and ploys is one of the rituals of the day. It's a male thing.

By the time I've put the phone down, Julia's toast is rock hard and the coffee has an unsightly scum of congealing milk on the top. But it'll have to do, especially as I've yet to discuss with Les Sweeney whether he wants to bat at five or six this afternoon. Julia will understand. She ought to be getting up anyway: my whites are still in the tumble dryer and someone has to go to Sainsbury's for some bloater paste and orange squash. Although I wouldn't mind some nookie this morning. Funny how that single white strip of light at the window can provoke carnal desire that all the porn manuals and imagined depravations can no longer muster.

What was that gag that Ken Dodd always tells?

'My wife said, "Let's make love." I replied, "Hang on, I haven't thought of anyone … "'

Obviously not a cricketer.

Imperial War Museum

It's Sunday morning. Seven days later. The Baldwins' second match of the season, and the day I've been looking forward to ever since stumps were drawn in our match last week against the W.G. Gracefullys and I left the field with a gutsy twenty-seven-not-out to my name. There have been times since then when I've thought today would never come. This is the moment. I hardly dare look.

But instead of last Sunday's snappy white line, today there is only a dull grey blur, an undefined, lustreless shroud, and the only noise in the street is the patter of raindrops on the window pane. And that tiny sprinkling sound breaks me.

All those phone calls, that bulk purchase of jam tarts – what's the point? We might as well cancel the whole bloody season if it's going to be like this. Powerless to intervene, I have nothing to look forward to except the phone call at 11.30 from the opposition captain confirming that he's had a look at the pitch and there's no way we can play on that without waders. Or, as the War Museum's skipper pithily described it when it rained just as hard before the corresponding fixture last season, 'The fucking fucker's fucked ... '

The very sight of that blurry grey line beneath the curtain provokes something dark and frightening deep within me, and I resort to the only solution left to disappointed males of the species. I crack the back of my skull against the headboard as hard as I can.

Staring out of the bedroom window at the swamp that was once our road confirms the worst. On the opposite pavement that oleaginous prat Sandy is loading that ozone-destroying gas-guzzler with those two twee kids. They're all dressed in blue sou'westers and bright yellow gumboots. He sees me standing at the window and gives a rueful wave. Hamish and Esme are stamping in the puddles and laughing with the sheer delight of it all. Scottish gits.

Julia stirs momentarily.

'Is it sunny?' she murmurs.

I break wind.

'Is it sunny?' she asks again, more anxiously this time.

This time I don't answer. Within seconds Julia is sitting bolt upright in bed. She knows what the silence portends. It's going to take all her efforts now to prevent the miasma of doom from descending and destroying my, and therefore her, one day off.

She makes me a bacon sandwich with tomato sauce. She tries to make me laugh by coming out of the shower doing a Carmen Miranda impression naked except for a towel round her hair. She doesn't utter a word of complaint when most of my first pee of the day misses the toilet bowl and streams all over the floor. She doesn't even complain when I drop globules of Gibbs SR on our new Conran bath mat.

But it's no use. The War Museum skipper calls to break the news for a second consecutive year that the fucker's fucked. And like every other occasional cricketer in the kingdom, I'm going to make sure that if my Sunday is ruined, then my partner's will be as well.

It'll all be done very subtly. It'd be too simple to say, 'Darling, I was so looking forward to this, here's fifty quid, go over and see your best mate and have a wonderful day, enjoy a meal out, I know it's stupid but I am so disappointed that I just want to sit here in a puddle of self-pitying misery and watch reruns of *The High Chaparral*.'

No. As we sit listening to *The Archers* I give meaningless assurances that I don't really mind, I'm already over it. I'm perfectly happy sitting here listening to Linda Snell's preparations for the fete and how Mike Tucker is coping with new silage quotas.

When Julia asks if I'd fancy taking Oona for a walk in the rain on Hampstead Heath I reply, 'Of course.' It'll be lovely, a nice change, after all we haven't done it for ages. When she suggests perhaps a movie later on, followed by a romantic meal, for which she'll treat me knowing how disappointed I must be to lose the cricket, I don't know whether to laugh or cry.

Because we both know the form. My mission is to squeeze any scintilla of happiness out of the next ten hours by walking beside her, eyes fixed on the pavement, grunting monosyllabically once every half an hour, falling asleep in the movie, picking an argument with the waiter in the Chinese restaurant, before the inevitable confrontation and recriminations explode just before midnight.

This is what now lies ahead. It's almost a tradition.

All part of the rich panoply of the best-loved game.

Match Report:
Harry Baldwins vs the Imperial War Museum.
Match abandoned.

Old Wokingham

In his masterwork, *The Art of Captaincy*, Mike Brearley, archi-
tect of England's 1981 triumph and generally considered to be
the keenest brain ever to turn his hand to the summer game,
cites meticulous preparation as the keynote of success. I copy out
this telling sentence on a Post-it note and attach it to the hand-
set of our telephone at the end of our first full season. We're
hoping to add the team of Old Wokingham to our fixture list for
the following summer, and if we are to triumph in our encounter
the spadework has to be done, not on the pitch in five months'
time, but now, on this chilly Sunday evening in November.
Meticulous preparation: I repeat the mantra three times and pick
up the receiver. I'm about to make my single most telling contribution to the entire game.

'Is that Dave? It's Mike Simkins here from the Harry
Baldwin Occasionals. I think we both know my cousin Pauline?'

Dave has been recommended to me by Pauline, whose son
plays in their team and who thought it would be nice to get the
two clubs together. Dave knows nothing about the Baldwins.
Thus Old Wokingham's entire preparation for the match is going
to be predicated on Dave's impressions gathered during the next
ten minutes.

'Mike, hi, good to hear from you, Pauline told me you'd be
calling. So you run a cricket team?'

I've already learnt a lot and he's only spoken nineteen
words. In these few brief seconds I've already assessed that the
prognosis is grim. I was hoping for a voice sounding wheezy

and out of breath, perhaps with a hint of smoker's asthma or fugged with the blur of claret. But Dave sounds young, sporty, one of the lads, the sort of man who prefers a game of squash and a Britvic to a rib of sirloin steak and a three-for-two offer from your local Threshers.

So I have two conflicting tasks to accomplish in the next few minutes. The first is to convince Dave that the Baldwins are worth them giving us one of the precious Sunday slots in their crowded itinerary. This is easily done – he's merely looking for a few assurances, namely that we'll turn up on time with eleven players, each with a full complement of arms, legs and heads, and that once on the field we'll provide an afternoon of competitive, vital, combative cricket: keen, energetic and purposeful.

The second (entirely conflicting) aim is to suggest that although we are competitive, keen and purposeful, we are at the same time fragile, lacking in ability, reliant on one or two key individuals whose attendance I cannot guarantee, and that unless they field their weakest side it will be a disappointing mismatch which will end soon after tea with a general feeling from every-one that we've wasted our one day off.

This is to ensure that when we meet them on Sunday 12 May 1991, we beat them by over a hundred runs.

Any club which has the name of an actual town in the title spells trouble. And Old Wokingham has a particularly chilling ring, suggesting committees, bank accounts, close-season dinner dances, nets, sight screens and boundary markers, showers with hot and cold running water and a proper tea urn. We prefer teams with names like the Ravers, the Contemptibles or the Stragglers, names that at least provide a shred of hope by suggesting that they, like us, will be composed of a motley collec-tion of overweight men in various stages of marital breakdown.

'So tell me a bit about yourselves,' says Dave. 'Pauline says your team plays every Sunday. Good standard?'

'Not bad, not bad.' Not bad is an all-purpose expression that could cover anything from a decent county side down to a knockabout on the local rec. I haven't found out enough about Dave yet to want to reveal my hand, so I get him talking and adjust to taste. 'What about you?'

The phrases I'm looking for are: 'Occasionals like yourselves.' 'One set of pads.' 'Pub team.' And, 'Sometimes we let our youngsters have a go.' What I don't want is what Dave now describes.

'Well, Mike, we have a very active set-up. We turn out three sides on a Saturday; our first eleven play in the North Hants league, then we have a second eleven, and a third eleven which tries to blend in kids from our junior colts team by mixing them up with some of the old hands who are turning forty and thinking of calling it a day. It'll be that side, really, that you'll be playing, plus one or two first-teamers just to give it all a bit of stiffening. That sound good?'

Well, no, Dave, it doesn't sound good. It sounds bloody awful. His description of what we are likely to face at Old Wokingham has already caused a slight but instinctive bowel movement deep within. We don't want multiple elevens, we don't want leagues, and we certainly don't like the idea of their oldest players thinking of retiring at forty when if they played for us they would still be in the vanguard of our youth policy. As for the word 'colts' ...

Youngsters are one thing. I was a youngster once. Colts are another. Youngsters mean ten-year-old boys who lumber out in their dads' pads, falling over every twenty yards or so, who once at the wicket have to be told which way to face, who aren't strong enough to lift the bat unaided, and who you can patronise with a few underarm lobs to please their mum gazing on adoringly from beyond the boundary before dismissing them with the first decent ball you choose.

Colts is a very different word. Colts are fifteen-year-olds who have attended colts coaching courses. Colts come to the crease in helmets and with emblems of past festivals stitched to their pullovers, whereas youngsters spend their time at the crease trying to stop their box falling out through their trouser legs. Colts spend their time driving savagely between extra cover and mid-off. Youngsters are happy enough to survive a single ball against the fastest under-sixteen bowler in the south-east. Colts are already shouting, 'Push, Darren, push,' as they turn for the second.

'So how would you describe yourselves?' says Dave. 'Just so I get an idea?'

What I should say is something like this.

'Well, Dave, we're a load of florid-faced broken-down men whose delusions of grandeur are matched only by the complete bankruptcy of our ability. We have a couple of opening batsmen who are terrified of being hit, our main stroke maker, on whom we rely for most of our runs, only plays one match in four because he spends most of his spare time networking with film producers at Soho House, we've got an opening bowler whose main claim to fame is that his mum used to run a launderette in Scunthorpe to which Ian Botham brought his washing, and between us we can muster three ruptured hernias, a slipped disc, a case of shingles, and on the evidence of my eyes in the showers last August, an undescended testicle. Our youth policy consists of a single individual under thirty who might or might not turn up on time, and our spin-bowling department consists of a sixty-year-old bloke from Cork called Pat Rafferty who, on the rare occasions that the ball actually reaches the other end, usually bowls wides … '

What I actually say is something like this.

'Well, Dave, we're essentially a wandering team, but we play twenty or so matches a year, we like to play to win but make sure we have a bit of a giggle along the way, and I like to think we're as good a bunch of blokes as you'll find in a midsummer day's march … '

It does the trick. I've disarmed him by using the phrase 'a bit of a giggle', the standard male currency of the warehouse canteen or factory production line, and then thrown him completely off balance with the slight rhetorical flourish: 'midsummer day's march'. It sets us out as something a bit special, and it also taps into any slight sense of inferiority he might be feeling. I've reckoned that because he's called Dave and he lives in Wokingham, chances are he's not been to university, is stuck in middle management, perhaps in a double-glazing firm or working for the council. Hearing 'midsummer day's march' carelessly tossed off down the phone makes him wary about asking too many more questions and showing himself up as an ill-educated oik.

It's time for the clincher.

'And after all, Dave, all we really want is quite simply a bloody good game of cricket ... '

Dave murmurs his approval. This is language he understands. All that clubs ever profess to want is a bloody good game of cricket. Which is true, if only partially. I'm not actually lying, just not completing the sentence. In fact, what we want is 'a bloody good game of cricket, at the end of which we humiliate you'.

'One last thing, Dave – oh dear, hang on, I've lost the piece of paper ... ' I put down the receiver momentarily and rustle the nearest piece of paper to hand, in this case a back copy of the *Pug Dog Rescue & Rehoming Quarterly*, which is lying on the desk. But the mere sound of rustling paper persuades Dave that we have files, contacts, sheets of A4, rotas, duties, responsibilities. 'Ah, here we are. I think Pauline mentioned you'd be looking to have us on Sunday, May twelfth.'

'Is there a problem?'

'Well, it's the Battersea Park Charity Fun Run. Any other day there wouldn't be an issue, but we have a bit of a tradition in our club that one or two of our boys like to run in it to raise money for various charities who have helped them out when they've needed it. Mountain rescue, the lifeboats – there's a potholing foundation in the Derbyshire Dales that one bloke on our team owes more than his batting average to, I can assure you. We like to repay our debts of gratitude.'

The only charity the Baldwin squad has any need of is Age Concern. But no matter: the notion of our being, were we only to be available, young, lithe and athletic, has been effortlessly dropped into his subconscious.

'Good on you,' says Dave sympathetically.

'So we'll probably be fielding a pretty under-strength side on that day. I wanted to mention it in case you wanted to look elsewhere for another opposition before committing—'

'No no,' says Dave. 'Of course not. Quite understandable. Thanks for mentioning it. I'll stand some of our better players down then. Glad you told me.'

'After all, the main thing is that we have—'

'A bloody good game of cricket,' we both chant together in fraternal unison.

'It's been great to talk to you. See you next year!'

'Actually, Mike, I may stand down myself in the light of what you've said. But I'll certainly do some umpiring.'

'Well, look forward to sharing a beer with you at Pauline's barbecue afterwards.'

'To be honest I don't drink,' says Dave. 'But I'll certainly have a Britvic … '

Match Report:
Harry Baldwins vs Old Wokingham.
Baldwins 213 all out.
Old Wokingham 89 all out.
Baldwins win by 124 runs.

Henfield IIs

By the following year the increased time and energy I'm devoting to the running of the team is beginning to affect my relationship with Julia. With the ever-expanding number of matches in the calendar (we're now up to fifteen) it's becoming more difficult to get a side together on a weekly basis, and Julia has only recently been complaining about the soaring phone bill and the fact none of her friends can ever get through after 7pm.

I've told her she's being unreasonable. And the eighty-five calls I've made in the last week have at least resulted in a grand team for this coming weekend's match against Henfield. It's a fixture we're thrilled to obtain, as the ground is one of the oldest in the country and the teas are apparently legendary.

The side includes five decent batsmen including the lecturer and Wordsworth expert Adrian Knapp, the toff Jason Buckingham, a specialist wicketkeeper in social worker Neil Oates, Pat Rafferty our token spinner, plus our opening bowler and one-man insurance policy Les Sweeney, the grizzled and hard-drinking itinerant session musician with a fondness for Carlsberg whom I know will keep us in the game even if everyone else has a shocker. I've sent out photocopied maps and directions to the ground to all eleven players, I've arranged who's bringing the match ball, who's got the kit bag and who collects the match fees at the end of play.

So now I can sit back with a gin and tonic and watch a video on the box, one I got on my way home this evening so Julia and I could enjoy some quality time together. But no sooner has

187

Greatest Benson & Hedges Zonal matches 1980–85 started rolling its opening titles than the phone rings.

A player whom I haven't heard from since before Christmas has rung to remind me that he's flying in from Bahrain on Sunday morning so can I fax him directions to the ground as he'll be hiring a car to drive direct from Gatwick. I apparently promised him he'd be selected for this match some time last season, as his brother-in-law plays for the opposition and they're having a family meal afterwards. He gives a fax number for the reception desk at the Bahrain Sheraton Hotel.

So. I've got a problem. Someone is going to have to stand down at short notice to make way for him. But who? The fairest way is simply to work out who might have played most, ring them up, point out you'd completely forgotten about your promise to Bahrain and ask him to step down. He'll understand. He's a Baldwin.

Unfortunately he's also my main fast bowler, Les Sweeney. The grizzled muso who never misses a game, the one man I can count on to ensure the afternoon isn't an endless drudge of pursuing the ball to all points of the compass.

The other option is to elbow Keith.

Every team needs a Keith. Keith works in a quantity surveying business in Aldrington. He's extremely mild-mannered, is a Cub Scout leader, enjoys collecting historical beer mats and loves playing cricket. I can do what I like to Keith, chucking him out on the morning of the match if someone better turns up, and then hauling him back on board at the last minute if it all goes tits up, in the knowledge he'll accept without question.

'Keithy, it's Simmo. I know you were hoping to play this week but the fact is … '

By bedtime, I'm back to eleven.

* * *

By Thursday evening I'm down to nine.

Jason Buckingham, the toff who bats at number 4 and is

415th in line to the throne, has rung to say he's been offered a rehearsed reading of a new project on Sunday at Westcliff-on-Sea. A friend of his has written a musical about childbirth called *From Here To Maternity*, and they're a couple short for a reading of it to show prospective investors. Rumour has it Matthew Kelly is interested in playing the gynaecologist, in which case neither Jason nor his brother, who was also playing (and is 414th in line to the throne), can turn down the chance to be on board. They're both going to have to pull out. Work always has to take priority.

I call Keith.

'Keithy, it's Simmo. Sorry to bother you. I know I said there wasn't a place for you but I've completely miscalculated and in fact what I meant was … '

Thursday 9pm. I'm back to eleven. Keith is bringing his eldest son along with him. Simon is only twelve but is very excited and Keith will take him out to buy him a protective helmet for Sunday, which is doubly good as apparently Henfield have got a great burly farmer who likes to pull off the front foot, and we can stick the lad in at short leg for any potential bat/pad catch. I would field there myself but I've got an ad audition on Monday for Heinz Spaghetti Hoops. It's important I turn up with a full set of teeth.

By Friday evening I've got nine.

Barney Kent, failed actor and now head of drama at the posh school in Surrey, has twisted his ankle shinning up a drainpipe after losing his house key, and the bloke in Bahrain has rung up from the bar of the Sheraton Hotel to say he's just met a woman at a party thrown by the oil company he works for who has persuaded him to spend the weekend with her going scuba diving. But could I put him down for the same match next year?

And then I remember schoolteacher Brian Charters. A quick look at last year's scorebook reveals he played six times last year. He's talented, reliable, and usually turns up with his partner Angie who has one of those dirty Sid James laughs that are very popular with cricketers. For some reason he hasn't been returning close season calls. It's time to try him once more. Almost before the phone has started ringing, it's answered up at the other end.

'Bri, is that you?' says a woman's voice.

'Angie? It's Sim.'

I can hardly hear her for the sound of a baby shrieking in the background. And then I remember. Of course! Angie was waddling round the boundary like a Michelin Man last September, she even had to forgo her customary rum and blackcurrant and a ciggie in the pub after the match.

'It's old Sim, my darling, calling on behalf of the kingdom of Baldwinshire.'

'Simmo?'

'I'm just ringing to give you both belated congratulations on your new arrival, we're all so delighted for you both, you clever girl, that's a fair old pair of lungs on your new addition, isn't it? Look, I know you must be up to your neck in muck and nappies, but my reason for calling is to say a belated congratulations on your pride and joy, that's all I've rung to say … Though, in fact, now I come to think of it, would Bri fancy a game this weekend? We're all desperate to meet the little sprog and start showing her a forward defensive, and the gang say it's just not the same without you sunning yourself on the boundary.'

'He's left.'

'Eh?'

'He's left. That lousy pig has left me, Simmo. Just walked out last night. I've got a new-born baby, I haven't slept for seventy-two hours, he hasn't left a forwarding address, he's taken the car and he's not answering his mobile. I can't believe he's done this to me – how could he leave a new baby? He's met someone at work, he says he never loved me and the last few weeks have just brought it all home to him, he even swept our wedding portrait off the sideboard as he went out, it smashed on the floor right in front of Holly, I just don't know what I'm going to do … '

She descends into huge, heavy sobs. A great seismic wailing, like some primeval animal in intense pain. Not unlike the sound our treasurer Chris Buckle makes when he's been run out without facing a ball. That reminds me, I must check he's organised the teas.

'Angie, I'm so sorry … '

More sobs.

'Christ, that's awful.'

Gulping sounds.

'You say he just walked out on you last night? Just like that?'

A grunt.

'And he says he's not coming back?'

'That's what he said.'

'You say he's taken his mobile with him?'

A huge, choking sob.

'You don't know if he might be free this Sunday, do you … ?

Friday 10pm. Adrian Knapp, my neighbour and college professor, has had a brainwave. Dr Hymie Arronovich, a visiting academic who is conducting research into the early watercolours of Edward Lear and currently staying with him, is happy to make up the numbers. Dr Arronovich can't really run and won't be able to stop or catch the ball as he's a gifted clarinettist and has to protect his hands, but he's heard a lot about the game of cricket and is a great fan of *The Good Old Days* on cable TV back in Pennsylvania.

Friday 11pm. I'm back to eleven. Keith's younger son, ten-year-old William, is choosing his helmet, box, thigh pad, arm guard, gum shield and first ever pair of long trousers first thing tomorrow.

Saturday midday. I've now got ten and a half. Phil Coleridge, an archaeologist currently involved in a huge project to save a Roman mosaic from destruction by contractors in Spitalfields, as well as being a forcing bat and unpredictable bowler, has slipped on a dog turd while walking his Labrador in the park and badly bruised his coccyx on the gravel path. He thinks he can still bat but won't be able to field. Do I still want him to play?

Saturday 5pm. Nine and a half. We've lost our wicketkeeper.

Neil Oates is a social worker and committed member of the Communist Party, whose utter inability behind the stumps has led him to being dubbed 'The Ancient Mariner' because 'he stoppeth one of three'. He's woken to discover a flat tyre on his car. As he won't be able to afford a replacement at Kwik-Fit until his monthly pay cheque comes through, he can no longer get to the game unless we get him a lift.

I assure him he has to play. I'll arrange him a lift. Somehow I'll persuade Rex Scudamore, our first-change bowler and scorer, as well as being a celebrated naturalist and one of Britain's leading experts in parasitic worms, to pick him up in his Volvo on the way to the ground. This will involve a trip from his home in Dulwich to East Sussex via Surrey, a detour of some sixty miles. I ring Rex and his wife answers. She says she'll tell him and unless he calls me back I can assume it'll be no problem. I'm back to ten and a half again.

By Saturday midnight I've got eleven and a half. Bahrain has rung to ask where's the bloody map he was promised? When I remind him of his conversation cancelling his berth for the scuba-diving woman he claims no memory of having made the call. I get Keith out of bed to tell him there is no longer a place for his youngest son. He expresses mild disappointment as the child has bought all his kit and was wearing it in bed when he last looked in on him. I tell him not to put emotional pressure on me as it's a bloody difficult job organising a team. Keith apologises.

Sunday 7.45am. Bahrain has called from the airport to say his plane has been delayed by a faulty alarm light on the smoke detectors in one of the passenger loos. He's not going to make it.

Sunday 8am. Keith's youngest son is back on board.

Sunday 8.15. Phil Coleridge, the archaeologist with the bruised coccyx, thinks he'll be able to play the full match.

Sunday 9.15. Rex Scudamore, the parasitic worms man, rings to say his wife has only just remembered to pass the message on. Rex has phoned the AA route-finder service to discover that the journey to Hounslow to pick up Neil the social worker would involve a detour of over fifty miles each way so sadly he is unable to help out.

Sunday 9.20. Without transport Neil has to stand down.

Sunday 11.15. Professor Hymie Arronovich rings to ask if anyone in our side might be able to loan him a spare pair of cricket whites, waist size 52 inches. He also asks if it's OK if he wears flip-flops as his feet get very hot.

Sunday 11.20. Neil says his neighbour has offered to drive him down, but only on the understanding that he can have a game. His name is Baz, he's a bit of a rough diamond and his only descriptive adjective begins with f, but he's got a heart of gold as long as you keep him off the sauce. Neil says Baz hasn't got any kit as he's only recently come out of Parkhurst but he'll loan him a pair of his white denims and Baz has got a white cutaway T-shirt he can wear. What do I think?

Sunday 11.21. We have a full eleven.

Sunday 11.50. Leo Lorimer-Smith, the Baldwins' only decent slip catcher and owner of a gastro pub in Angmering which is striving for its first Michelin Star, calls. He's woken up to discover that his chef has absconded during the night with not only the entire Saturday night's takings and the keys to the deep freeze, but also a waitress from Lithuania. He's waiting for the arrival of an emergency locksmith, after which he'll be cooking and serving up a hundred and thirty roast beef lunches virtually single-handed. Sorry to let us down at such short notice.

Sunday midday. The phone rings just as I'm driving away from the house towards Sussex. I decide not to go back and answer it.

Match Report:
Harry Baldwins vs Henfield.
Henfield 214–6 (Colgate 81).
Baldwins did not bat.
Match abandoned after tea when Baz tells the Henfield president's wife to move her fuckin' car as it's boxing him in and he needs to nip down the offie.

Worthing Railways

One of the wonderful things about cricket is the way it throws up unlikely heroes: the elderly slip fielder who pouches the vital catch; the duffer who scores a century; or the substitute fielder who makes the crucial run-out.

Our match in 1991, away against Worthing Railways, is just such an occasion. Somehow I'd got it into my head that the Railways were probably a side of model-train-set enthusiasts and that we'd enjoy an easy victory against a load of blokes in NHS glasses and carrying duffel bags, but they turn out to be a fiercely competitive team comprising assorted ticketing and booking-hall staff from stations on the British Rail south-coast main line. The venue is Patcham Place, the very same ground on which I had my first fumbling encounter with Emma's mammaries all those years ago. I'm looking forward to spending time on the scene of my old triumphs.

The match is supposed to begin at 2pm, but by 3.15 has yet to commence. Of the eleven players who should have turned up for the Baldwins, so far we have four. A glance at the main road skirting the ground is all that's needed to see what the problem is. Patcham Place runs directly alongside the main A23 London to Brighton road, and today's match has coincided with the annual London to Brighton cycle rally, in aid of the British Heart Foundation. There are between 25,000 and 30,000 cyclists all approaching the town centre along a twenty-mile stretch of the A23, behind which founders a vehicle traffic jam, that is already stretching back nearly fifteen miles. Somewhere in the middle of that lot, cooking quietly on a low heat, is the cream of today's Baldwin team.

Phil Coleridge the archaeologist, his wife and six-month-old son Luke have been stuck in their car just outside a Little Chef at Pease Pottage since noon, waiting for the cyclists to pass. However, they've started moving again and are now making relatively good progress in that they've travelled nearly a hundred yards in the last quarter of an hour. Phil thinks his tot might be suffering heat exhaustion and the red light is flashing on and off on his radiator thermostat on the dashboard. He also has two large carrier bags with fifty rounds of rapidly warming sardine sandwiches on the back seat.

Six hundred yards further down the motorway James and Jason Buckingham, neither of whom were chosen for the pregnancy musical, have left their similarly stationary car and are sitting on the hard shoulder chatting up a couple of girls who have had to pull over on their bikes due to blisters. Sue and Elaine are staying the night at a small B & B in Kemp Town and have agreed to meet up with my middle order later this evening at Busby's nightclub.

A quarter of a mile further on, Rex Scudamore, the parasitic worms man, is having an impromptu picnic on the bonnet of his Volvo in the fast lane of the Hickstead bypass.

That leaves four others, one of whom is our star player, Jez Baker. 'Bakey', as he is known, a huge lantern-jawed beefcake of a man with biceps like hams and pecs you could swing from, is a swashbuckling personality with effortless charm and a lead-from-the-front attitude reminiscent of ex-England captain Tony Greig. If he doesn't exactly say, 'We'll make 'em grovel,' as Greig once infamously predicted before being blatted from arsehole to breakfast-time by the 1976 West Indians, he similarly likes to get stuck in: and his presence in Baldwin colours usually results in a keener cutting edge and a certain brio to the way we approach the game.

But he's also currently trying to forge a movie career, and

today has been delayed by having to attend a screen test in a private room at the Groucho Club for a new Hollywood film of the story of Noah's ark, starring James Garner as Noah and with Jim Henson providing the animals. He assures us he'll be catching the next train down the moment his interview is through, and is confident he'll be in plenty of time to bat second wicket down or provide first change with the ball.

Further north still, Barney Kent, the failed actor-cum-drama teacher, lies still asleep in his squalid bedsit in Tooting, next to a girl he thinks might be called Tina or Brenda, whom he met in a club in Soho at 3am. Barney is the wild man of the side, a bloke who turns up to matches in a succession of beaten-up old cars with a succession of beaten-up old girlfriends. His sexual exploits are so prodigious that other team members have clubbed together to provide him with his own box after being advised by their GPs not to share the communal one with him from the kit bag.

Which leaves Clive True, a mild-mannered hotel manager from Queens Park, and the ubiquitous Les Sweeney. True was supposed to pick up Sweeney, erstwhile musician and occasional barman at the Spotted Dog in Wealdstone, outside C&A on Wembley High Street at 11.30. But Sweeney, who has never been inside a domestic goods and clothes outlet in his life, has been waiting at the store for the last two hours without realising he's positioned himself outside See & Save, a supermarket specialising in tinned goods and comestibles for the Nigerian immigrant community.

He only realised his mistake after noticing that the main window display of one of Britain's leading department stores specialising in easy-care leisure garments had nothing in it but millet and tins of okra in brine.

Fifty yards down the street, Clive True had waited outside the correct location for nearly an hour. Now that Sweeney has phoned from a call box to notify us of his cock-up, True has been sent back for him, even though he was already at Roehampton. They're expected soon after tea.

Which leaves myself, Keith the Cub Scout leader whom I rang twenty minutes ago to whisk away from his youngest's birthday party at the Saltdean Flume Water Park, and finally our impromptu substitute, Gordon Quill.

Quill is one of the curios of the side. He readily admits to being entirely hopeless at the game but likes to come along and watch and afterwards enjoy a blackcurrant and lemonade in the pub with us all. He doesn't really play much, but because he deals in antique Victoriana and thus loves anything to do with the period, he's become enamoured of a team dedicated to a Victorian cricketer. On the infrequent occasions when he comes along to watch, he sports a waxed moustache and dresses in a straw boater and stripy blazer. In fact, he's only come along to today's match in order to show me his collection of antique seaside postcards he picked up at an auction in Lewes last week.

The Worthing Railways captain comes up to me. A large bluff man called Frank, he works as a ticket inspector on the Three Bridges to Arundel spur.

'How many are you now?'

'Well, if my friend Gordon Quill plays that'll help out a bit. And one of our players is already on a direct train from London Bridge and will get off at the stop just up the road from us, so with any luck he should be here within twenty minutes—'

'London Bridge to Waterloo East is closed for weekend engineering works. There's also a replacement bus service between Blackfriars and Norwood Junction, and in any case Sunday services don't stop at Preston Park. So I wouldn't count on him getting here before Tuesday if I were you. How many does that leave?'

'Um ... '

'Never mind. My boys have given up family barbecues for this and if we don't start now they're going home. Let's go.'

'Of course, of course. It's just that ... '

'What?'

'Well, it's just that we forgot it was the bike rally today ... '

'Tough.' In his professional life Frank is used to lame excuses and pleas of ignorance. 'We'll lend you a couple of fielders till they arrive. Let's go.'

He pulls on his batting gloves and summons his opening partner to join him in the middle. I call across to Quill who is just showing a first-edition postcard of Donald McGill's 'I Can't Find My Little Willy' to the Worthing Railways wicketkeeper.

'Gordon, you're going to have to open the bowling.'

Having Gordon Quill opening the bowling is a bit like asking my mum to front a twelve-part television cookery course. But the fact is there's nobody else. At least Quill can just about propel it down the other end. We'll get through his first over and then regroup. Perhaps somebody else might have turned up by then.

By the time we've all got out onto the pitch, it's nearly 3.30 and the human tide of cyclists on the London to Brighton road shows no sign of lessening. The Railwaymen have lent us three of their team, all of whom are standing sulkily in the outfield waiting to be positioned. I hand Quill the match ball provided by the opposition, a gleaming rock-hard cherry still in its tissue paper, and retire to mid-off to consider my tactical options. Opening your bowling attack with an antique postcard collector resembling Stuart Hall in *It's a Knockout* is a handicap I would defy even Mike Brearley's tactical acumen to surmount, but at least it fulfils his other dictum for successful captaincy, 'Always do what the opposition least expects.' Frank the ticket inspector marches to the wicket with his opening partner. In addition to the normal paraphernalia of pads and gloves, they're both wearing helmets, thigh pads and arm guards. They look like something out of Securicor.

Our team, by contrast, looks as if it's been kitted out by Mr Dranse. With an injection of cash in the winter, courtesy of an obligatory £10 subscription among the players, I had hoped to cut a collective dash on the field today, but the kit bag containing all our gleaming new accessories is in the back of Rex

Scudamore's Volvo. Consequently, quite apart from Quill, the only other indigenous Baldwin currently on the field, Keith, is keeping wicket in shorts, a T-shirt with 'Real ale enthusiasts do it on beer mats' emblazoned on the front, and a pair of motorcycle gauntlets. Suddenly I'm seized with an overwhelming sense of humiliation about it all, one I haven't experienced for many years. This isn't what it was supposed to be like. Dad bowling in a pair of swimming trunks and Mum eating a Cadbury's Creme Egg at cover point suddenly seem like Don Bradman's 1948 Australians by comparison.

But there's no delaying the inevitable. And at least I've persuaded Quill to remove his boater and blazer. He approaches off a run-up of about three inches, and whirls his arm over. The ball bounces three times before coming to rest just in front of Frank's motionless figure at the crease. Frank removes his helmet and stares over at me with a look of withering disdain.

'Is he taking the piss?'

'Not at all.'

'This is your opening bowler is it?'

I scan the roadside before replying. Just an endless crawl of slowly moving traffic. 'Just at the moment,' I reply.

'Right,' mutters Frank, simply. He picks up the ball and throws it back to Quill. 'Here you are, Dr Livingstone,' he says. Quill marches back to his run-up and sets off again.

Three seconds later, via a brief but violent interruption in its trajectory from Frank's bat, the ball soars over my head at extra cover, hits a tree on the boundary halfway up its trunk, ricochets into the road where it nearly decapitates a member of the Crawley Down Road Racing team, before bouncing off the far pavement and coming to rest against the wall of the Black Lion Hotel. Keith trots off to fetch it, but with the cyclists still surging past in an endless flood, the simple act of crossing and recrossing the road eats up a further five minutes.

The next ball is hit with such force that it breaks a security light outside the front door of the YMCA hostel at the far end of the ground. Quill looks nervously over at me, but I give him a thumbs-up sign to indicate he's doing just fine. Frank thrashes his next delivery as hard as he can straight back at the bowler, but fortunately it narrowly misses Quill and cannons into the far set of stumps beside him, not only preventing any runs from being scored but breaking one of the bails in the process. Further minutes tick by while some binding tape is found from the pavilion and the wicket is repaired.

Quill's fifth delivery is flayed over extra cover, where it strikes the hub cap of a Peugeot 406 travelling in the opposite direction from the cyclists on the main road, and rebounds back onto the field of play. My heart momentarily leaps: perhaps the driver will have noticed the collision and pull over, thus providing the opportunity for a long and involved altercation about insurance liability with the Railwaymen that will use up yet more time. But he drives on, oblivious. Funny how when luck's against you …

But at last fortune turns my way. Quill's last delivery is smashed for six high over the midwicket boundary, where it lands deep into a huge bank of nettles and fallen tree trunks brought down by the great storm of 1985.

After furious exhortations from Frank to the pavilion, his grumbling colleagues eventually rise from their deckchairs and begin a slow and painstaking search for the missing ball. Quill watches the Railwaymen swishing about in the undergrowth with their bats, his fingers twirling the ends of his moustache in silent despair. Then he turns to me ruefully. 'Sorry old chap,' he says. 'A bridge too far, I'm afraid…'

But there's no need for an apology. He's playing a blinder. Success on the field is all about percentage cricket, and with the current wage restraint being imposed on British Rail platform staff combined with a brand new cricket ball retailing at nearly fifteen quid a pop, there's no way this lot are going to give up the hunt for it easily. By the time the precious ball is found lying behind a rotting tree stump, the clock on the YMCA building is showing nearly 4 o'clock. The Railwaymen celebrate the discovery with a yell of triumph, but even as the ball is being thrown back onto the pitch, I spot Rex Scudamore's Volvo pulling into the car park at the far end. What's more he's already changed into his whites and is ready to play. Phil Coleridge's Renault is only thirty yards behind. I celebrate by giving my emergency bowler a huge hug of gratitude. The hits into the cyclists, the broken bail, and the disappearance among the nettles: Quill's single over may have conceded thirty runs, but crucially it has occupied nearly half an hour. He's got us through our crisis. Mafeking has been relieved. Game on.

Match Report:
Harry Baldwins vs Worthing Railways.
Worthing Railways 103 all out off 18 overs
(Quill 0–30, Scudamore 5–22)
Baldwins 104–4.
Harry Baldwins win by 6 wickets.

Buddhists of England

The philosophy of Buddhism is concerned with respect for life in all its forms. It contends that each individual, through consistent Buddhist practice over many lifetimes, can transform darker sides of human nature into enlightenment, and that in every situation, however unpromising, the state of Buddhahood may be drawn to the fore.

And this evening, Guy McKenzie is about to go from dark to light via every shade in between in one transcendental delivery.

Our fifth match of the 1991 season is against a team calling themselves Buddhists of England, at their retreat near Saffron Walden. It wouldn't be possible to believe that a fixture against a group of individuals whose firmly held faith espouses peace, non-aggression and a desire for enlightenment in this lifetime could be so ill-tempered. But in fact Buddhists of England are about as combative a lot as we've ever played against. Already the match has featured several angry exchanges between individual members of the teams, and now, with the contest boiling up to a tight finish in the gloom of an overcast July evening, the match is threatening to bubble over into open fisticuffs.

Six to win. One wicket left. And Guy McKenzie is on a hat-trick.

In the pub before the match the Buddhists were explaining that their faith is about developing an acceptance that suffering is an inevitable condition of human existence. I point this out to their captain when he refuses to leave the pitch upon being given out LBW first ball, after claiming he got a thick inside edge onto his pad.

'But I hit it,' he cries.

'You merely think you hit it,' shouts Jez Baker from second slip. 'In fact that's just your ego pain-memory. Your dad obviously abused you as a child.'

'Aren't all things transitory?' shouts Barney Kent from gulley.

'What if they are?'

'Well fuck off then!'

Their captain, a publisher in his early thirties, appeals silently to the ring of smirking fielders grouped round him. It's difficult not to feel sorry for the bloke: he may espouse Buddhism as a life philosophy, but it's difficult to see how anyone who was truly enlightened could think it was a good idea to come out to bat wearing a green-and-maroon striped cap.

From halfway down the pitch, my star bowler, Australian Guy McKenzie, points the captain's way back to the derelict shed that serves as the changing rooms. 'Go on, off you go, Dalai,' he shouts. 'You're out, my old China. Go and meditate about it. In any case, I don't know what you're worrying about. Don't you lot believe in reincarnation?'

'It's a central tenet of our faith.'

'Well, you can come back in as number eleven and have another go then, can't you?'

The publisher imagines what he'd like to do with the handle of his bat before trudging off.

It's been a tight attritional game of cricket. The Buddhists have responded well to our innings of 118 on a dodgy track and are now only six away from victory. We in turn require one further wicket. And with muso Les Sweeney having ricked his ankle in the first over, Guy McKenzie has had to shoulder the entire burden of our fragile hopes. He's responded magnificently. An archetypal Aussie with a sunny smile and a laid-back approach to life, he delivers huge banana away-swingers to order. So far today he's taken each of the nine wickets to fall and now stands on the threshold of a remarkable achievement in Baldwin annals. All ten in a match. And this track suits him perfectly.

Unfortunately it doesn't suit Camilla, his wife. The only track she wants to see is layered with tarmac and fringed with signs saying M3 and the south-west. She's only allowed Guy to play this afternoon on the understanding that they'll be away by 6pm in order to drive down to Lyme Regis for a romantic few days together to repair the parlous state of their marriage. In fact, this is Guy's first game for the team since packing the sport in completely in order to win her back after a long and acrimonious separation.

Allowing him to play at all today represents a hugely magnanimous gesture on Camilla's part. Their relationship only foundered in the first place because he was playing five times a week and was starting to turn down offers of sex as he didn't want to be tired for the next afternoon's match. It's remarkable she's given him another chance.

Guy and Camilla are due to be at their candlelit table in a swanky restaurant overlooking the Cobb by 8pm. I've promised Guy on my dad's grave that he'll be on the road by six. No ifs, no buts. This brief holiday is make-or-break for them; indeed, she has deliberately allowed him to play this afternoon as both a trial and a gesture of faith that he will no longer abuse her time or trust.

It's now just past seven.

I trot up to the bowler's end and press the ball back into McKenzie's hand. The final Buddhist batsman, a primary school teacher from Epping, is already marking his guard. On the boundary Camilla turns on the ignition of her Saab and pushes the accelerator, the noise of furious revving shattering the silence of the Essex evening.

McKenzie gazes despairingly towards the boundary and pushes the ball back into my hand. 'That's it, Simmo, I'm going. I can't even finish the over. Sweeney will have to bowl on one leg. Look at her. She's going to put the accelerator pedal through the floor of the car in a minute. I've let her down again. We should be past Winchester by now.'

The Saab is now inching back across a pile of discarded grass cuttings, sending flurries high into the air. Camilla is normally a pretty young thing but even I have to agree that now, here in the gathering gloom and with her features contorted by fury, she looks like the Wicked Witch of the West.

This is when the true leader shows his mettle. In any walk of life, this is when the great ones show their true skills in man management. After all, it's not just about field placings and corridors of uncertainty. Sometimes you have to know about underlying humanity to inspire and relieve those around you who are suffering. No wonder Mike Brearley became a psycho-analyst and the Dalai Lama spent time as bowling coach at Leicestershire.

I slip my arm round McKenzie's shoulder – this simple ritual, a basic act of physical connection between man and man, one used to enormous effect by Mike Brearley on both Ian Botham and Bob Willis. Now I'm trying it for myself.

'Guy, Guy, Guy … ' I continue this mantra soothingly for some seconds until at last he looks up at me. Poor bloke, his eyes are full of divorce courts, maintenance orders and removal vans. Buddhism states that you can change poison into medicine. This is what I must do now.

'Guy, just think.' I take his face between my hands and regard him with a look of the most profound love. 'You've taken all nine wickets. You're on a hat-trick. This would be the first time in club history a bowler has taken all ten. Imagine it for a moment. You'll have your name for eternity in our hall of fame, eclipsing forever Sweeney's 7–56 against the Weekenders. Think of it, Guy … '

'Simmo, I—'

'Just one more wicket, Guy.'

'One ball, Simmo. That's your lot. Take it or leave it.'

'Imagine it, Guy – your name above Les Sweeney's. You'd like that, wouldn't you?'

'Simmo, I can't.'

'At least finish the over. Three more balls. That's all I need.'

He looks across at the car. 'One ball, Simmo. That's it.'

'Two. Give me two—'

'One ball.'

'OK. One ball it is.'

But he's already grabbed it and is pounding in. His sudden approach catches both teams unawares. Our communist wicket-keeper Neil is blowing his nose and has only one glove on. Barney Kent is lying on the ground and Phil Coleridge is in the middle of a long and steaming urination into the far bushes. Even the batsman is polishing his glasses. But McKenzie is already approaching the popping crease.

Camilla reverses into a patch of nettles, sends the car lurching forward again and begins accelerating round the boundary towards the exit gate to the main road.

Moments later Guy releases the ball. Without stopping he charges past the batsman in pursuit of the Saab, his arms stretched out like an aeroplane in a mixture of triumph and supplication, as the primary school teacher surveys his shattered wicket. And it strikes me that Guy McKenzie has undergone a profound Buddhist experience this afternoon.

Many life states can combine in a single moment, or so the Buddhist scriptures state. Guy has taken all ten wickets, the club's first ever hat-trick, and with his future disappearing over the horizon his features display all possible life conditions, from the Hell of Incessant Suffering to Nirvana, in a single expression.

As the car reaches the gate back onto the road, Camilla glances in her rear-view mirror and catches sight of him, still in his whites and gaining ground on her rear bumper. His quest seems hopeless, but then the car slows momentarily and suddenly McKenzie is level with the front offside door. A moment later it swings suddenly and violently open, and he dives straight inside to the sound of massed cheering from the Baldwin ranks. Even the Buddhists of England manage half-hearted applause.

A second later the car slews drunkenly out of the field and is lost from view as it heads towards the Maidenhead bypass. And with it goes Guy McKenzie's final ever appearance in Baldwin colours.

Match Report:
Harry Baldwins vs Buddhists of England.
Baldwins 118.
Buddhists 112 (McKenzie 10–56).
Baldwins win by 6 runs.

Stonegate Mariners

If you find a new recruit who can actually play a bit, someone who knows how to hold a bat and perhaps even play the odd shot, you're a lucky man. If they can also bowl on a decent line and length, you can consider yourself blessed. If in addition they prove to be a lithe and graceful fielder with a safe pair of hands, you're allowed to think all your Christmases have come at once.

But if they're also capable of undertaking minor surgical procedures on the pitch, you've really hit the jackpot.

I can't recall how or where we picked up NHS employee Steve Sarstedt. I think our club treasurer Chris Buckle met him at a parents' and teachers' evening at the local school. He makes his debut for the Baldwins in a match against a minor public school eleven, which I'm unable to attend because of a day's work on a TV drama, and thus I miss Sarstedt's sensational start midway through our 1992 season.

He plays what by both sporting and humanitarian standards is an absolute blinder. Not only does he score a brisk half-century and follow it up with three wickets with some probing left-arm swing, but according to those who were there to witness the incident, he also saves the life of a drowning infant whom he's called upon to revive after the child gets into difficulties in the school swimming pool.

I meet him the following week in our fixture against the Mariners, an occasional pub side from the village of Stonegate, which nestles in the lee of the South Downs. I'm originally destined to miss this match as well as I've managed to get a pair of tickets to the *Ken Dodd Laughter Show* in Eastbourne: Doddy is one of the few performers I'd cancel a cricket match for, especially as I've never yet seen him live and rumour has it he's not looking so well these days. But then it's pointed out to me by Jez Baker that the recreation ground on which we're playing is only ten miles away from the front stalls of the Congress Theatre. If the match finishes on time at 7.30 I can be well in my seat by curtain up at eight.

And with our new hero on board, there's never a question of missing my favourite comedian. Stephen Sarstedt is a real find. A burly bloke with thinning hair and an expression of amiable kindness, he weighs in with a very handy thirty-odd in the middle order, then breaks the back of the Mariners with a controlled spell of left-arm seam up.

More than that, his occupation as a senior male nurse in the casualty department at East Grinstead District Hospital ensures that his reputation as comforter of the distressed and friend of the sick and dying continues. As well as all those runs and wickets, he alleviates a severe bout of cramp in Pat Rafferty's big toe, resets Jason Buckingham's right index finger after he dislocates it attempting a steepling catch, and is able to offer comprehensive pre-operative advice to Barney Kent, who reveals he's thinking of having several unsightly moles removed from his back.

The match is over by 5.15, plenty of time for me to shower and be off for the opening chorus of 'Love Is Like A Violin'. Even as we cheer him off the field, Sarstedt responds with commendable modesty, receiving the slaps of congratulations and hearty handshakes for each new triumph with a shy shrug of the shoulders.

'Does he never get worked up?' I ask Chris Buckle as we follow him off the pitch and back towards the changing rooms. Ahead of me Sarstedt is literally having to be pushed to the front to take his rightful place at the head of the phalanx. This man is a saint.

'Not really,' replies Buckle. 'He really is the most amiable chap imaginable. Though if ever he does get upset or excited, you'll know about it.'

'How's that?'

'He develops an instant and prodigious stutter.'

'Well, he's a real find,' I observe as we climb the concrete steps to the changing rooms. 'We've got to hang on to him. He's played like a veteran.' But as we enter the room itself, Sarstedt's lack of experience in club cricket is suddenly and shockingly revealed.

Anyone who plays cricket in municipal parks soon learns not to leave valuables in the changing rooms. Unattended and insecure, they offer the opportunist thief the easiest of targets. Open to the general public, their dilapidated corridors peopled by transient hordes of anonymous men, they're a honey pot for thieves and ne'er-do-wells. The Baldwin regulars have been cleared out of our valuables more times than we can remember, which is why we learnt to take our wallets, car keys and anything else we'd rather not lose with us to the side of the pitch at the commencement of the match.

Today the dank and windowless changing room immediately confirms yet another invasion by unwelcome visitors during our long hours out in the field. Our trousers have been flung in all directions, coats and jackets have been removed from their pegs and lie in piles on the floor, even our surplus kit has been strewn around as if someone has been told to pad up in four seconds to save his life. The culprits are obvious: a couple of weasely teenagers with acne and shifty looks whom I now recall encountering in the corridor mid-afternoon and who, when challenged, asked rather stiltedly if they could use the toilet.

Little enough has gone: the odd clutch of pound coins, a cigarette lighter, and it seems Chris Buckle has lost his special-issue Swiss army knife. But he has a spare one at home so even that's not the end of the earth. Not so Sarstedt. He still thinks the world is like him: modest, self-effacing, honourable, anxious to assist the common man, and whose every thought is instinctively filled with the milk of benevolence and altruism. Consequently he's lost all his credit cards, his car keys, various photographs of members of his family and nearly eighty quid in cash.

He goes very quiet.

I feel terrible. As captain it's my responsibility to hang on to him. A genuine all-rounder with surgical and massage skills doesn't come along every day. With his own vehicle now rendered useless, the least I can do is to offer to run him to the police station so he can report the theft. It'll make it a bit tight for the opening set, but apparently with Doddy's reputation that will last about four hours anyway.

By 6.45 we're both sitting on a long wooden bench in the reception area of Eastbourne central police station. Sarstedt has gone strangely quiet. I'd been hoping to dump him here and get off to the theatre, but after explaining the bare facts of the incident to the desk sergeant I too have been asked to remain here for a short while. The minutes are ticking away. Eventually a tired-looking constable in shirtsleeves appears with a report book and a pen.

'Sorry to have kept you both,' he says wearily. He opens a fresh page and begins writing his name along the top in a cramped hand. 'I'll take down your statements now.'

'What, me too?' His request for my inclusion in the procedure takes me by surprise. In fact, I've already stood up and am fumbling for my ignition key.

'Yes, sir. You as well.'

'But surely there must be some mistake.' I seem to be responding to the situation by even talking like a suspect in a police drama. 'It's really nothing to do with me.'

'I understand you were both victims of the robbery, sir?'

'Well, technically,' I reply. 'But I had nothing to steal. All I lost was a bag of Minstrels and some tissues.'

'That's as maybe, sir.' He casts a sideways look at the desk sergeant before continuing. 'But I understand you're the only one who obtained a clear view of the likely suspects?'

'Well, yes, but—'

'We'll try to get through this as quickly as possible.' He turns to Sarstedt. 'Let's start with you, sir.'

'Excuse me, constable, but could I possibly go first? I'm a bit short of time.'

The officer stops writing. 'Perhaps you would like to conduct the interview yourself, sir?'

'No, of course not, but—'

'But you have an important engagement. Yes, you said. What is it, may I ask?'

'I've got tickets to see Ken Dodd at the Congress.'

He gives me a fatigued look of infinite contempt, takes a sheaf of witness statement forms and writes the time and date in a box at the top.

'Now then, sir,' he says, turning again to the Baldwins' favourite son. 'I'll begin with your personal details and then record your statement. Include anything you think may be relevant. First name?'

'S-s— – s – s-s-s-s s-s s-s-s-s–'

'Stuart?'

Sarstedt shakes his head.

S– s-s – s – s-s s-s -s -s -s -s -s –s–'

'It's Stephen,' I say, interrupting. The desk sergeant raises both hands this time. 'Let him answer for himself, please, sir. It's his statement we're taking, not yours. Stephen, is it?'

Sarstedt nods.

'Surname?'

'S – s- s- s – s- s- s- s- s- s- s- sssssssah – sah – sah–'

'Sanders?'

'Look, it's Sarstedt!' I interject. I may have paid to see Ken Dodd but it feels as if I've wandered into a *Two Ronnies* sketch. The constable jabs his ballpoint in my direction. 'Please be quiet and wait your turn. Your address, Mr Sarstedt?'

I stifle a groan. The *Ken Dodd Laughter Show* begins in less than forty minutes and I've just remembered the Baldwins' newest recruit lives in Sissinghurst.

Doddy's reputation is well deserved. He ends his Sunday laughter show at just before midnight. And just as well he does. It means that I'm able to catch nearly the whole of the last thirty minutes.

Match Report:
Harry Baldwins vs Stonegate Mariners.
Baldwins 167–8 declared (Baker 56, Sarstedt 37*).
Mariners 78 all out (Rafferty 5–40, Sarstedt 3–31).
Baldwins win by 89 runs.

Farleigh Wallop

The playwright Harold Pinter once wrote, 'Everyone knows which comes first when it's a question of cricket or sex.'

The 1993 season looks for a while as if it might be our best so far, with five consecutive victories in May and June. Much of our success is down to vice-captain and team-toff Jason Buckingham, who leads from the front with a series of match-winning innings against a variety of opponents. There's even talk of him succeeding me in time as captain. But just as the summer looks as if it might confirm his credentials as heir apparent, Jason gets struck down without warning. A victim of Silvikrin.

It's Les Sweeney who first notices the problem. Les Sweeney has been Silvikrinned more times than he's bowled a wide and is particularly good at spotting one. Standing on the boundary, or gliding gently back and forth on the kiddies' swings at the far end, her newly washed hair blowing in the breeze, she waits for her lover out on the field of play, the guy she met only last week at a dinner party or nightclub, who told her that he plays cricket at weekends and would she like to come down and watch. So there she is. She's decided he's the one and is going to use his obsession with the best-loved game as a Trojan horse in which to inveigle herself into his citadel.

My Julia was like that once. Sitting on that swing, looking longingly out at me, saying how much she's always fancied men in cricket whites. Try inviting her to a match now and she'll tell you that she's got better things to do with her one free day a week than watching 'meaningless encounters between groups of sexually inadequate middle-aged no-hopers'.

But even if she's correct, the fact remains that Jason is one of our most valuable sexually inadequate middle-aged no-hopers. He turns out nearly every week, makes a stack of runs and has his own car. Yet as Les Sweeney and I pull into the ground at Farleigh Wallop near Winchester soon after eleven for our only all-day game of the year, the eagle eyes of my travelling companion spot the crisis even as he's hauling the crate of lager from my back seat.

There she is, a previously unidentified Silvikrin, that girl who's nibbling Jason's ear as she unloads a magnificent bespoke picnic hamper from his car. She comes in the trademark garb: large straw hat and simple summer cotton dress decorated with illustrations of wild flowers and designed to show the shape of her pert young breasts and her sturdy, child-bearing hips.

Jason sees us and shepherds her over.

'Simmo, I'd like you to meet—'

The girl reveals a smile. A beautiful, melting smile, gleaming white teeth framed by lips the consistency of ripe strawberries, every inch of it designed to stimulate maximum psychological and sexual response in her new partner.

'Pleased to meet you, Simmo,' she says, giving me a furtive peck on the cheek. As they wander off to the pavilion, Les and I study her departing frame. The freckles and nearly-see-through-linen-dress combo, it's all contrived. She couldn't have done more to excite his interest if she'd arrived in a dominatrix outfit, clutching a bottle of baby oil.

'He's got it bad,' remarks Sweeney.

'Should I say something?'

'He wouldn't hear you,' replies Sweeney, taking a long drag from his roll-up. 'He can't hear anyone. You could hire Brian Blessed to bellow through a loudhailer and he wouldn't flicker an eyelid. Leave it, skip. Maybe he'll pull out of it. I've known it to happen.'

He's right, of course. In any case, we have a match to win. I call correctly at the toss and decide to take first knock. A good captain must put larger concerns out of his mind until the contest is over. And the first priority is to decide on a batting order.

'Jason, I'd like you to bat number five. You happy with that?'

Jason isn't listening. Silvikrin has removed her hat, and she's even washed her hair. There it is, in all its natural glory, the colour of chestnut, blowing freely in the breeze and inundating Jason's nostrils with a scent of warm, sexy summer luvvin'. With the scent of Silvikrin.

'Jason, is number five OK?'

But Jason is already helping her to unpack her picnic hamper. She's turned up with a huge cool box full of fresh produce from her local deli. No Mother's Pride smeared with Cross & Blackwell sandwich spread. Instead fresh crusty bread and Ardennes pâté, containers full of salad with her mother's own-recipe vinaigrette, bottles of rosé wine, proper napkins, and just in case all this fails to nail her prey, there's a home-made date and walnut cake wrapped in tinfoil.

In a show of Baldwin solidarity, Les Sweeney deliberately stands next to them with his own picnic: a meat-paste bap and a Londis own-brand lemon-flavour slice.

'Jesus, where did you get this? It's delicious!' splutters Jason through a mouthful of dates and walnuts.

'Jason, did you hear me? You're batting at number five.'

'I made it, silly,' she smiles back at him: a big fond smile, peaches and cream cheeks and eyelashes bleached by the sun. She leans across and pulls the brim of Jason's cricket cap before plucking a slice of fresh peach from the fruit bowl on the rug and popping it in between his lips.

'Jason, the match is starting. You're batting at five. Can you get your pads on?'

Silvikrin looks up. 'Oh, do you need someone to help operate the scoreboard?' she coos, and before I can stop her she's sorted out all the tin numbers into little piles on the grass and is running back and forth to the scorebook to check she's put up the correct number of leg byes. She's putting out a clear message: that although this afternoon she's only hanging up Jason's score, one day soon she'll be hanging up his pants.

But in order to succeed she must gather allies. If she's to survive she not only has to become hypnotic to my vice-captain, she has to get the entire team on her side. Once she's got our collective validation there'll be no reason for Jason to hold back. He needs twenty-four-hour suicide watch. But I can't monitor his movements for the entire day. I'm batting first wicket down.

The match commences. Adrian Knapp and Phil Coleridge get us off to a solid start, and going in first wicket down I tuck into some insipid second-string bowling and compile a patient 42, mostly through midwicket, made in over an hour. But every moment I'm out here in the middle is a moment when I can't be back in the pavilion protecting Jason from his fate. I find myself scanning the boundary between deliveries. Where are they now? What is she saying to him? Who else is she casting her spell over while I'm marooned out here on the pitch? I'll have to hope that Les is overseeing developments. But then, I realise, Les is out here himself doing some umpiring. Jason is utterly alone and unprotected.

Eventually I'm out. I remove my pads and wander over to the trestle table by the pavilion to check my total in Rex Scudamore's pristine scoring book. Dear old Rex, he at least should be immune from her charms: after all, he's a leading authority on parasitic worms.

'I must say I like Jason's new companion,' he pipes up as soon as he sees me approaching.

'Oh her?' I reply nonchalantly. 'I hadn't really noticed her. Bit of an airhead, I thought. Anyway, Jason's going to be useless to us once she gets her claws into him.'

'Oh I don't know.' He smiles self-consciously. 'She's very enthusiastic,' he continues, blushing slightly as he spots Silvikrin a few yards away stooping to pick up a number 8 and showing a flash of chaste, sun-kissed cleavage. 'I think she's throwing herself into it with wonderful energy. She certainly seems to be enjoying her day out, doesn't she? She even asked me to teach her the rudiments of scoring.'

As he speaks I notice a mist of cake crumbs spattering the scorebook.

'What are you eating?'

'She kindly offered me a piece of her date and walnut cake,' says Rex, blushing an even deeper crimson. 'I must say it's jolly good.' Rex, too, has succumbed.

A yell of triumph from the middle confirms Knapp's downfall for 60. It's Jason's turn to bat. Silvikrin kisses him and as he walks to the middle she kneels attentively on the rug, looking out at him. I experience a twinge of acute melancholy that catches me unawares. I remember those times. My wife Julia was like that once.

Julia even used to put down her newspaper in case she missed something. She didn't seem to twig that she could probably complete a course in media studies at the Open University before I attempted anything even resembling an attacking shot. Her belief in me used to break my heart. Which of course was her precise intention.

'Well done,' she'd yell encouragingly, every time I actually hit the ball off the cut square. In between overs she'd give me the thumbs-up sign, and when she did decide to go for a wander round the boundary it was always by herself, as if she needed to be alone to cope with the frenzied kaleidoscope of emotions that were crowding in on her at the mere sight of me in a pair of stained cricket whites. And when, after forty minutes or so, I limply swatted my first aggressive stroke straight into the hands of cover point, Julia would shout 'Hurrah!' from her perch by the boundary rope, thinking that hitting the ball for the fielders to catch must be the whole point of the game.

Those were the days.

Jason is soon out without scoring. As I knew he would be.

He's already a busted flush, his mind elsewhere. But at least it brings nearer the moment of the acid test. As if by magic Les Sweeney joins me with a can of Diamond White. He too knows this is the moment of truth. If Silvikrin is deadly serious, this is the point when she'll have to stick her neck out. If she stays on her rug we may be all right, but if she runs out towards him, then ...

'Then he's fucked,' says Sweeney, as if reading my thoughts. His conclusion is devastating in both its accuracy and brevity.

It has been statistically proven by police records that along with discovery of an infidelity and anxiety about imminent bankruptcy, the most likely time for any man to murder his partner is when he's trudging back to the pavilion having been given out and she's run out to console him. Is she really willing to put her own life at risk in order to show him just how much she has fallen under the spell of this crazy, wonderful game? Does she not realise she's about to get a Gunn & Moore Crusader Powerspot shoved handle-first down her pretty little throat if she as much opens her mouth for the next half-hour?

'She's getting up,' snarls Sweeney next to me.

She is. Even before Jason is halfway back she's arm in arm with him, nibbling his ear and telling him how proud she is of him. Even Julia was never brave enough to attempt this. You have to feel a sneaking respect for this girl. And the terrible thing is, it works. Despite the fact that Jason has wasted three hours in a foetid car getting to this God-forsaken fixture and now his afternoon is over with a big fat zero to his name, he's smiling and content with this creature from Paradise wrapped round his now redundant thigh pad.

'The girl's got guts, I'll give her that,' says Sweeney.

The game finishes some time around 7pm and the two teams pile into the local pub. I was hoping that Silvikrin would demand to return home as soon as stumps were drawn, but my opponent is formidable. After nearly eight hours of entirely forgettable inaction she announces that although it's her mum's birthday and Jason swore he'd get her back to town by nine so she could share a glass of champagne with her family …

'Of course we can go to the pub,' she grins, chucking Jason under his chin. 'You don't have to ask. Do you want me to drive so you can have a few drinks?'

Two hours later she's still there nursing her fifth orange juice, and even though she doesn't know anything about the game she seems genuinely thrilled to be surrounded on all sides by twenty-two blokes all with differing levels of body odour, all poring over old statistics in the scorebook and trying to stand behind her at the table so they can get a shufti down the top of her dress.

Her laughter fills the snug, and she squeezes Rex Scudamore on his arm when he asks if she'd like some of his nuts, which only makes him go even more crimson than he was already, given that he's bowled fifteen overs off the reel and is nearly sixty.

'It's disgusting,' says Sweeney from the fruit machine.

'We should be going,' says Jason at last. Thank God. Our torture is nearly over, at least until next time. 'No no,' she grins. 'Let's stay a little bit longer. That friend of yours – what's his name?'

'Les Sweeney.'

'Les says he's got a very funny story to tell about the time he put a pair of left-handed batting gloves on instead of a right-handed set. I don't want to miss it. He's just gone to the loo. Please let's stay and hear it.'

'Really?'

'Really.' She kisses Jason on the cheek, just allowing the moist point of her tongue flick his skin as she does so.

We finally stagger out into the darkness of the pub car park at just gone 10pm. By now there's a queue of players waiting to say goodbye to her. 'Bye-bye. See you again, I hope,' says Clive True, the hotel manager.

'Bye-bye,' say Barney Kent, Jez Baker and Pat Rafferty.

'Bye-bye,' says the opposition captain, kissing Silvikrin on the cheek – the one who laughed the loudest when you holed out in your innings, the one who screamed, 'Drop It!' as I was about to catch him off a skyer at point.

'Bye-bye, lovely to meet you,' says Les Sweeney. That's when I know we're in trouble.

'See you later in the season, I hope,' says Rex, winding down the window.

'I hope so,' says Silvikrin, throwing a dazzling grin in his direction. 'You're playing Pulborough Thirds next week, aren't you?'

'How did you know that?'

'I've inked all your fixtures in my Filofax,' she explains bashfully.

This girl is just too good to be true. She has effortlessly made every one in the team fall in love with her. With her eyes, her dress, her breasts, her picnic, but most of all with her apparent instinctive love of the game, of all its idiosyncrasies and oddities. Poor old Jason. Once the mortgage is signed, the date fixed and the in-laws approved of, she will turn overnight into Ena Sharples. I know it. Les Sweeney knows it. Probably deep down even Jason knows it. But like most of life's seminal experiences, he can't learn by listening to his elders. He's just got to make his mistakes himself.

Of course it won't last. Ask Sweeney. Ask me. Ask Julia. But in the meantime I'd better put Jason higher up the order next week. Because this season may be his last.

Match Result:
Harry Baldwins vs Farleigh Wallop.
Baldwins 180–7.
Farleigh Wallop 112–6.
Match drawn.

The Orang-utans

The amazing thing about sport is how it brings out the primitive animal in the male of the species. Take my brother and now distinguished academic Pete, for instance. A kinder, more gracious soul you couldn't wish to meet. Having relocated to Suffolk with his family, along with our mother in an adjoining granny flat, he's revered for the balance and discretion of his opinions. But put him in the stands at Portman Road with an Ipswich Town shirt on his back, give him a disputed penalty to worry about and he becomes King Kong.

Or my other brother, Geoff. At the age of nearly fifty, a typical jazz musician, taciturn, solitary, uneasy in front of the microphone, and a man of remarkably few words, preferring to let his music do the talking. But an evening in front of his beloved baseball on Channel 5 and watch him turn from Bix Beiderbecke into the Incredible Hulk.

It's something deep and primeval about men and sport. We can't deal with real life at all, so we revert to our evolutionary roots by beating our chests, putting our fists through walls and chucking our food about.

Chris Buckle is in many ways the most important member of the Baldwin team. As well as being a senior accountant with a firm of stockbrokers and a close personal mate, he's also treasurer of the club, a labour of love for which he receives little thanks and, when things occasionally go wrong, considerable opprobrium. He's also a committed Christian, a tireless fundraiser for charities both at home and abroad, a leading member of the local

Rotary Club and the Campaign for the Protection of Rural England, and one of the most reasonable and compassionate men I have ever met. An old-fashioned gentleman, the sort of person who would instinctively offer his seat on a bus or try to talk someone down from a window ledge.

He also loves his cricket. Chris Buckle loves it. He loves watching it, playing it and talking about it. Charts, tables, endless diatribes about team selection and field placings, his enthusiasm and dedication to the Baldwin cause makes Steve Waugh's decision to take his Australian squad to Gallipoli for a bonding session prior to the forthcoming Ashes appear positively slipshod in comparison.

And here's the problem. Because Chris Buckle is a spectacularly inept cricketer.

In all his years with the team he's scored a total of 311 runs in just over a hundred innings. Which works out at an average of just over 3.1. And yet his desire to succeed burns incandescent somewhere deep within him. Put him in a pair of whites, stick a bat in his hand, light blue touchpaper, stand well back and enjoy the show.

Not that he's selfish with it. He knows he's not exactly Viv Richards. All Chris Buckle asks for is a few minutes at the crease and a run or two, and when he's safely back in the changing room he won't offer anything more than a Penny Sparkler.

'Sorry, chaps, disappointing to get out when I did, I was feeling pretty good. Still, I made a couple and that square cut felt nice, even if I didn't score with it.'

But if the failure is more stark, which it usually is, his reactions increase proportionately through Roman Candle, Catherine Wheel, Squib to Mount Vesuvius. And if – no, when – Buckle is out first ball, as he is several times a season, playing some inept shot or being LBW on his big toe, or, as happened recently, after spearing himself in the ribcage with the handle of his bat mid-pitch while attempting to run his bat in, it rises to the intensity of a small nuclear device on one of the smaller atolls of the far Pacific. I've seen an entire changing room of grown men clear in thirty seconds at the news that Buckle is on his way back from the middle after a duck. In fact, the Firework Safety Code is a perfect metaphor for how to cope with Chris Buckle on the cricket field.

1. Keep in a sealed box or tin.
2. Never put in your pocket.
3. Ensure all children are well supervised.
4. Keep all pets and animals indoors.
5. Wear gloves to handle when spent, and douse in a bucket of cold water as soon as possible.
6. On no account return to the object, even if it seems to have gone out.

The Ceremony of the Dismissal is a feature of Baldwin cricket and as inviolate as the Changing of the Guard. Only recently a mate of one of our team who was producing a film for Channel 4 on animal behaviour surreptitiously drove down to one of our matches and secretly filmed Chris Buckle with a video camera through the passenger window of his car. The ritual begins with the customary throwing of the bat through the changing-room window, followed by the flinging of the pads into the air, the stomp round the boundary, the hour of solitude with occasional recurrences of ear-splitting expletives, then at last the slow sheepish return.

We then reach the real core of the event: the public declaration on the steps of the pavilion from his wife Bella that if he ever behaves like that again in public she will not only ban him from ever playing a cricket match again but will divorce him immediately and forthwith, and burn his whites on a bonfire, perhaps with him still wearing them. The pageant ends with the solemn oath from Chris to each individual on the ground that he will definitely control his temper from now on and that we need never fear an outburst like that again.

Until, of course, the next time.

The match against Tony Quirke's Orang-utan Relief XI is a new innovation in 1993 and one we've been looking forward to. Tony, a close colleague of Buckle's, is passionate about wildlife and has started his own charity to provide funds and support to those beleaguered conservationists attempting to stem the inexorable destruction of the orang-utans' natural habitat in the jungles of Borneo. Today's game will involve a raffle and increased match fee for all concerned, and in his capacity as leading light of the Rotary Club, Buckle has persuaded a local firm making garden furniture to sponsor every run scored in the match. The resulting profit will hopefully save a tree or two on the other side of the world.

Because of Buckle's increased commitment and the jovial nature of the encounter, I'm keen to ensure he gets a decent innings as reward. So is Tony. In fact, we all are. Because we like him. Because he deserves it. Because he's helping to save the rainforests.

It's a simple enough matter to arrange. In a conversation between myself and Tony the night before the match, we agree our strategy. For the first couple of overs Chris faces, Tony will ensure that his bowlers pitch it up, not too fast outside off stump, (so that Buckle can get off the mark without fear of being bowled or LBW), and that the fielders won't try too hard to catch anything that comes their way. Once he's got ten or so on the board we can play properly again.

It's about 4.40 on a perfect summer's afternoon in August. The Baldwins are batting, and we're four wickets down for plenty with only twenty minutes to go before the break. The Orang-utans are serving up a mixture of decent quality along with friendly right-arm filth, and God is in his firmament. Bella's celebrated teas (including her orgasmic meringues, today priced at £1 a pop) are being laid out ready for the teatime declaration, and the air is sweet with the smell of freshly warming scones and home-made elderflower cordial.

Chris Buckle is walking to the wicket.

It couldn't be a better moment for his entrance. Both the bowlers are aware that Buckle is to be given a few to be getting on with. After all, with a total of 160 already on the board, he deserves a boundary for the sponsorship alone.

As Chris walks to the wicket, flailing his bat round in the classic windmill pattern he's seen so often purveyed by his hero Ian Botham, Tony Quirke leads the Orang-utans in a gentle round of friendly applause to greet his arrival. I'm watching from the pavilion steps with Adrian Knapp, the college lecturer and Wordsworth specialist. We agree it's all unfolding beautifully for our plan; in fact, double beautifully, as Buckle's arrival has coincided with the end of the over. He'll be non-striker, which will give him a chance to scrutinise the bowling from the other end before receiving.

Around us the remaining Baldwins take up various vantage points. Jason sits on the steps in the sun with his back against a wooden post, Rex Scudamore sits at his customary berth over his scorebook, Steve Sarstedt and Barney Kent peer out of the open window of the changing rooms. Jez Baker interrupts his mobile-phone call to Los Angeles, even Les Sweeney stops rootling round in the coolbox for a can of Carlsberg and looks intently out at the middle. We're all rooting for Chris Buckle. Not only for him, but for the ground. This is a fine old pavilion. It would be a pity to see it destroyed.

Buckle stands quietly at the far end while a lanky middle-aged Orang-utan called Arthur lollops in and sends down a friendly half-volley to Phil Coleridge. Phil only needs four more for a fine half-century and is seeing it like a football. Without even bothering to move his feet he crashes it away towards the extra cover boundary where a young Orang-utan gallops after it. But no need to run for that one. It was four from the moment it left the bat.

Both sides break into spontaneous applause for Coleridge's landmark. Buckle ambles down the pitch, hitting his bat against his glove to denote applause, and congratulates his senior partner with a hearty pat on the back. The bowling is undeniably friendly.

'Even Chris should make runs today,' says Adrian.

The following events seem to unfold in slow motion.

The ball just hit is about three feet from skimming across the boundary rope when it strikes the indented handle of a drain cover concealed in the outfield. By some extraordinary chance of physics, the act of hitting the sunken handle stops the ball dead in its forward motion, sending it instead about three feet into the air, from where it drops gently back onto the grass, all momentum spent. Nobody spots this freak of physics except the young Orang-utan galloping after it.

The young Orang-utan is a member of Tony Quirke's church. But he's only been brought in this morning when his dad, a churchwarden, had to pull out with a sudden attack of rheumatism. The young boy doesn't know about Borneo. He doesn't know much about orang-utans. He doesn't know much about the Baldwins. And he sadly knows sod all about Buckle and the tacit understanding between the two sides agreed before the match.

He picks up the ball a matter of inches from the rope, turns and sends in a murderous return towards the non-striker's wicket, where Buckle is still eleven yards down the pitch thumping his partner warmly on the back and telling him how much he'd enjoyed watching such a classic exhibition of stroke play by one of the team's most popular players, and reminding him that this is his highest score in seventeen innings since his sixty-one against Clymping the season before last.

At the last moment Buckle looks round and realises his plight. The return throw is already hurtling towards his end like a tracer bullet. He makes a desperate lunge back for his crease, resulting in his falling flat on his face as if he's been felled by a stun gun. The ball hits the wicket on one bounce about halfway up middle stump with a direct hit.

'I'm afraid that's run out,' says the umpire in tones of indescribable regret. 'Terribly sorry. I'm so terribly sorry.'

Buckle picks himself up with all the grace and care of an elephant recovering after being tranquillised. He carefully bends back the arm of his glasses and places them carefully on his nose where they hang lopsidedly like an impromptu tribute to Eric Morecambe, and begins walking off.

Of course the Orang-utans would call him back. We all would. After all, it's a freak dismissal, the sort of thing that any friendly game would allow to pass without comment. But we can't. Because Buckle won't let us. He's out fair and square, and once we start patronising him by allowing him to score runs when he's already lost his wicket, that means the whole thing's obviously bollocks, all the careful planning and the match stats and the post-match discussions about whether to play an off-spinner in the next game and whether Sweeney should bowl round the wicket more often. It's all meaningless crap if we don't follow the rules.

And Buckle doesn't want it to be all meaningless crap.

As he begins the long limp back, the occupants of the pavilion begin shifting uneasily like a herd of wildebeest sensing the gradual approach of a lion. Adrian Knapp scrambles to his feet and sets off for a long walk, Steve Sarstedt remembers something he needs from the boot of his car, and Rex Scudamore announces he needs a shower. For several moments the silence is deafening. Then the first rocket goes up.

'FUCK FUCK FUCK, FUCKING FUCK!'

Back in the pavilion it becomes a frenzy of activity. Phil's partner Rachel begins shepherding their young son towards the door, Sarstedt's wife Yvonne gathers up Bella's meringues and returns them to the safety of the kitchen, while Jez Baker runs into the changing room and opens all the windows. Within seconds the entire building is a cricketing *Marie Celeste*, with doors swinging on their hinges, still-smouldering cigarettes and beakers of squash abandoned where they were left. Even Les Sweeney has forsaken his freshly opened can and has gone for a pee in the bushes.

'Now, Chris, Chris, remember your promise?' Bella rushes out in her flip-flops to meet him halfway and try to stave him off before he demolishes the entire arena including the grounds-man's hut. But it's no good. A sound of tearing Velcro and seconds later a pair of pads sail high into the air like two huge, white birds flying in formation, twirling in elegant patterns before falling gently back to earth.

The display is under way. And it's going to be a big one. There's nothing left but to wait for it to run its natural course. So sit down. Pull up a chair. Got your video camera? Good, so much the better. After all, you might as well enjoy it. Who knows when there'll be another one?

Match Report:
Harry Baldwins vs The Orang-utans.
Baldwins 245–7 (Coleridge 70, Buckle 0).
Tony Quirke's Orang-utan Relief XI 219–8.
Match drawn.

Wandsworth Cowboys

A man phones his doctor in the middle of the night.

'Doctor, come quickly. My wife seems to have a cricket ball stuck down her throat.'

'Really? How's that?'

'Don't you bloody start,' replies the man.

A gale of drunken laughter drifts in from the beer garden. Good old Sweeney, he always tells that joke after the match, and to be fair to him he tells it well. The assorted ranks of Baldwins and Wandsworth Cowboys gathered round the rustic tables certainly enjoyed it. Mind you, you could get a gale of laughter out of that mob by reading the telephone directory just now. It's amazing what a couple of hours in a beer garden will do for a weak gag.

Saturday, 19 June 1993. My new friends the Cowboys and my old friends the Baldwins are enjoying a balmy summer's evening in a pub near Tolworth after a stupendous game of cricket that went down to the very last ball. The pub is doing a huge barbecue, with racks of plump sausages, honey-drizzled spare ribs and aromatic charcoal fumes wafting across the revellers. The beer is Shepherd Neame, and the highlights of the day's play in the Lord's Test between England and Australia are showing on the telly screens at the bar. This is what I call a pub. Fantastic.

The Test may not make pretty viewing, with England holed at 193–9 in reply to the Aussies' 632–4, but apart from that this couldn't be a better place to while away a summer's evening. I could stay here for ever, talking about today's match, drinking

Shepherd Neame and boring the Cowboys about old matches we've played so that they can bore us back about old matches they've played. This is what cricket's really about. Twenty-odd blokes boring each other to death while we get slowly pissed.

There's only one problem. I'm supposed to be taking Julia out for dinner.

Julia and I met exactly nine years ago today, and I'm supposed to be taking her out for a meal. She's currently appearing in a play in the West End, a robust comedy from the pen of John Godber called *On the Piste*, a satire on skiing holidays. It being Saturday she has both a matinee and an evening performance, which is why I've been allowed to play cricket on this, the day of our special celebration. But at 10.15pm sharp I must be at the stage door of the Garrick Theatre in Charing Cross Road, showered, aftershaved, suited and booted, with a bunch of flowers in one hand and a reservation for a table for two at the Ivy in the other.

The clock now shows 9.27. I'm in danger of cutting it a bit fine. I wonder if I left now whether I could do Tolworth to Charing Cross Road in forty-two minutes? I'll just get this round in and then I'll go; with any luck the South Circular will be clear at this time of night. It won't matter too much if I'm not there dead on time.

Mind you, these three pints I've had are a problem. Plus the one I've just ordered. I'll just have a sip. Les Sweeney can have the rest. He doesn't have to watch his intake since he lost his licence.

Someone's calling my name from outside. It's Barney Kent. 'Simmo, come here and tell us that story of your getting pissed in the commentary box with Brian Johnston and how you convinced Len Hutton that you were James Hewitt.'

Ah. The Len Hutton story. It's one of my best, and with thirty-six pints of Shepherd Neame between them I'm sure to get a good response, particularly the bit where I set the clock-work feet running across the top of Henry Blofeld's bald head.

I'll just tell that one and then I must be going. Come to think of it, I really ought to change out of my whites as well. And have a shower. Perhaps I'll be able to freshen up in the Ivy toilets. They have swanky sachets of hand-wash and fresh towels in the bogs there too. I can spruce up while Julia's ordering the cocktails. Perfect.

I grab a handful of pints and follow Barney out into the warm air. Someone has brought me a plate of sausages. God they look good, lying there surrounded by mounds of coleslaw and long lazy curls of tomato ketchup. I suppose a couple of bangers couldn't do any harm, just in case I'm delayed in traffic. And the service at the Ivy can be notoriously slow.

And there's still so much to talk about. The match, the final over, Clive True's catch on the boundary, Barney Kent's run-out; and then there's the Test match to dissect. What I'd give to be going to Lord's tomorrow, for the Sunday of the Test, to see England's beleaguered batsmen trying to save the game in front of a full house and with this new Aussie wunderkind Shane Warne bowling at them. Apparently Graham Gooch, the England captain, is now under severe pressure to step down after yet another disappointing personal performance. The newspapers are claiming that his loss of form is to do with the recent break-up of his marriage and his public liaison with a new mystery woman.

What a dark horse! Difficult to believe, really. It's a funny old world. And a drink with the Cowboys in a beer garden is just the sort of evening when life's absurdities are best discussed.

'So what happened, Simmo?' shouts one of the Cowboys. 'Barney tells us you had a water-pistol fight with Trevor Bailey live on air.'

* * *

Twenty minutes or so later I'm dimly aware that something's vibrating in my pocket. It's my pager. The message is simple. Ring Me.

I run to the payphone by the serving hatch and call the stage door of the Garrick Theatre. The doorman answers and puts out a call over the tannoy for Miss Deakin to come to the payphone. After several minutes I recognise the sound of her footsteps approaching down the echoing corridor.

'Where are you?' she says without waiting for pleasantries. 'You said you'd be in the dressing room when I came off stage. We've just finished the curtain call – are you nearby?'

'Well—'

'Don't say you're running late, you'll kick yourself if you're not here now.'

'Look, Julia—'

A huge burst of Nordic laughter erupts in my left ear. Sweeney is telling his cricket-ball-down-the-throat joke to a party of Swedish tourists sitting at an adjoining table.

'Where are you? Are you on your way?'

'Well—'

'Are you still in the pub?'

'Look, Julia—'

'If you've let me down on our anniversary, I will never forgive you.'

'Julia—'

'I'm all tarted up. I've got my new dress ready and my stilettos. I've washed my hair. I didn't have anything to eat between shows because I knew we were eating later. Are you telling me you're standing me up?'

'Look, it's slightly complicated—'

'Give her a bite of your sausage,' shouts Barney into my phone as he passes on his way to the toilet.

'Look, the fact is—'

'Just tell me. Are you nearby or not?'

'No. I'm still in Tolworth. I'm running late.'

There's a long, long silence. In the background I can just hear the show relay system. The running times for tonight's show were first act 1 hour 6 minutes, second act …

'Julia, let me explain—'

'Have a good weekend, everybody. And, Miss Deakin, you have guests.'

'I'll never forgive you for this, Michael.' She's obviously about to finish the conversation. I've got to think fast. Luckily there is one maxim that all errant husbands can make use of. As Harold Macmillan once said: 'Greater love hath no man than this. That he lay down his friends for his life … ' This is such an occasion.

'All right, Julia. The fact is, if you really want to know, the fact is that Barney thinks his relationship is going belly up. He's absolutely worried sick and he doesn't know who else to turn to for help. Poor bloke, he's got hardly any work at the moment, he can't even afford to pay petrol money, his hair is falling out, and now he reckons Nadia is about to leave him. He says I'm the only bloke he can talk to. All he's asking for is a shoulder to cry on and someone to listen to his troubles. What am I supposed to answer? Sorry, mate, but I've got a warm tart with wild blue-berries and dusted icing sugar with my name on it? We're supposed to be buddies, for Christ's sake. Men have emotional needs as well. And if I can save their marriage and stop him throwing himself off Waterloo Bridge by giving the bloke a shoulder to cry on on a Saturday evening, I reckon that's the least I can do. And you too, come to think of it.'

Barney, returning with some pistachio nuts, shouts, 'Hello, Deaks!' down the phone, followed by a loud raspberry.

'Who was that? That sounded like Barney.'

'I told you. He's overwrought.'

'He sounds pissed to me.'

There's a commotion on the other end of the phone. 'I've got to go, there are some VIPs who want to meet me. Don't say I didn't warn you.' She hangs up.

This is going to be a difficult one, no doubt about that. If I set off now and buy her some flowers on the journey, that usually helps. There's a BP garage up by Roehampton, they usually do them outside on the forecourt and at this time of night I might even get them reduced. I'll just tell my *TMS* story and be getting off.

* * *

Up in Charing Cross Road Julia puts down the receiver and returns to her dressing room. Moments later there's a knock on the door. She checks her make-up in her dressing mirror.

'Come in.' The company stage-manager's head appears round the doorframe.

'Are you decent?'

'Yes, thanks.'

'Sure it's OK?'

'Yes, yes, of course. I'd be pleased to meet them.'

The manager looks behind him and nods. 'Please come in,' he says. He opens the door to its full width and ushers in the England cricket captain and his new partner.

I suppose when the national team you're skippering has just been taken for 600-odd in under two days you want a bit of light relief after close of play. And what better way to escape the miseries of your responsibility than attending an uproarious live comedy, particularly one by John Godber.

A brisk taxi ride down Baker Street has ensured they've made it from St John's Wood to the Garrick in plenty of time for curtain up. Having recognised the England captain as a VIP, the company manager arranges for free drinks at the interval and asks if they'd like to meet the cast at the end of the evening. Graham's partner, who is also called Julia, says she would love to. One by one they've been introduced to the entire company of six. Julia is their final stop.

'We've had a great evening,' says Graham, shaking Julia's hand.

'We mustn't stay long,' says his Julia. 'Graham has another big day tomorrow and it's an early start again.'

My Julia nods. She hasn't even pretended to follow cricket

for over five years now, but has a hazy suspicion Graham has got something to do with the game.

'Are you interested in cricket?' asks Graham.

'No, Graham, I'm afraid not. In fact, I couldn't fancy it fried.' My Julia always lapses into Lincolnshire colloquialisms when she's tired. 'But my partner's bloody cracked on it. He talks about it from morning till night, sometimes he goes entire days without mentioning anything else. He bores on about it so much sometimes I don't know whether I'm on foot or 'ossback.'

Graham and Julia love this. Foot or 'ossback. It's an expression neither of them has ever heard before.

'What a pity he's not here,' says Graham's Julia, still chuckling.

'Isn't it?' says my Julia. 'If he were in the room now meeting you two he'd be like a dog with two dicks.'

Graham and Julia love this expression. A dog with two dicks. Marvellous.

'What a shame,' says the other Julia.

'Isn't it?' replies my Julia.

'Is he around tomorrow?' asks Graham.

'I haven't decided yet,' replies Julia.

'What I mean is, I'd be happy to offer you a couple of free tickets for tomorrow's play at Lord's,' replies Graham. 'I have a pair on me now.' He fishes out two tickets for row H of the new Mound Stand.

My Julia takes a sip of wine. Her party dress for the Ivy, bought specially for the occasion from Karen Millen, is hanging behind the door on a hanger, just above where Graham and Julia are sitting. The stilettos, purchased between performances earlier today, are still in their tissue paper on the floor. And something in her knows that ten miles away I'm probably handing over £4.99 for a pack of two-day-old dahlias wrapped in greasy cellophane.

'Would you like a day at the Test match?' he continues.

'To be honest, Graham, just now I'd rather have my arse scraped with a brick.'

Graham and his Julia burst into fresh laughter. My arse scraped with a brick. It's another expression neither of them has ever heard before.

'Never mind then, I know what it's like,' says Graham, glancing at his Julia. 'Cricket can be a long old haul if you're not passionate about it.'

'You said it,' replies my Julia. She's rather taken with Graham and his partner. She turns to her new friend and smiles ruefully.

'What a coincidence we both have the same name,' she says. 'I suppose you're a cricket widow as well, are you?'

* * *

When I get back home just after midnight, via a BP garage at Tolworth, a diversion on the Kingston bypass due to an overturned lorry, a locked theatre and a maître d' who explains that our table was reallocated soon after eleven when nobody had appeared, our flat is in darkness and Julia is asleep in bed. But there on the mantelpiece are two tickets to the Sunday of the Test. Julia is nothing if not generous-spirited. And we have a wonderful day: one I'll remember for ever.

Not that the tickets are free. On the contrary. As well as rescheduling our trip to the Ivy, I'm required to pay for an MOT for her car, accompany her round every shop in Hampstead High Street without complaint, take out the rubbish for the next six months and agree to her mother staying with us during the entire Oval Test Match.

Match Report:
England vs Australia.
Australia 632–4 declared.
England 205 and 365.
Australia win by an innings and 62 runs.

New Delhi Gymkhana Presidents XI

Every club player who has ever picked up a bat in the lowliest knockabout harbours fantasies about what it might be like to face a world-class bowler. Eavesdrop on any group of cricketers in a pub and you'll hear us endlessly speculating on how we'd fare against Derek Underwood, Bob Willis or Ian Botham. Even now, thirty years later, I still fantasise about facing Wes Hall at Lord's.

Watching them on television or even in person from a grandstand seat in the ground gives no hint of what it might actually be like out there in the middle. That's why crowds at cricket matches always gather behind the batsman when professionals are conducting a net practice. We're not watching them facing the bowlers at the far end – we're imagining it's us.

How fast would they be? A bit quicker? A lot quicker? Would we even see the ball? And what about facing a spin bowler? Might it be possible to read his action out of his hand, or even, and whisper it softly, perhaps score a run or two? A true occasional's belief in his ability to survive against the world's best will inevitably rise exponentially according to the amount of beer he's consumed. We all secretly fancy ourselves to score a few before the inevitable clatter of stumps. True occasionals, whatever else, are eternal optimists.

On 12 January 1996 I finally have the chance to find out for myself. Just after 4.30 in the afternoon, in the concrete furnace that is the Jawaharlal Nehru International cricket stadium in the suburbs of New Delhi, I walk out to bat for the Gaieties Cricket

Club of London in their match against the New Delhi Gymkhana Presidents XI. At the far end, about to bowl the next ball, stands one of the greatest bowlers in the history of the game.

The match, and indeed the entire tour, is in its closing moments. A day of withering one-sided cricket reduced to the simple equation of me versus possibly the greatest slow left-arm orthodox bowler ever to come out of the subcontinent. At one end the founder of the Harry Baldwins and scorer of nearly 750 runs in Sunday-afternoon village cricket in only a decade. At the other Bishan Singh Bedi: the bowler who has taken over 1,500 first-class wickets, including 266 in Test matches at an average of 28.7: a bowler of whom it was said that the purity and perfection of his art was a connoisseur's dream, a man who could lure the most gifted batsmen in the world into giving up their wicket as if entranced by some necromancer's spell. Twenty-five years since watching him torment and humiliate the Sussex batsmen at Hove, years spent imagining what it might be like to face him in a proper game, it seems I'm about to find out.

He stands twenty-two yards away, spinning the ball lazily from hand to hand as he studies his latest quarry, his trademark sky-blue turban on his head as if some celestial oil-colourist had dropped a blob of paint onto the monochrome canvas of concrete and parched outfield enveloping us.

The odyssey, which is about to reach its stark climax, started on a dark December evening a few weeks previously with a phone call from Jez Baker. One of the other teams he plays for, a louche outfit of media types and theatricals called the Gaieties, created by Lupino Lane and currently overseen by the brilliant and baleful playwright and author Harold Pinter, was due to embark on a short cricket-playing tour. Almost before the last cracker had been pulled and the piccalilli put away for another year, they would begin the first of twelve planned fixtures across northern India. A space had come up in the team.

Since arriving on New Year's Eve, the trip has been an exotic medley of joy and farce. We've played on everything from Test match grounds to virtual building sites, competed against every-one from children to gnarled ex-pros. We've taken the field against the Maharanah of Udaipur's XI to the accompaniment of 'Sussex By The Sea', played by his personal fife and bugle band on a distant hilltop. We've had our railway carriage invaded by eunuchs, we've seen the Taj Mahal and the Red Fort at Agra, we've experi-enced cocktails at midnight at the top of the highest building in Bombay, and in one extraordinary scenario we've found ourselves leaping a hedge to avoid clouds of tear gas and a battalion of lathi-wielding policemen in Connaught Square at midnight: the only piece of athleticism most of us have shown all tour.

If we've spent most of our evenings downing vast quantities of booze, on the field of play it's been a sobering experience. We've been trussed and basted the length and breadth of Rajasthan. A long English winter followed by nearly two weeks of scales-buckling meals has proved piss-poor preparation for an itinerary of ten matches in twenty days in soaring temperatures, and the original squad of sixteen are now reduced to a Dads' Army of nine semi-fit crocks with the remainder hobbling like cripples or slumped over the toilet bowl in their hotel bedroom. To top it all, our best batsman has just returned home to London after being bumped off his rickshaw by a speeding car, and the remainder are now hanging on grimly while team after team perform a jig on our lifeless corpse.

We face our customary hopeless position again today. After having been taken for 379 in our allotted forty overs in a limited-overs contest, we require a further 267 for victory in six overs with only me left. Which works out at a run rate of 44.5 per over.

This being the final match, I've decided to go out with a flourish. It's been a fantastic, exotic, wonderful trip, but I've barely made a ripple on the field of play. After an initial knock of twenty-three against a warm-up game of twelve-year-olds, I've barely got it off the square. Too many Bristol Creams, too many Cheese Footballs, too many small cigars. My contribution to the trip can be summed up in one deadly word. 'Forgettable.'

But now is my chance to do something – anything – that will linger in the memory. Tomorrow we fly home and the tour will be over. I may never get this chance again. And I'm determined to go out with a flourish. If I do nothing else on this tour (and I have done nothing else), I'm going to play the most audacious of all cricket shots, the one that no self-respecting amateur would dream of playing against a legend of the sport. A reverse sweep.

The dictionary definition of a reverse sweep is: 'A cross-batted sweep shot, but reversing the blade of the bat halfway through the swing and thus sweeping the ball around to the off side from the leg side.' It's considered a suicidal stroke to attempt by all but the most gifted batsman, as it involves momentarily letting go of the handle mid-air in order to rearrange the hands. Mike Gatting's reputation never recovered from fatally attempting it in a World Cup semi-final on this very continent. But for me it's a question of Hobson's choice.

The awful truth is that after a summer of diving headlong through a fireplace in a long-running farce, the reverse sweep is now my only scoring shot. With a dickie left elbow as a result of my twice-nightly exertions, my only two scoring shots, namely the cover drive and the smear into the window display through midwicket, are now impossible to play. All last season and into Rajasthan I've been confined to playing ugly little nurdles through square leg or patting the ball meekly back to the bowler. But the reverse sweep is the only stroke entirely unrestricted by my afflictions, so much so that I've come to rely upon it exclusively to move my score along.

I take my familiar guard and step away for a moment to survey the fielders with an extravagant 360-degree gaze. Even now I have no idea why I bother to do this, as the fielding positions have never had the slightest influence on my shot selection. Any stroke from my bat that bisects diving fielders has sadly always been entirely coincidental. Still, Bedi won't know that.

He looks hard at me, scrutinising me like I'm an insect pinned to a card. Is it my imagination, or has he already uncovered my myriad shortcomings just from the way I'm crouched over the bat, tapping nervously. The way my hands are too close together on the bat handle, the way my head is already falling over to the off, the way my eyes aren't parallel to the ground. He appears to know all about me.

With a wave of his hand he makes a few minor adjustments: gulley pushed a bit deeper, mid-on brought in a couple of yards and square leg pushed to just backward. Each minute repositioning of his fielders is indicated by the smallest of finger signals. Does he know the shot I've already decided to play? How? I haven't told anyone. Not even myself.

Bedi is ready at last. A final twirl of the ball, the umpire calls play and he begins that short loping approach, the one I've seen so many times on telly over two decades. He approaches the wicket and releases the ball. I'm about to find out what it's really like to face a top-class bowler.

It hangs there in the air.

And suddenly all those discussions in the pub about the gulf between amateurs and professionals have been answered. Because it's like something Dad would have lobbed up to me when I was a kid in Brooklands Park: not too quick, not too slow, not too anything, merely spinning innocuously in the blue sky like the illustration on the front of Mr Fitchit's beach cricket set.

I'm appalled. I was expecting something horrendous, a delivery so far beyond anything I've ever faced before as to confirm my decision all those years ago to forsake a career in the game. But as it hovers there in the blue sky, I'm seized with the realisation that the chasm between us and them, amateur and pro, is no more than a crack in the pavement. If someone bowled a ball like this to me in a Baldwin match, I'd probably stop it with my glove, sling it back to the bowler and tell him, 'Never mind, have another go … ' In fact, I might say it anyway, once it's been retrieved from the far stands.

I lift the bat high, let go and in a trice have grasped it again the other way round. Perhaps age has caught up with the Indian master. Or perhaps he was never quite as good as we all thought. Perhaps none of them are.

But then something inexplicable occurs. The ball, having seemed suspended in the air from some invisible string with the words 'Hit Me' on it, suddenly dips and loops at the last second. It pitches just short of a length, spits like a cobra and climbs at a scientifically unfeasible angle. Striking the outside edge of my bat it balloons gently into the air and is caught with pathetic ease by the wicketkeeper.

My tour is over.

Even as the catch is pouched, Bedi is marching down the pitch towards me. His face is wreathed in an expression of delight and disbelief. Last time I made a mess of such an important moment, the cold, cruel eyes of games master Dave Bunker were staring back at me. But this time it's impossible to feel depressed at the warm, spluttering laughter issuing forth from Bedi's lips.

'Michael, I think that must have been a spur-of-the-moment shot.'

'On the contrary, Mr Bedi,' I reply. 'I've been planning it since 1971 ... '

Match Report:

Bombay Gymkhana Presidents XI vs The Gaieties.
Bombay Gymkhana Presidents XI 379–8.
The Gaieties 113 all out (Bedi 4–20).
Presidents XI win by 266 runs.

South Africa 'A'

At the end of the 1997 summer I announce to my team-mates that I've bowled my last over. During the countless Baldwin matches over the years I've tried hard to remodel my action and become a genuine contributor with the ball, but it's remained stubbornly stuck in its old mode, the subject of gentle derision. My news is greeted with a howl of disappointment. The Baldwins assure me they love me bowling the odd over: it livens up the day, brings a smile to their lips and reminds them that there are more things to cricket than winning or losing. Like having a good laugh.

But I'm resolved. The guffaws are starting to wear thin, and at the age of forty it's time to acknowledge that Les Lenham was right after all. Nobody with my bowling action is ever going to get a wicket. There's only one claim I can make about those years of futile effort: my bowling action may not be any good but at least it was unique.

A few months later, on Sunday 9 November, the visiting England team under the captaincy of Mike Atherton are playing the final warm-up match of their tour before locking horns with South Africa proper the following week. The opposition for this final four-day practice match in Kimberley is South Africa 'A', a team of talented players on the fringes of national selection and with plenty to prove.

It's been a tough first day and a half for the tourists, with South Africa 'A' eventually declaring on a massive 470–9. Midway through the second afternoon, England openers Atherton and Stewart pad up to begin the long wearisome reply.

In the commentary box at the far end of the ground my old mate Chalkie White, second-in-command at Everyball and occasional ringer for the Baldwins, sits at a microphone. He's recently emigrated to Johannesburg to pursue a sports-journalism career and is now working as summariser for national radio, providing regular updates to the nation's sports-mad fans. His Gloucestershire burr provides a soothing counterpoint to the guttural tones of his commentary partner, a bloke named André from Durban whose acquaintance he has only made at the start of the match.

Much of the media interest in the game is due to the unexpected inclusion of an eighteen-year-old mystery leg spinner, Paul Adams. Completely unknown, words like 'freak' and 'one-off' are already sticking to him. The selectors are backing what is commonly called 'a hunch' …

At approximately 4pm, eight overs after the tea interval, Adams comes on to bowl. In every part of the ground binoculars are raised, sandwiches are dispensed with mid-munch, newspapers are put down on nearby seats. The biggest mystery bowler since Spedegue the asthmatic schoolteacher is about to deliver his first ball in the spotlight.

His first attempt is greeted with a wave of laughter that ripples round the stadium. Not because it's a terrible ball – it's right on the button – but because of his bowling action. It's something indescribable, a shower of windmilling arms, his head jerking violently downwards as he bowls so that at point of release he's actually looking underneath his own chest towards deep long on. When he looks up again Alec Stewart is staring open-mouthed back at him.

His second delivery clean bowls Stewart with a perfectly pitched googly. Up in the commentary box André from Johannesburg rocks back in his seat and pushes his headphones further up his forehead. 'Well, for once I'm lost for words,' he says. 'It's impossible to describe this young man's bowling action. He looks … well, he looks like a frog in a liquidiser.'

André turns to the expert summariser beside him. 'I've never seen anything remotely like it. Have you, Chalkie?'

My old Everyball mucker and occasional Baldwin leans into the microphone.

'Well,' he begins, a faraway look in his eyes. The fact is, Chalkie's been missing England a lot lately: the pubs, the traffic, the London buses, *Fifteen to One* with William G. Stewart ...

'In actual fact, I have.'

His brow crinkles into a fond memory of Baldwins versus Merton Park Casuals at Palewell Common ...

'There's this actor I know in London ... '

Match report
South Africa 'A' vs England.
South Africa 'A' 470–9 declared and 148–4.
England 308 (Simkins 4–65).
Following on 309 (Simkins 5–116).
South Africa 'A' win by 6 wickets.

Nuthurst

Cricket is an extremely delicate mechanism. Like the finest quartz watch, it works only when every component part is in place and combining in perfect harmony. Start tinkering with an extra centimetre on the bat, a thicker seam on the ball, wider stumps, a longer pitch or the use of substitutes, and before you know where you are you've got people in pyjamas playing rounders to the sound of 'We Are The Champions' and half the crowd watching from portable jacuzzis on the boundary. Leave well alone if you want the game to work.

Which is why I'm horrified when Jez Baker tells me that for our 2001 match against the village of Nuthurst, both teams have agreed to play twelve a side.

Playing with twelve rather than eleven is perhaps the most profound possible example of meddling. The game evolved for eleven a side, no more or less. At a pinch you can get away with fewer, but having any more has a disastrous effect and inevitably disrupts the contest, guaranteeing a wretched afternoon for all concerned.

But even as I protest down the phone I know I'm on a sticky wicket. Bakey is match manager for this fixture and has already done the deal with his opposite number. He assures me that the Nuthurst captain, a huge and amiable man called Dave Butler, was very understanding about the sudden request, made only this morning. Dave even thought of a twelfth man that Nuthurst could bring in to even things up again. No worries apparently.

But how have we got twelve? I was with Bakey until 3am this morning at Theatros nightclub. I dimly recollect we spent most of the evening talking about how parlous the acting business is just now and lamenting the fact we never get to meet anyone powerful enough to turn things round for us, but I distinctly remember him confirming as I poured him into the minicab that we had a full eleven for today's match.

Bakey explains. He received a call only this morning from an old university mate who's just back in the country for a long week-end and really fancied a game of cricket. Bakey said he just couldn't say no. It will probably be the bloke's only game this year.

'To be honest I thought you might be able to find room for him in the car as well,' he continues. 'His partner has to borrow their only wheels and can't join us until later in the afternoon.'

'I'm not interested. We never play with twelve. I don't care who he is, it's absolutely against everything we stand for to add in make-weights who ring up on spec when we're already full just because they're old college mates of yours. It's an absolute violation of your position as match manger and frankly I would have expected better of you. So you can ring him back now and tell him there's no room either in the car or the team. Sorry, Bakey, but your attitude really takes the biscuit.'

'You feel that strongly, do you?'

'I do. I really do. Who the hell is he anyway?'

'It's Sam Mendes.'

'The Oscar-winning director Sam Mendes?'

'That's the one.'

'What time are we picking him up?'

* * *

Sam Mendes is, of course, not only an Oscar-winning film direc-tor but also one of the greatest theatre directors in the country, head of the internationally acclaimed Donmar Warehouse in London and one of the three or four most influential Englishmen in the entire world of theatre, feature films and showbusiness. He is also going out with one of the most ravishing and gifted actresses of our generation, Kate Winslet. As Alan Ayckbourn once wrote, 'Some people are born with silver spoons in their mouths. Others have an entire canteen of cutlery.'

The chance of spending time with one of the most powerful and influential creators of jobs in this miserably overcrowded industry is just too much to resist. Particularly as things have been unusually quiet recently. Apart from three lines as a crooked florist in *The Bill*, I haven't worked for nearly three months. And rumour has it that Mendes is soon to be directing his second movie, a gangster picture set in 1920s Illinois starring Paul Newman and Tom Hanks.

We pick up Sam from his Primrose Hill apartment soon after eleven. Despite his meteoric rise to international stardom, he remains exactly as I recall him from previous encounters with him at parties and suchlike. He's jokey, self-deprecating, hugely appreciative of a chance to play a game he loves and has already popped out to get some sandwiches for the ride down. But he also carries with him a huge and intimidating cricket bag, known in the game as a coffin, and universally regarded as the sign of a seriously good cricketer.

We stop briefly at a petrol station on the A24 near Dorking so he can run in for the Sunday papers. His latest play has opened to raves in the dailies, and rumour has it today's broadsheets are even more spectacular. While he's waiting to pay, I take the opportunity of his momentary absence to tackle Bakey again.

'Are you sure Nuthurst know what they've agreed to?'

'Yes, yes, stop worrying,' replies Bakey, opening a carton of mung beans and alfalfa sprouts. He has got to do a scene in a jacuzzi for a forthcoming TV movie being filmed next month, starring Dyan Cannon and Mickey Rooney, and is on a detoxification programme. 'He'll fit in perfectly. You can see for yourself he's the best company.'

'It's not his company I'm worried about,' I hiss. Mendes is already emerging through the automatic doors with a ton of newsprint. 'I Googled him before we set off. He was nearly a Cambridge Blue at cricket and taught the game at some swanky school in Oxford before taking up directing. What's more he opens the batting for some village that got through to the final at Lord's the other year, and said in an interview recently that he's met Mike Brearley several times and tries to integrate his theories on captaincy into his directing.'

The rear door opens and Mendes climbs in. 'Thought I'd get us some sweets,' he says, distributing jelly babies, Twix bars and Kettle Chips in all directions. It's impossible not to like this man.

As we approach the ground, I tell myself perhaps we'll be all right after all. Perhaps the disruption to the game won't be too substantial. Nuthurst is a charming group of blokes who have played on the same village green since the late nineteenth century. We can't afford to sour relations and lose the fixture.

Their captain, Dave, is waiting to greet us at the car park when we arrive soon after 1pm. We introduce him to our twelfth man, whom we merely call Sam.

'Good to see you all,' says Dave, beaming. 'We always enjoy this match. The Baldwins play in such a good spirit, not like some of the shysters we've picked up over the years. We're always so evenly matched. You can guarantee a close encounter between Nuthurst and the Baldies.' He offers to help me in with the kit bag.

'You're sure you're happy to play twelve-a-side?' I ask nervously as we lumber up the steps of the pavilion.

'Absolutely. Glad to give your friend a game. Though your match manager says your mate hasn't played much in recent years. So we've hauled in someone to balance things up. In fact, here's our twelfth man arriving now.'

He points across the green to a line of horse chestnut trees in the distance. A boy of no more than eleven or twelve and carrying a Tesco's bag containing a pair of gym shoes is approaching us.

'My nephew Warren,' says Dave proudly. 'Hasn't played

much except for Kwik Cricket but apparently has good coordination and has been wanting to play with the big boys for a couple of years. You've made his day.'

We win the toss and I decide to bat. And I'm delighted to see that Sam Mendes is nothing if not self-effacing. He insists on batting no higher than number nine, offers to do a stint of umpiring while we start our innings, and even fields for the opposition when one of them has to pop home to check he turned the gas off.

Perhaps it's the inevitable tension and nerves of being in the presence of quasi-royalty, or perhaps it's just our usual incompetence, but we manage to make a complete Horlicks of our innings. Jez Baker is caught on the boundary essaying an extravagant drive, Barney Kent treads on a stray bootlace mid-pitch and is run out, I swat limply to mid-off for three, and Chris Buckle is hit on the instep and has to retire hurt. Even by Hollywood standards it is a spectacular flop. Mendes enters with us holed at thirty-seven for seven, and with Buckle with his foot in a bowl of iced water and unable to bat.

Mendes's innings lasts a mere forty minutes. After a carefully played over of classic forward defensives, he unleashes a VistaVision array of shots to all parts of the boundary, bombarding neighbouring rooftops and sending twigs and leaves cascading down on passing cars. His entire century occupies forty-three balls, his last scoring shots being six, six, four and six. The Nuthurst opening bowler, whose figures had stood at eight overs, five wickets for eleven runs, finished up with twenty-one overs, five for 179. The Baldwins' total of 265 for nine is our highest in the club's history.

'Quite handy your extra man, isn't he?' says Dave with a forced smile as we leave the field for tea.

The break passes in what can be best described as a mood of simmering cordiality. The communal tea table, normally a scene of friendly mingling between the two teams, is now one of stilted politeness. Nuthurst's opening bowler, the one who now has the most expensive bowling figures in the club's 103-year history, sits outside on the steps eating his sandwiches in silence. Mendes is adamant that he won't bowl, not after he had such a big innings.

Whether it's because of nerves or just that the combined age of our bowling attack is two hundred and fifteen, but we bowl like drains in the two-hour session after tea. Despite our monumental total, by six o'clock, Nuthurst have filled their boots against what is known in the trade as cafeteria bowling, a help-yourself offering of juicy half-volleys and feeble long hops, and are now only thirty runs short with five men – six including Dave's nephew, young Warren – still to bat. We've tried all other ten players, including Neil, our communist wicketkeeper, but to no effect.

There's only one place left to turn. I summon Mendes up from deep fine leg and throw him the ball.

He carefully marks out his run-up and practises a warm-up delivery: a short, rather languid approach, with a slight burst of adrenaline into the delivery stride.

'Any thoughts, skipper?' he says.

Well, yes, but none about the cricket. Plenty of thoughts about whether there might be a part for me in his next film, what it must be like to wake up with Kate Winslet, whether the chip shop in Dorking will be open on the way back and how much a round of drinks for the entire opposition team might set me back – but, as usual, precious few on how to win the game. But I need to come up with something now, if only to save face with a potential future employer.

I launch into an assortment of half-digested phrases I've heard professionals use during recent post-match interviews on the box: 'letting the batsman sniff the leather'; 'pitching it at the stumps so that if they miss he'll hit'; making sure the ball 'goes big on them'. I'm just about to add that he should remain 'absolutely still until the last possible moment' when I realise that was goalkeeper Ray Clemence talking about the art of saving penalties. To my relief Mendes seems to accept my words of wisdom without comment. He trots back to his mark.

But my words of wisdom obviously do the trick. Over the next five minutes he takes four wickets for three runs, including an unbelievable caught-and-bowled requiring him to leap high into the air in his follow-through to pouch one-handed a murderous drive that otherwise would have taken out the lounge windows of a distant bungalow – a hit from the bat of the simmering opening bowler, naturally. With only one wicket to fall, Dave's nephew Warren begins tottering on. The match is near to its climax. And even nearer to my next problem.

The sight of a child coming in to bat at a crucial point in an autumnal Sunday afternoon's cricket match stirs up a hornet's nest of conflicting priorities. On the one hand you don't want to be brutish by decking him with a beamer or splaying his stumps first ball and crushing his spirit for ever. On the other hand, we want to win. And they're only a couple of meaty blows from victory. Even before Warren has reached the crease, I spot Mendes returning for some more expert guidance. I'm going to have to think of something else to say.

But what? I've already used my stock of all-purpose phrases. If I begin droning on about corridors of uncertainty I'll be rumbled in an instant. But thankfully Mendes is only approaching to make a suggestion of his own.

'Let's take it easy, shall we?' he suggests. 'I'll get him down the other end and then we'll throw everything against the other batsman.'

I nod sagely. Mendes returns to his mark and shortens his run-up. But even as he's measuring his revised approach, Les Sweeney sprints up from deep long off. I haven't seen him move this fast since we arrived at that pub just as they were calling last orders. My authority as captain is being stretched to its limits.

'What are you going to do?' he asks anxiously.

'Les, you can see the boy's only eleven or twelve. I've told Sam to give him an easy single and get him down the other end.'

'Have you seen what he's wearing?' Sweeney nods in the direction of the incoming batsman. And then I spot it.

Warren's wearing olive-coloured trousers.

One of the Ten Commandments of Sunday cricket is: 'Thou Shalt Beware The Batsman In The Olive-Coloured Trousers.' Bitter experience has shown that the scruffier and more ill-prepared the batsman appears, the more likely it is that he'll be some superhuman cricketing prodigy who'll batter you to all parts of the county and who, by the time you've realised his talent, will have his eye and consequently be unstoppable.

What to do? Sweeney beckons Mendes back over and a frenzied three-way discussion with Britain's greatest young filmmaker, me, and the man whose mum used to wash Ian Botham's shirts ensues. An amended strategy is agreed: Sam will stick to our opening gambit for his first ball and see what happens. If it disappears back over his head we'll consider the head-high beamer next up.

At last Warren is ready. Sam ambles in off a few gentle paces and sends down a juicy half volley well wide of the off stump. Warren lifts the bat and attempts a mow in the direction of extra cover. More by luck than judgement he manages to connect with the very toe end of the bat. The ball zings off in the direction of third man.

Our third man is Chris Buckle.

Fielders stationed at third man are habitually among the poorest in a team. The position, far away from screaming catches and meaty biffs, is one in which you can hide those players who can neither run nor catch. Or who are carrying a debilitating injury, such as a badly bruised instep. In any Baldwin side at least half the team would qualify for this sort of special dispensation, but today Chris Buckle is in the team, and in addition to his batting average of 3.1, he is a notoriously poor fielder even by our standards. To my knowledge he has never actually managed to cling on to a catch.

Warren's toe-end mow comes straight at him. Unable to get out of the way because of his injured left foot, he shoots out a vast pair of claw-like hands to protect himself. The ball goes straight through his splayed fingers and hits his breastbone with a loud smack. Before it can drop to the ground, Buckle somehow manages to clasp it to his jersey. Disbelief gives way to orgasm as he realises he's completed his first catch. He lets out a bellow of joy that can be heard at Gatwick airport, and throws the ball in ecstasy into the air.

* * *

In the changing room afterwards, frigid cordiality soon gives way to seething resentment. Their captain Dave asks to see me in my capacity as club president in the car park. His once jovial features are set in a mask of disappointment and anger. His lips are pulled back into a snarl and his rubicund cheeks are now pinched and white. Adge Cutler has turned into Sid Vicious.

'Mike—'

'Dave, I know, I'm sorry, it's just that—'

'No, Mike, let me speak. The boys have asked me to point out that although Sam was a lovely bloke it was obvious to any fool from the first ball that he's a supremely gifted cricketer and leagues above anything we could offer up.'

'Dave, I know—'

'No, Mike, you don't know. We've always enjoyed our matches with you, but the fact is the boys have given up their one day off for this game and all we ever ask is a fair and even contest. So as far as we're all concerned this afternoon has been a complete—'

He flicks a glance over my shoulder.

'A complete …'

He seems to have lost his train of thought.

'A complete …'

His features are already reassembling themselves into something more familiar, more comforting. The set mouth is upturning at the edges. The rubicund complexion is returning to those frostbitten cheeks. His eyes start to twinkle.

'A complete pleasure,' he continues happily. 'We've enjoyed meeting Sam enormously. And what a cricketer!'

'You think so?'

'Absolutely. A pleasure to watch. Those six successive boundaries will live long in the memory, I can tell you.' He's still peering over my shoulder at something with a huge, beaming Ainsley Harriott grin.

I turn around and follow Dave's eye line.

Kate Winslet is standing by the door of a small sports car on the boundary edge. The star of the movie *Titanic* and one of the most beautiful actresses in world cinema is being introduced individually by Sam to both sets of players, who are queuing up like schoolboys at a graduation ceremony. The Nuthurst bowler, the one who looked as if he wanted to line us up against the wall and shoot us, is asking her to write her autograph on the blade of his bat.

'In fact, can't wait for next year,' says Dave, still looking dreamily across. 'That's what we love about the Baldies. You always give us an occasion to remember.' With that he does something I thought only ever occurred in the pages of a Thomas Hardy novel. He spits onto his giant farmer's hands and smears his hair flat with the accumulated spittle, before resuming his gaze into middle distance with a look of hopeless enchantment.

'Well?' he says. 'Aren't you going to introduce me?'

Match Report:
Harry Baldwins vs Nuthurst.
Baldwins 265–9 declared (Mendes 165).
Nuthurst 242 all out (Mendes 5–5.)
Baldwins win by 23 runs.

Rolvenden

By 2002 almost all the Baldwins are on email, and suddenly organising a cricket match becomes much much easier. No more frantic phone calls and garbled messages left on answerphones that cut out before you've left the directions. Just a flick of a switch and you can send maps, aerial views, weather forecasts and up-to-date averages and team news. But you have to be careful. The internet is very much a two-edged sword. As the humorist Patrick Murray observed, 'The problem with computers is that they're replacing masturbation as a leisure activity.'

I'm upstairs in my office retrieving my overnight emails one Monday morning when there's a knock at the door. I've only been up for twenty minutes and am still in my pyjamas. Who on earth is calling at this time of day? Obviously nobody who knows anything about actors. Unless it's the thing I bought on eBay, Jack Hobbs's 1924 book entitled *Cricket For Beginners* – special delivery often calls around this time.

It takes me longer than usual to hobble down the stairs to answer it as I still haven't fully recovered from yesterday's match, an end-of-season fixture in fading September light against the village of Rolvenden in Kent. With the final few overs played out in torrential rain and our car headlights trained onto the pitch as impromptu floodlighting, it proved to be a miserable last couple of hours. We lost the match, got drenched in the process and it was a long drive in steaming dank clothes back to London at the end of it. Despite a hot bath I'm not sure that I haven't caught a chill.

To my surprise there are two policemen staring back at me from the doorstep.

'Yes?'

'Are you Mr Simkins?' asks the elder of the two constables.

'That's right.'

'Mr Michael Simkins?'

'Yes. What seems to be the problem?'

'Is your wife at home at the moment, sir?'

'No, she's not. She's away for a few weeks visiting her sister in Australia.'

The older policeman gives a knowing look to his younger companion, a teenager with spots who's wearing a helmet at least two sizes too large. He looks like Benny Hill as his alter ego Fred Scuttle.

'Can we come in for a moment, sir?'

'I told you she's not here.'

'It's you we wanted to have a word with, sir. If you don't mind.'

'You'd better come in.' I shepherd them into the lounge where we stand awkwardly staring at each other for several moments. The principal policeman's younger spottier companion seems to be scanning the inside of the house. Why does he keep peering up the stairs?

'So. What can I do for you?'

The older policeman removes his helmet. 'Do you have a computer, sir?'

'Yes, I do.'

'And are you connected to the internet at all?'

'Why do you ask?'

'We've had a complaint, sir. Apparently you have been traced as being the source of sexually explicit emails sent from this address to local government employees.'

Sexually explicit emails? Chance would be a fine thing.

'You've come to the wrong address I'm afraid, officer. There must be some mistake.'

'Yes, sir, that's the reaction we usually get in such enquiries. But you'd be surprised how quickly people's stories change when confronted by the evidence. Speaking of which … '

The older constable clicks his fingers and Fred Scuttle produces a piece of folded A4 paper from his tunic pocket. He hands it to his superior who unfolds it and studies it for a moment.

'This offending email was picked up by automatic internet screening software, sir, installed in the computer system at Bromley and District Council. The device scans all incoming correspondence and sends an automated warning to the local education authority of any correspondence containing offensive words and phrases. Such as this one, sir. This one giving explicit descriptions of male ejaculation.'

'But that's ridiculous. I can assure you—'

'There's nothing ridiculous about it, sir. It's very serious. If convicted, an individual can be given a suspended prison sentence and be placed on the sex offenders' register—'

The room swims in front of my eyes. I've fallen through a trapdoor into a tragic case of mistaken identity, but already seem to have been tried and convicted without my knowledge.

'You have my word, officer, that whatever you have in your hand is nothing to do with me.'

'Are you saying that you are not the author of this email, sir?'

The older constable hands it to me and waits in silence. 'Is that what you're saying?'

'No, I'm not saying that,' I reply after a long pause.

'You are the author then?'

'Yes, I am.'

Older constable turns to Fred Scuttle with a barely concealed look of triumph. 'Get your notebook out, Pete,' he says. 'Looks like we'll need to record this conversation.'

The document I'm holding in my hand is my emailed match report for Harry Baldwin Occasionals versus Rolvenden.

The weekly match reports are one of the many customary

duties of whoever is captain on any given weekend. It was decided last year at our AGM that writing up a short resumé of the fixture, with statistics and a few highlights along with the odd bon mot, would be a good way of keeping the extended family of Baldwin Occasionals scattered throughout the south-east up to date with how the team were doing.

The report in question was one I wrote up on Sunday night. A couple of hundred words, and as befits a club dedicated to the memory of a rotund stalwart of the Golden Age 1890–1914 (particularly one with such a fine moustache and impressive waist-line), I have done what all match reporters are required to do, namely to write up the weekly despatches in an artificially grandil-oquent style appropriate to the memory of our hero. A slight Edwardian flourish to the account, in other words, just to help the whole feel of the thing and make it a more enjoyable read.

Which is why the penultimate paragraph of my email describing Baldwins versus Rolvenden has been ringed in red biro with the words 'Please investigate' next to it in the margin.

' … the principal bowlers Mr Les Sweeney and Mr Barney Kent both performed with spunk but weren't able to penetrate the opposition.'

'Well?' says Fred Scuttle.

It's immediately obvious what has occurred. One of our team, a tall bloke with ginger hair called Darren, works in Parking Solutions for the London Borough of Bromley. He doesn't currently have email at home as he's just moved into a rented flat after splitting from his girlfriend, so had requested that the weekly reports be sent to his official email address at the town hall.

Of course. Such a simple explanation. But easy to see the mix-up. I let out a loud guffaw of relief.

'You find internet grooming a humorous matter, do you, sir?' says Fred Scuttle.

'No, no, you've got hold of the wrong end of the stick, offi-cer.' But his bleak stare reminds me that I'm on very thin ice here. With a suspended sentence and a future consisting of having my lounge windows stoved in by bricks from crowds of angry female traffic wardens, it's important I get my explanation right. One false word and I could yet be in a very deep hole.

'You see, I run a cricket team dedicated to an old sportsman, and we tend to communicate in slightly obfuscatory language so as to replicate the whole period milieu.'

Both constables are now frowning. My references to old sportsmen, spiced with words like obfuscatory, period and milieu, are, I suspect, only compounding their suspicions.

'Come upstairs and I'll show you.' I begin climbing the stairs to my office. The two constables follow me at a safe distance.

'There we are.' Throwing the door open to my office I point to the far corner above the computer. 'That picture will explain everything.' I usher them into a room in which theatre posters and prints of old cricketers jostle for space on every wall.

'There he is. Over there in the corner. Our hero and godhead. See what I mean? Harry Baldwin. That's what this is all about.'

The older constable steps gingerly forward and scans the large sepia print: our Harry, standing erect, holding up his trousers with both hands, his huge walrus moustache spilling over his top lip.

The older constable stares suspiciously for some moments.

I never realised it till now, but in fact Harry does look rather shifty. As if he's just been caught doing something he shouldn't. That umpire standing beside him doesn't look very happy to be there either. And those trousers: they do look terribly big for him. Funny, I never noticed it before. I suppose that's what living in a climate of fear does to people. Everyone starts to look like a refugee from the *Crimewatch* CCTV gallery.

'Now do you see?' I ask hopefully.

The elder policeman chews his lip thoughtfully for a moment. Then he looks at the print again. Then at the email. Then at his companion, who is scrutinising a large framed picture on the far wall, that of the actor Henry Irving in tights and a codpiece, holding a skull.

'Perhaps you should come and see this one, sir,' he says, pointing to the codpiece. 'Looks like there might be a whole ring of them.'

The older constable loosens his tie and looks at me wearily. 'Perhaps you should begin at the beginning,' he says, flicking a glance back at our hero on the wall. 'You say you know this man. A Mr Harry Baldwin, did you say? And does he have access to the internet?'

Match Report:
Harry Baldwins vs Rolvenden.
Baldwins 155 all out.
Rolvenden 156–4.
Rolvenden win by 6 wickets.

The Old Spring

In a recent interview, England opening batsman Mike Atherton observed with crushing simplicity, 'You cannot make runs unless you first learn to occupy the crease.'

It's equally true that you cannot make runs if you are not physically able to lift the bat.

The 217th match in Baldwin history takes place in the beautiful city of Cambridge, on one of its loveliest grounds, Emmanuel College. Our opposition are a team of ex-undergraduates called the Old Spring in tribute to a nearby watering hole that was their second home during their former salad days. Today marks my 170th appearance at the crease.

In the decade and a half since the Baldwins were formed, I've made a total of 3,818 runs at an average of just over twenty-two. I've completed a clutch of fifties, and also gathered enough ducks to start a poultry farm. Fifteen summers, three different bats; I've travelled over thirty thousand miles, played in monsoon and drought, I've gone out to bat with a brass band playing 'The Dead March (From Saul)' in an adjoining field and returned from a second-ball nought to Elaine Paige singing 'Don't Cry For Me, Argentina' at a nearby open-air concert. I've done it all, seen it all, heard it all, been called it all.

Well, of course there's one thing I haven't yet done. I've yet to score a century. In all 176 visits to the crease, I've still yet to accomplish the big three figures. A couple of seventies, an eighty or two, I've even managed ninety-nine. In fact, I've managed it twice. On both occasions we were on grounds on which there was no scoreboard to keep me informed of just how near I was to achieving the Holy Grail. And mental arithmetic was never my strong point.

I'm now resigned to never knowing that one moment of batting ecstasy, the pump of the arms, the bat aloft, the blade presented to all points of the compass and the kiss of the cap badge. Sometimes the one thing you most want is denied you.

And yet on this baking Cambridgeshire evening in August, I find myself only three runs away. The afternoon has unfolded in a fashion I could only have dreamt of. The signs were there: a peerless track, an outfield like glass, a failing attack of paunchy barristers and crusty professors who'd already spent several hours getting pissed at their old alma mater before the commencement of the match, and, crucially, a scoreboard. And with even the most pitiful forward defensive skimming away like a billiard ball across a marble floor, the scoreboard shows I'm on ninety-seven. I'm nearly there. And I'm completely, utterly bollocksed.

The reason is simple. I've never batted this long before. I've been at the crease now for over two hours in baking August heat, and for much of it using Jez Baker's huge bludgeon of a bat, a weapon so formidable as to be almost impossible for a weakling like me to lift. It's all right for him: he has a personal fitness trainer and works out in a high-tech gym at Chelsea Harbour. But in my hands it now feels like a tree trunk. I didn't know it was possible to feel so tired and still be alive. My legs ceased to work about twenty minutes ago, my arms are hardly capable of even patting the crease with my bat, and my feet feel as if someone has attached them to the crease with a giant staple gun. For the last quarter of an hour I've displayed all the sparkling footwork of a tailor's dummy.

Another ball cannons into the two lifeless pillars of suet with attached pads which rumour has it are somewhere beneath my waistline.

'OWWWASSTTHAAT???!!!!!'

Not out. Going down leg side.

Back in the pavilion it's a picture of happiness and content-ment. Jez Baker seems to be decanting a jug of Pimm's into some glass tumblers. I can hear the ice cubes clanking gently together as he lifts the jug, the slow, leisurely outpouring of gin and lemon slices and mint, the drink foaming into the tumblers. Sweeney is asleep in a deckchair. Phil Coleridge the archaeologist is sitting on the grass with his son Luke, helping him crayon in a large drawing book. Jason is dozing on the grass with a straw hat perched raffishly over his face. Barney Kent is flicking absent-mindedly through a stash of porno magazines. Look at them, they couldn't care less—

OWWWAASSTHAAAT?????!!!!!

Jesus, what was that? It's another ball. Thudding into me, this time my thigh pad. I hadn't even noticed the bowler running in.

Not out. Too high.

The bowler trudges back again. He turns and begins his approach. The first faint fingers of cramp twist up my calf muscle. Bring it on, say I, whatever it takes: a heart attack, renal failure, falling debris from the space shuttle – anything to allow me to lie down.

'Just a moment.'

It's my batting partner and friend, the mild-mannered lecturer, Adrian Knapp. Something's wrong. He's stopped the bowler mid run-up. Perhaps there's a speck in his eye. Perhaps his box has slipped. Perhaps he's noticed one of the fielders surreptitiously moving position while my back is turned. I no longer know. I no longer care. I just want to be allowed to lie down.

'Sim, could I have a word?'

He walks down the pitch, prodding the pitch thoughtfully as he does so. He looks troubled. For my part I'm not sure even sure I've got an eleven-yard walk left in me. But somehow I manage to lift one foot, then the other. Someone has put diving boots on me while I was looking the other way.

'Sim, can I ask you something?'

'What is it?'

'How long have you waited to score a hundred?'

'Well … '

'I'll tell you. Just under two decades. One hundred and seventy innings, if I recollect. One hundred and seventy attempts. And I've been at the other end of the wicket for most of them. I've been doing a little mental arithmetic in the past few minutes and I estimate that I've spent just under seven entire weeks of my time on this earth standing twenty-two yards away watching you trying to score your century. I could have done a lot of other things in those seven weeks: travelled round the world, learnt to windsurf, written a short novel … So now your century is here for the taking, and I'm wondering to myself, have you been wasting my time?'

'What do you mean?'

'Have you been wasting my time?'

'Of course not but—'

'Have you?'

'I already said—'

'Have you?' He grabs my wrist with his gloved hand and squeezes it with fierce intensity.

I've never seen Adrian like this. The most diffident and fastidious man I've ever seen on a cricket field, a gifted professor, he normally shows no more anger or dissent on a cricket field than a slight crinkling of the nose. But this man before me now I no longer know.

'Well, then, may I suggest with all due deference that you get a bloody grip on yourself and stop fannying around. We've all waited too long for you to prat about like this.'

'I'm too tired.'

'You can sleep the rest of your life,' he snarls. 'Just do it.' Releasing my wrist, he turns without further comment and walks smartly back to his crease. 'So sorry for any delay,' he says amiably to the umpire.

And he's right. Perhaps I'm hallucinating, but as I wander back to resume my stance an entire gallery of the game's legends swims before my eyes – Dad, Colin Milburn, John Bodkin Adams, Paul Herring, Kevin Draper, Mr Fitchit, Abdul Hashish-Orandi, Shaggerarder, Les Lenham, Rayleigh G. Strutt, the third most dangerous man in London, Bishan Singh Bedi – even Sam Mendes is there, still clutching his Oscar, his head poking out between Nancy and Mongey. And they're all repeating the same mantra. You can sleep the rest of your life.

Fifteen seconds later I plant my diving boot straight down the pitch, swing the tree trunk in a lumbering arc and send the ball skimming away across the green baize. A huge cheer goes up from the pavilion. Sweeney is clapping his hands above his head, Jason has thrown his straw hat into the air, and Barney Kent and Steve Sarstedt are dancing what seems to be a Highland reel. Even Rex Scudamore is leaning drunkenly out of the scorebox window and pointing enthusiastically at the three figures he's just rattled up against Batsman Number 2. All around me the fielders applaud politely, while at the far end Adrian Knapp nods his head up and down with quiet satisfaction as if appreciating a finely turned pottery urn or piece of modern sculpture.

Phil the archaeologist runs onto the pitch with little Luke, who's clutching a sheet of paper newly ripped from his drawing book. He gathers me up in his huge hairy arms and swings me round. 'Well done, skipper, we knew you'd do it one day!' He returns me to earth and ruffles his son's head lovingly. 'Lukey's got something for you,' he says, ushering his son forward. 'Go on, Lukey, show Simmo.' His seven-year-old son shyly holds out his sheet of paper for inspection. 'He's been working on it for the last half an hour,' explains Phil proudly.

Luke has drawn a rudimentary figure of a man with huge red cheeks and thick felt-tipped streaks of matted hair. The figure has what might be wicker baskets or possibly just cricket pads strapped on his legs, and holds what looks like a cricket bat aloft in one primitive hand. Apart from the customary two pinprick eyes and triangle nose that are the trademarks of any seven-year-old artistry, the main facial feature of the figure is a huge thick inky smear of a mouth. And it's smiling – literally – from ear to ear.

Below, in a variety of garish colours, is crayoned the phrase: 'simo 100'.

'OK, we'll get off,' says Phil, picking his son up in his arms. 'Lukey will look after the picture and you can have it at the end of the innings. Glad you liked it – he was insistent he finish it in time to give to you for the big moment.'

Luke scrutinises me from the safety of his father's embrace. 'Dad?' he says, tugging at his father's shirt collar. 'Simmo's crying.'

'Are you OK?' asks Coleridge anxiously.

'I'm fine, thanks, Phil. Just some sweat got in my eyes.'

Match Report:
Harry Baldwins vs The Old Spring.
The Old Spring 228–9 declared.
Baldwins 230–6 (Simkins bowled 101).
Baldwins win by 4 wickets.

Burpham

I'd been looking forward to our match with Burpham. A charming village a few miles from Arundel in a sleepy corner of West Sussex, the ground boasts a bucolic aspect, stunning views and a simply fantastic pub at the end of the lane after stumps are drawn.

But on Sunday morning I get a call from Juanita, the small, bustling matron of the nursing home in Felixstowe where Mum now resides. It's only a couple of days since I was last there, sitting in the cramped and baking room overlooking the seafront where Mum spends each day from mid-morning until early evening. Juanita's tone leaves me in no doubt that I should get up there.

* * *

Mum has been in and out of various hospitals and nursing homes ever since January when she suffered what the authorities believe to be heart failure. Since that dank winter morning when she was stretchered out of her granny flat and into a waiting ambulance she hasn't walked again. After a time spent at Ipswich General Hospital she's been squeezed through a giddying series of rehabilitation centres, special-care units and halfway houses, each serving terrible food, and in one case even managing to lose her false teeth for over a fortnight.

With each successive month her condition has slowly but inexorably declined, until now, late summer 2004, she's been washed up here in this suburban villa-cum-care-home on the outskirts of this small Suffolk seaside town. It's the same villa, if a cement plaque set into the wall of the car park is to be believed, in which Wallis Simpson spent the weeks waiting for her divorce to come through thereby allowing her to marry Edward VIII.

Best not tell Mum that. She was never a fan of Wallis Simpson. The woman suffered the same unforgivable genetic trait in Mum's eyes as Harry Carpenter and Neil Kinnock: she had thin lips, the one misdemeanour Mum always found impossible to forgive.

Between us the three brothers have managed to get along to see her most days in her new abode, but Mum has been insistent throughout that we should take the weekends off. She was already a pale shadow of the Peggy Simkins I'd always known, the woman I recall heaving bundles of papers about, weighing out sweets, sharing a gin and it with Ida Wackett and laughing at Kendo Nagasaki. The vast visceral powerhouse of working-class vigour and good humour that had always been Peggy Simkins was already 90 per cent gone, leaving just a skeleton staff carrying out essential functions and little more.

In the last couple of months she'd started regurgitating her food. Whatever she consumed found its way back up her gullet within twenty minutes, until the point where she was hiding bits of pork chop and chocolate éclair in her handbag so as she wouldn't have to eat them and put into operation the resulting melancholy process of quietly vomiting it all back up again over her cardie.

We'd spoken to experts, visiting nurses, social workers, specialists in geriatric care. Everybody had a theory. There were any number of reasons why this could be happening, they explained: her drug dosage; a viral infection; somebody even suggested that she might even have become an anorexic. The idea of my mum, the only person in the world who could demolish a family-size bar of Galaxy even more quickly than I could, suffering from the same emotional malady as a teenager showed just how much we were in uncharted territory. Mum wouldn't have known anorexia from Annapurna.

But whatever it is, it's killing her. She can no longer keep any sort of food down, not even a bit of mashed banana or a Nuttall's Minto, with the alarming result that her already frail body is starting to wither. Her dentures are now so big for her that she can't use them to eat, and when she does wear them she looks like David Ward, the Surrey batsman principally famous for his Herculean set of gobblers. During my last visit only a couple of days ago she tried her best to rally, asking for a plate of freshly fried fish and chips from a nearby café, and something she's never asked for in her life – a half-pint of Guinness.

I sat with her in a foetid lounge for much of the afternoon among the ever-present wailing and groaning from other sick, unhappy or unhinged residents arrayed round us in all directions, gently spooning morsels of rapidly cooling cod in batter and congealing chips onto her chapped lips as she attempted desperately to force them down her past her swollen tongue and into her parched throat. Neither worked. As on every other occasion since mid-June, she sat stoically enduring the embarrassment and indignity of having her youngest son clean up her waves of sick as, piece by piece, each morsel of food came flooding back up through her digestive tract and out between her dentures onto her freshly pressed blouse.

As if this wasn't enough indignity to suffer, all the while she was throwing up, a visiting duet of entertainers, Denise and Co, stood barely five feet away singing 'Get Happy' at an ear-splitting volume to a room full of trapped and pitiable geriatrics.

'I'm so sorry, Mikey,' she'd croaked as I'd pushed her up the corridor to her room.

'Never mind, Mum, it's not your fault, your stomach's playing up.'

'Bugger my stomach; I meant that bloody duo.'

Now, two days later, Juanita is at her wits' end. Mum hasn't been able to keep down a single cornflake since Thursday, and is in the middle of the rapid, debilitating process of quietly starving to death. Juanita is thinking of having her admitted back into hospital. My brothers are also on their way so that someone can be there to reassure her when the ambulance arrives. I tell Juanita I'm on my way.

I phone Jason, who's organising the team for Burpham, and inform him of my withdrawal from the side. Within half an hour I'm driving along the A12, trying to clear my head for what I sense is going to be a painful and frightening twenty-four hours.

It's a blazing hot late summer's day, one of the hottest of the year. Until Chelmsford my mind is marginally distracted by the comforting buzz of *Test Match Special* on long wave: England are slowly prevailing against the visiting West Indians at Old Trafford, and the tourists face a gruelling two-day rearguard if they're going to have any hope of saving the series. With Henry Blofeld describing hampers full of pork pies and batsman hitting balls like kicking horses, I can almost forget the purpose of my journey for a few miles.

But once we approach Colchester the AM frequency rapidly peters out, and I'm forced to listen to BBC Radio Essex, who are holding a phone-in general-knowledge quiz to win a ceramic mug in the shape of a pirate. For the final stretch of the journey even this doleful broadcast breaks up, and I turn the radio off and allow my subjugated miseries to have their own airtime.

Even as I press the bell on the main door, I can smell the deadly aroma of cabbage and bedpans that has now become such a feature of my weekly visits. I can only hope the residents no longer notice. Juanita answers the door and gives me a wan smile. I'm the first to arrive. She tells me she's just called the ambulance and that Mum will be going back into hospital for further tests. She'll be in the same ward she was admitted to ten months ago after my brother found her marooned and exhausted on the toilet at five o'clock on a freezing January morning.

Except, of course, she's about five stone lighter.

'She's very weak, I'm afraid,' says Juanita, leading me through the maze of corridors. 'She hasn't really kept a thing down for nearly a month now. If we can't persuade her to eat ... '

Her voice tails off. The end of the sentence hangs in the air between us.

We pass the dining room, where half-eaten trays of stew remain where they've been left since lunch. A couple of the carers are sitting round, eating sandwiches and laughing in hushed tones at a dog-eared copy of *Hello!* magazine on the table. Mum's chair is empty, though her handbag still hangs from the armrest.

All the familiar residents are in their usual places: Mona, who paints watercolours with her mouth because her limbs no longer function properly; Margaret, who spends each day looking out at the sea with silent tears of uncomprehending misery coursing down her cheeks; Della, who writhes and flails in her wheelchair in violent and uncontrollable reflexive lurches, all the while displaying a long flailing tongue, the surface of which is coated with a thick carpet of bright custard-coloured bile.

Juanita leads me up the back stairs to the first-floor bedrooms. As I follow her down the landing I glimpse vignettes of the lives of other, anonymous residents who never make it downstairs and whose lives I'm too preoccupied and frightened to investigate. The crumpled frame of a figure, no longer recognisably female, perpetually hunched in her bed. Another woman methodically crying out for help every twenty seconds or so each and every day. Olive who eternally sits in her room waiting for her favourite John McCririck and the Channel 4 horseracing.

Eventually we reach Mum's room. Somebody has written Mrs Sunkins in a spidery biro and pinned it to the door. I've kept meaning to replace it, but I suspect now is not the time. Juanita turns the handle, then stops and glances back at me.

'I told her you might be coming. She knows she's waiting for collection. I'm sure she'll be all right.'

I wouldn't have thought it possible for Mum to have got any thinner than she was on Thursday. Certainly not in a mere forty-eight hours. But she has. What seems like every bone and sinew in her body is now revealed clearly through the thin translucent skin stretched across her frame like that Silvine tracing paper we used to sell at sixpence a roll. She's awake, yet when I peer down at her she doesn't seem to register my presence.

And then I notice why. This woman who once chased a yobbo down our street because she saw him pinch a pint of milk off our doorstep, corralling passers-by to 'stop that bloody doings' until he was eventually manhandled to the ground by a friendly labourer in front of Dranse's second-hand clothiers, is now unable to find sufficient power in her wasted muscles even to turn over in her bed. One frail claw-like hand, with brittle yellow nails on each finger, is gripping the side rail. The skin hangs off her wrist like folds of bread dough. She looks so tiny now I feel I could crush her between my forefinger and thumb.

'Hello, Mum.'

The sound of my voice seems to halt her efforts. She stares up at the ceiling. After several seconds I lean over into her view and her eyeballs swivel to meet mine. Red and staring, too big for their receding sockets, they resemble those false ones on springs we used to sell at Christmas.

'Hello, Mikey,' she rasps. 'Is it Sunday?'

Her voice reminds me of shredded coconut matting. I give her what even she must be able to identify as a bogus facsimile of a smile, and clasp her nearest hand, the one still welded to the side rail. It already feels like that of a dead person. Cold and waxy. But she manages to will the appendage to squeeze me back.

'Juanita says I've got to go back in for a few tests,' she says.

'That's right.' I do something I would never dare have done when she was in her pomp: I put my hand on her glistening fore-head and stroke her hair. 'Just to find out why your stomach's upset. So we can get you well again. I thought I'd just come and make sure you didn't take over the ambulance.' Despite this feeble joke she seems to register my misery, and she squeezes my hand again.

'Don't you worry,' she says. 'I'll be all right.' She too attempts a reassuring smile, though her efforts are even more horrifying than mine, a mere stretching of skin across bone, the look of nothing more than a moving death mask.

'I can't get comfy.'

'Try and rest. It'll be here soon.'

'Are you staying a bit?'

'Yes, Mum, I'll be here as long as you want.'

'Haven't you got a show to get back for?'

'No, Mum, it's Sunday, you're all right.'

She spends several moments processing this information. The necessity of remembering the meaning of individual days and weeks faded with admission into hospital last January. At length she draws back her lips again and stares up at me.

'Sunday?'

'That's right.'

I retrieve an easy chair from the other side of the room and draw it level with the bed. Through the single window onto the street I can glimpse an oblique view of the sea, bright blue in the afternoon sunshine with fluffy clouds. Somebody is windsurfing. A framed photograph of Dad stares back at me from the wash-stand, next to another one of me and Julia at our wedding.

Then Mum speaks.

'Aren't you playing cricket today?'

'No, Mum. I've come to see you. Pete and Geoff are on their way. And the Baldwins can do just fine without me.'

'How are they all?'

'Fine.'

'Jason well?'

'He's fine.'

'Bakey?'

'He's great, Mum. They all send you their love.'

'I'm sorry you're missing your cricket,' she says. 'Put the doings on.'

'It's all right, Mum, I don't need the telly.'

'Go on. There'll be some cricket.'

'It doesn't matter.'

'Put it on. I'd like you to.'

My mum, who wouldn't know one end of a cricket bat from the other; my mum, who can't even raise herself any longer from the horizontal, whose view of the world is reduced to that of a magnolia ceiling rose and a fringed lampshade, wants me to switch the telly on so I can watch the Test match.

I reach for the remote control. It's greasy to the touch. Atop the ageing set in the corner are a couple of free-standing photos in decorated frames, including one of some long ago cricket match in which Pete and Geoff both came along to umpire. There we are, all thinner and younger, me in whites and pads with an arm round each of each of my siblings, standing in white coats like a gathering of butchers. Apart from a tiny snapshot of Dad playing the saxophone, it's the only sign of Mum's personal history. Only last week we found a Get Well card to a previous occupant of the room still on the window ledge.

I press the On switch and the set shudders into life.

Slowly through the mist the figure of Michael Vaughan appears. It looks like a nice day there at Manchester. Brian Lara and Chris Gayle are both batting in shirtsleeves.

'Have you found it?'

'Yes, thanks, Mum.'

I lean over the bed guard and stare down at her. I can see each tiny vein in her forehead. Her eyes are still staring at the ceiling rose. She licks her lips.

'Would you like a drink, Mum?'

She shakes her head and squeezes my hand with her bony fingers.

'Thanks for giving up your cricket,' she rasps.

'It's OK.'

'Is the telly on?'

'Yes. The telly's on.'

'Have you found the cricket?'

'Yes, Mum, I've found the cricket.'

'Who's winning?'

'England are, Mum.'

The news seems to comfort her. She closes her eyes and her breathing becomes more regular. I sit down next to the bed with her hand in mine and stare blankly at the screen, while two hundred miles away Steve Harmison bowls to Chris Gayle.

At about the time Brian Lara scores his ten-thousandth run in Test match cricket, the ambulance arrives. Two smiling men in uniforms remove the guard rails from Mum's bed and wheel her back along Mum's own corridor of uncertainty, down in the lift and out to a waiting vehicle in the car park. As they load her gently into the back I squeeze her hand one last time, promise her I'll be along in the morning to the hospital, and watch as the ambulance disappears out of the gates and back towards Ipswich.

Back in her room the television is still on. I retrieve my jacket from behind the door and spend a few minutes gathering up an impromptu collection of things to take with me tomorrow, things I'm hoping against hope she might still need. Wet Wipes, tissues, even a tube of Rowntree's Fruit Pastilles, even though I know she hasn't been able to eat them for weeks.

At last I'm ready. But I'm reluctant to leave. The room still smells of Mum, of her talcum powder and Blue Grass eau de cologne. Her sandals are still by the bed. I pick them up, put them gently to my nose and inhale. Finally I sit down in front of the television with them on my knee.

Up at Manchester the West Indies are in free fall. Another smart catch from Andrew Strauss off the bowling of Flintoff accounts for the mighty Brian Lara, and the living legend turns with an air of resigned finality and walks back to the Old Trafford pavilion for what will probably be the last time. As he reaches the step he glances momentarily over his shoulder for what seems to be a final look back.

I wonder if this is it.

W.G. Gracefullys

At the end of his book *Cricket For Beginners*, the great Sir Jack Hobbs, England's finest batsman and Dad's inviolate hero, devotes his last chapter of his manual to a brief homily. A gentle morality tale, if you like.

His story, a cricketing equivalent of Shakespeare's 'The Seven Ages of Man', tells of the four ages of a cricketer. The individual in question, a young man whom Hobbs refers to simply as 'Jones', starts out as a gangling youngster, until, 'having gained a more athletic figure, and with his face tanned by long days in the sun', he finds himself playing regularly for a team. 'Let him persevere,' writes Hobbs, 'for there is no knowing to what heights he may eventually attain.'

The second phase finds Jones at the height of his powers, with crowds of well-wishers following his every movement. People passing him on the boundary often say 'Good old George' or slap him on the back as he leaves the ground. As star of the side, his wicket is considered the most prized scalp by the opposition bowlers.

The third phase is short, says Hobbs. A few years further down the line, Jones's name now appears sixth or seventh on the card. It seems to be a different side altogether, for older friends have dropped out and younger ones taken their places. Jones has even been left out a few times, and finds himself 'scanning the team sheet anxiously to see if he has been selected'.

The fourth, writes Hobbs, is a sorrowful affair. Like nearly every once-popular man, he is now largely forgotten. Instead of a respectful greeting and a smile, he finds his views dispensed with and his opinions ignored. 'That's Jones,' says someone nearby on the boundary, and the reply hurts more than anything. 'Who's Jones? What, one of those old players? Those old fogies always think they know better than anyone else.'

By the summer of 2005 I've largely given up playing for the Baldwins. The reason hasn't only been to do with wanting to go out on a high, although I was never likely to surpass that single extraordinary innings against the Old Spring if I played till I was a hundred myself. But after fifteen years spent sitting on the M23 with Les Sweeney and the rest, I've discovered other ways to spend a Sunday afternoon: all manner of possibilities that had never previously occurred to me.

Things like weekends by the sea with Julia. Things like foreign holidays, with long lazy days swimming in the Aegean before sitting watching the sun going down at a local taverna with a Greek salad and a glass of Ouzo. Or going for walks, or to the pictures, or even relaxing over a glass of wine with Oona our black pug and watching *Ice Cold in Alex* on the box. Funny, these things once had no attraction for me. And yet now …

But there are other reasons too. I noticed recently how odd things seemed to be happening, things I couldn't quite explain. Catches I used to hold on to at gulley were hitting me in the breastbone before I had a chance to get my hands together. Balls seemed to be sliding through my hands for four more often than they used to. When batting I found the ball was through me before I'd managed to frame a shot, and I could no longer read the scoreboard from the middle of the pitch. And attempting a quick single in my only match last year I was run out by several yards more than I would once have deemed possible. Is it my imagination, or are bats becoming heavier, outfields bigger, drinks breaks shorter, balls harder and my flannels tighter?

But I still instinctively respond to an urgent plea for recruits from Les Sweeney. The Baldwins have been struggling to raise sides during the long hot days of August and Sweeney is on the verge of having to cancel this week's match for lack of players unless we rally to his call. Scratching a fixture owing to insufficient numbers is the final shaming ignominy in Sunday club cricket, and Sweeney's SOS does the trick. Of course I'll play: never let it be said the Baldwins couldn't raise a side ...

Thus I find myself driving for the first time in several years down the road to East Grinstead to take part in our annual clash against the W.G. Gracefullys. Once famous for their collection of beards, they now, like the Baldwins, have morphed into a loose confederation of friends and acquaintances far removed from the founding tenets of the side. But I have happy memories of my many afternoons there. With its rustic pavilion, nearby pub and preserved steam railway just over the far hedge, it's an ideal spot for a game of cricket.

But the drive down the old A22 south of Croydon isn't as I remember it. In my memory it was a pleasant run through the countryside of East Sussex on a road largely free of traffic and fringed by massive trees and open fields, culminating with a glorious view out over Ashdown forest and the borders of Kent shimmering in the distance. But things have changed in the years since I made my annual pilgrimage. The route has been widened in places to dual carriageway, and the tiny villages and hamlets that once dotted its route are now swollen with acres of suburban sprawl, with convenience stores and garden centres fringing the roadside.

Yet despite its apparent upgrade, the route is now clogged with traffic, and I'm so busy trying to make up time so as not to be late for the 1.30 start that I miss the secluded fork to the village of Isfield and waste further precious minutes having to double back. Or perhaps it's because the official signpost indicating the ground is half hidden behind a Day-Glo poster advertising banger racing on a nearby estate.

The village itself has largely escaped the ravages of progress, but even here the passing years have left their mark. Last time I visited the quaint local pub opposite the ground, the only food available was a traditional roast dinner, and only from one till two. Today an impressive notice in the forecourt advertises a wide range of Thai and Indian cuisine available all day, as well as vegetarian options. There's even a climbing frame for children in the garden, set into chips of soft tree bark, which should have the Health and Safety Executive purring with pleasure. The once quiet public bar is showing an early season football championship match on a wide-screen TV set into the wall.

Even the ground is different. The gloomy hut that once served as the pavilion and smelt of linseed oil and sawdust has disappeared. In its place stands an impressive structure resembling a modern community centre. Instead of the dank lean-to round the back that once constituted the Gents', there are now proper interior cubicles with reliable flushing mechanisms, and a set of working showers with proper thermostats.

Some figures in the distance are already practising on the outfield. Not recognising them I assume the Gracefullys have overhauled their pre-match fitness regime, which, as with us, once consisted of three pints of Shepherd Neame over at the pub. But then I recognise the familiar figure of Les Sweeney knocking up catches with a bat in the centre of the throng. These are obviously my colleagues for today.

Les greets me warmly and shows me into the visitors' changing room. Where once the bare floor would fill an unprotected foot with enough splinters to start a sawmill, it's now covered in shiny hard-wearing composite lino, and the rusty nails in the wall that once served as coat hooks have been replaced by proper aluminium ones.

One by one Les introduces me to my team-mates. Chris True the hotelier needs no introduction, of course, and the archaeologist Phil Coleridge is also delighted to see me again, though his son Luke doesn't accompany him any more, preferring to attend junior football coaching back in north London. Rex Scudamore, our first-change bowler and resident scorer, is as ever outside helping the Gracefullys to put out the boundary markers.

So where are the others? Well, Chris Buckle is on holiday, Jez Baker has moved to Los Angeles to pursue his career, Adrian Knapp is over in France negotiating the purchase of a second home with his long-term partner, and Jason is now settled with a wife and family, which takes up most of his weekends. Steve Sarstedt has moved out of the area as part of his work, and Gordon Quill no longer plays, having suffered a hiatus hernia while lifting a box of old sheet music covers he'd purchased in an auction in Lewes.

Their replacements in the ranks seem a nice bunch of blokes who greet me warmly, but they're from a very different mould: younger men with definable waistlines, state-of-the-art equipment and trendy haircuts. I'm paraded before them as if a fragment of porcelain from the Ming dynasty.

'Gavin, this is Simmo.'

'Sinno?'

'Simmo. He founded the club.'

'Good on yer,' says Gavin, turning back to his copy of *GQ*.

'Tom, this is the founder of the club.'

Tom is watching Fulham versus Manchester City on a miniature TV screen. He breaks away and flashes a welcoming smile.

'Great to meet you. You're Harry Baldwin, are you?'

'No, in actual fact—'

'COME ON!!!!' Tom is already back at Craven Cottage where Luis Boa Morte is speeding up the touchline.

'Gary, this is Simmo.'

Gary turns his iPod off and winks.

'Hello, Simmo. Nice to meet you. Make yourself at home. Played for us before?'

'Once or twice, Gary.'

'They're a great lot of blokes. You'll like them. Do you bat or bowl?'

'A bit of each.'

'Well, let's go out and get 'em.'

I change into my straining trousers and ferret in my dusty kit bag for some boots. The last time I played was on a ground covered with rabbit droppings and my outfit is now suffused with the musky scent of animal dung. It somehow seems entirely appropriate. The team I once captained, that I've played for nearly two hundred times, filled with people with names like Knapp and Quill, the team that saw the latter bowling in a sola topi and Sarstedt leaving the field to resuscitate drowning infants, seems suddenly as rustic and far off as Harry himself: both of us trapped in sepia from a bygone age.

As the afternoon unravels in the buttery autumnal sunshine, I find myself becoming mildly anxious. Something else has changed – but I can't put my finger on it. And then I realise. Whenever we've played here in the past we've always had a spectator: one of the residents of the numerous bungalows fringing the far side of the ground who always comes out to watch the match, whatever the weather.

An old gent with a military gait and a pair of binoculars, he pitches his picnic chair in the same spot in front of his leylandii hedge at 2pm sharp and watches till stumps are drawn. His presence is as much a part of the ritual of the day as the tossing of the coin or the traditional Baldwin middle-order collapse. We've never spoken to him except to offer breathless thanks on the numerous occasions when he's offered to retrieve the ball from his garden – but he's always there.

Except today. The hedge in front of his bungalow is flourishing, and the tiny wooden gate leading through it into his house has been newly painted. But the Gracefullys' own Father Time is nowhere to be seen.

Never mind. It's a lovely afternoon. I'm down to go in at number seven, but the innings goes so well that it doesn't look as if I'll be needed, so I spend much of the afternoon sitting in my pads at the scoring table, dozing in the sunshine and regaling the other waiting batsmen with tales of past glories and disasters from my mental archives.

Luckily I've got the photo of Harry with me as an aide memoire to why we're all here. The club are planning a swanky fixture card for next year and Les asked me to bring along today the original photograph in the *Gallery of Famous Cricketers* so it can be scanned and copied onto the cover for next season.

About ten minutes or so before tea, Gavin approaches. He's just been out for forty-eight made in even time, including shots to all points of the compass and audaciously sprinted singles. He slumps down in the seat next to mine with his beloved *GQ* magazine. It's a particularly good edition this month, he assures me, with seven pages of Abi Titmuss naked. Frankly I would rather see seven pages of Fred Titmus naked, but that's progress for you.

'Looks like you might not get a bat today, Sinno.'

'Simmo. No, it doesn't. Still, 240-odd for four is wonderful. We've done jolly well.'

'Creamed 'em,' says Gavin.

He holds up the centrefold and carefully removes the offending staples. Then he checks his score. He reckons he got a faint nick on the four leg byes that were given while he was batting, in which case he reckons he should have been credited with a half-century instead of the forty-eight he's down as having scored.

'Scuse, Sinno,' he says as he leans across.

It's then that he spots the *Gallery of Famous Cricketers*. The walrus moustache, the blancoed pit boots, the sailcloth trousers. An old man hitching up his flannels and squinting out across the century.

'Who's that twat?' he says.

* * *

Sir Jack Hobbs finishes his story of Jones thus.

'One cannot expect even the greatest players to remain long

in the memory of the public. Each man has his innings, and when he is dismissed he must abide by the decision of the umpire and retire.'

That'll do for me.

Match Result:
Harry Baldwins vs W.G. Gracefullys
Baldwins 247–4.
W.G. Gracefullys 166 all out.
Baldwins win by 81 runs.

TWENTY OVERS IN THE FINAL HOUR

Sackcloth

Woody Allen once said, 'If you want to make God laugh, tell him your plans ... '

It's early September 2005, and things are a bit quiet up there in the celestial heavens. The Almighty has been overdoing the bad news recently – the tsunami, earthquakes in Turkey, the death of Richard Whiteley – and the assorted angels and archangels gathered around him are in need of a laugh.

'Tell you what,' He says, 'this coming Sunday looks like it's going to be the most important day for fans of English cricket in the last fifty years. It's the Ashes decider at the Kennington Oval and England are clinging on to a two–one lead. Every cricket fan will want to be there. The poor Poms haven't had a look-in for ages, the whole match was sold out months ago, tickets are at a premium, I reckon we can have some fun here ... '

'What do you suggest?' says a winged messenger sitting nearby, the one wearing the silver helmet, who looks like a member of the Bulgarian fire brigade.

'You see that bloke down there in north London?'

Bulgarian fireman squints down through the clouds. 'Which one?'

'That one, the one living just off Mill Lane at number 36 ... That one there, sitting there at the kitchen table surrounded by unpaid bills.'

'What, you mean the actor? The one who hasn't worked for nearly six months?'

'That's the one. Cricket fanatic. Talks about little else. He can clear a room in thirty seconds if you get him on the subject.'

'What about him?'

'How about this for a laugh?' continues God. 'He's blown a stack of decent job interviews recently, he can't get arrested, he's going under a bit, rumour is he's having a few problems with his mortgage and wifey's putting a bit of pressure on him to get a real job delivering sandwiches. What about if we … '

He takes his lyre and idly picks out a version of the Channel 4 cricket theme, 'Mambo Number 5', while he thinks for a moment. An image of a charging Andrew Flintoff trampling somebody's picnic flashes through His mind.

'How about this? We arrange for him to be offered a seat. Out of the blue and without warning. Best seat in the ground for the most important day in English cricket in three decades. England two-one up, with the Ashes in the balance and only a day's cricket left in the game. The whole works.'

'What do you mean, the whole works?' says the Bulgarian fireman.

'Corporate hospitality box, grandstand view, free bar, three-course meal, waitresses in pretty frocks, TV set on the wall for slow-motion replays. Good?' He leans forward gleefully. 'But then we make it interesting. We ensure the asking price is something ludicrous, something that really puts his priorities on the line … '

'Go on,' says the Bulgarian fireman.

'And then at the last moment, just when he's decided to go for it, we offer him a part on a TV drama … '

God allows himself a smile of satisfaction at this exquisitely torturous conundrum. Even He has to admit it's one of His best.

'Good?'

'Good. But fiendish,' says the fireman.

* * *

For any cricket lover, there's only one place to be on the planet on Sunday, 18 September 2005. All summer long the Ashes series has swung back and forth. From the very first – no, the very second ball of the opening Test match, when a ball from England's opening bowler Steve Harmison ripped through Justin Langer's defensive prod and smashed his elbow – the contest has spontaneously combusted, and with the final deciding match now approaching its climax, the entire nation is gripped by Ashes fever. And the Oval is the only place to be.

What I'd give to be there in person. In the ground. Savouring the atmosphere, biting my nails to the quick, cheering every last run and wicket. But of course I can't. The match has been sold out for months. The touts are having a field day.

But then I get a call from Chris Buckle.

'My firm has a corporate box for the Sunday,' he says. 'We booked it months ago before we had any idea how important a day it was going to be. Thing is, one of the junior partners has had to drop out and I was wondering if you'd like to take the berth. Best seats in the ground. There's even a TV set on the wall offering slow-motion replays.'

'How much?'

'Free bar all day.'

'How much?'

'Three-course lunch … '

'How much?'

'Coffee and Dorset knobs on arrival.'

'How much?'

'Five hundred pounds.'

'Chris, I can't. I'm even answering adverts in the back of *The Stage* for work as a lookalike. That's how desperate I am.'

'A lookalike for whom?'

'The golfer Nick Price actually.'

'Who would want to hire a lookalike of him?'

'Nobody. That's why I'm skint.'

'I could let you have it for four hundred and fifty if that would help.'

'Chris, Julia would kill me.'

'You could pay me some of it next year when things look up?'

'Sorry.'

'Oh well. I'm sorry too. The press are describing the Sunday as probably the biggest day in English sport since we won the football World Cup. Never mind, I'll bring you a commemorative tea towel.'

A series of marriage-wrecking arguments and three sleepless nights later I tell him I'll have it. No matter that I can't afford it, I have to be there. I'll take a delivery job, I'll squeegee car windscreens on the Marylebone Road, I'll get a job as a vaccine tester, anything. The possibility of seeing Michael Vaughan lift that tiny urn … it's a once-in-a-lifetime experience.

Up on the clouds, God allows himself a tiny chuckle. 'Stage one complete,' He says. 'Time to activate stage two.'

'I'll do it now,' says the fireman.

The next day my agent rings. It's a day's work on a new drama series. This coming Sunday. A thousand quid. She'll bike round the script for me to have a look.

I ask for an hour to think about it. I phone Chris back, instruct him to offer up his ticket to his next candidate, and shuffle off to the pub with the script and my bank statements to do some urgent calculations. The script suggests I've got nothing more onerous to attend to than to walk up a hospital corridor, approach a weeping Martine McCutcheon standing outside the door to the private ward where her husband, Art Malik, is dangerously ill, and break the news that it's only a matter of time before his brain sac explodes causing instantaneous death.

Six set-ups. Two hours tops. I may no longer be free to enjoy Chris's all-inclusive de-luxe package, but once filming is over, a quick taxi ride from the location and by late morning I could be in urgent negotiations with a ticket tout outside the Hobbs Gates.

I call my agent back. I'll take it.

'Looks like he's hoping he can get away quickly and still catch the climax,' says the Bulgarian fireman.

'So he's still not suffering much?'

'Doesn't seem to be. Delusion can get you a long way in life.'

'Very well. Let's turn the screw. Send him the filming schedule.'

The filming schedule arrives and confirms my worst fears. My approach up the hospital corridor is scheduled for 9am, but the bit of dialogue with the grieving McCutcheon isn't down to be shot till six. Or to put it another way, I'm in the first and last set-ups of the day, thus requiring me to spend eight hours in between times at unit base in the car park of the Shepherd's Bush Tesco.

'Do you still want to do it?' asks my agent.

Outside I can see Julia deadheading some roses with a pair of razor-sharp secateurs.

'I think I'd better.'

If I've blown my opportunity to partake in a moment of cricketing history in order to fumble in the greasy till of commerce, I may as well enjoy it. I'm picked up by the unit driver soon after 6am and deposited at location base by the Tesco delivery gate. With no prospect of getting to the Oval, there's going to be little else to do except wait to be called and tuck into the free catering. I gorge myself on fried bread and hash browns, plum tomatoes, bacon, sausage, fried and scrambled egg and black pudding. Someone has left a large container of sunflower seeds for any passing vegetarians. I grab a handful. The Ashes are being decided in the next eight hours and I've forsaken them for a few hundred pounds and three free meals. Might as well make them doubles.

Walking silently along a linoleum corridor was always my strong point at Rada, and the first set-up passes without incident. By 10am I'm back in the tiny partitioned caravan that serves as my dressing room. Surely they can do without me for the next few hours?

The third assistant director, a young man with black frizzy hair, looks in. 'You wanted to have a word?' he asks amiably.

'Gideon ... when do you think you'll be needing me next?'

'It's gonna be a while,' he replies, flicking idly through the call sheet. 'God, I hadn't noticed. You're not needed again till the final shot. Sorry about that. Bloody awful scheduling. I'd put your feet up, try and relax. Can't see us getting to you much before seven.'

'Seven?' I exclaim with as much mock surprise as I can muster, throwing in a bogus glance at my wristwatch for good measure. The watch is a dummy one provided for my consultant to wear as part of his costume, but no matter, Gideon won't know that. This is going to be my best performance of the year.

'That'll be nearly nine hours,' I observe breezily. 'Almost time to go home for a bit ... '

Gideon's walkie-talkie is crackling. It's now or never.

'Don't you think?'

'No can do, I'm afraid,' he replies distractedly. 'Haven't got any free drivers.'

'I can catch the tube!' I plunge on. If only I can get dispensation to disappear for a while, I might catch most of the day's play and still be back in time to break the awful news.

'Can't do it,' says Gideon. 'It would only need a signal failure and we'll be stuffed ... '

'Look, I'll be back by five. Promise. It's only a few stops back to my home and my wife isn't feeling too well, food poisoning I think, she was throwing up when I left her at five, she'd really appreciate a couple of hours of TLC.'

'Mike, I can't sanction it,' says Gideon. 'If they bring your scene forward and you're five miles away watching *EastEnders* or shagging in the bath I'll get fired.'

Shagging in the bath. How quaint. I forget how young these third ADs are. He'll learn.

'The fact is, she's not too bright at the moment, Gideon. We went to see a consultant yesterday and, well, it's been a bit of a shock, she's going to need a lot of support—'

'Mike, I'm sorry. No can do.' Over the radio someone is summoning him back to set. Martine is having a fag break outside and needs her mules brought. 'We'll call you as soon as we can,' he continues with an apologetic look. 'Sorry, Mike, I know it must be tough. Must go.' He swings the sliding door shut with what can only be regarded as a gesture of finality.

The day's play will be starting soon. If the weather clears up, that is; at the moment it's as dark as Hades. Fortunately there's a radio in my cabin so at least I can follow the day's progress. I begin fiddling with the tiny AM radio set into the plasterboard partition. Any minute I should be warmed by the fruity tones of Henry Blofeld and Vic Marks.

This was supposed to be my day of days. And yet I'm entombed in a freezing-cold plywood booth in my socks in a supermarket car park, with only the noise of one of the supporting artistes farting in the next cubicle for company. They've even hung another actor's name on my door; obviously somebody to whom the part was offered before me. I wonder why he pulled out? Probably because he decided to go to the Oval instead. It's the final degradation. Can things possibly get any worse?

At which point the tuning knob comes off in my hand.

* * *

By the time I've found a pair of pliers and some superglue and managed to get a semblance of Radio 4 long wave on the radio, Australia are all out and England are now a mere eight runs ahead with Strauss already back in the pavilion. Any one of four results are still possible by close of play. It's lunch.

Speaking of which …

The catering wagon in the car park has assembled a mouth-watering array of dishes for the cast and crew. I select a Caesar salad and bridge roll to start with, followed by roast lamb with all the trimmings, treacle sponge and custard, cheese and biscuits and several more handfuls of sunflower seeds before waddling back through the car park to continue my long sojourn.

I'm just skirting a particularly fancy-looking trailer parked next to the portable toilets when I hear the roar of 20,000 spectators echoing out. A glance through the open door reveals leading actor Art Malik reclining on a luxurious couch with the remote control in one hand and a kiwi fruit in the other, watching live Channel 4 coverage on a portable colour television set perched on the fridge. The afternoon session has just commenced. He sees me peering in and smiles warmly.

'Sorry, just wanted to check the score,' I mumble. But Art Malik is nothing if not the perfect host. He invites me in, commands me to take my ease in a sumptuous recliner and insists that I tuck into the vast bowl of fresh fruit thoughtfully provided for him by the producers. We settle down to Vaughan and Trescothick peering through the gloom at the advancing Aussie bowlers.

We watch in silence for several minutes.

'I've never really been into cricket before,' he says at last, 'but this summer's really gripped me. Can't take my eyes off it. Have the Ashes been around for very long?'

I launch into a brief but what I hope will prove an interesting description of the last hundred or so years of Anglo-Australian cricket, beginning with the burning of the stump in 1882. After twenty minutes, I've just got to the 1902 tour by the Aussies with particular reference to Fred Tate's crucial dropped catch at Old Trafford, when there's a knock on the door.

'Whoever it is, come in,' he says.

It's Gideon. 'Sorry, Art, you're wanted back on set. We're doing a shot through the ward-room window of you asleep in bed.'

I get up to leave. But Art is having none of it. 'Mike, sit down. Relax. No need for you to go. I'll be back in an hour.' He hands me the zapper, pulls on his bed gown, wipes some mango juice from his cheek and steps out onto the dank concrete. 'Treat the place as your own,' are his departing words.

Treat the place as my own? Presumably those Crunchie bars in the top-of-the-door compartment of the fridge are fair game? And what about that stash of Diet Cokes by the daybed? There's even yet another stash of those sunflower seeds in a large bowl on the table. I settle back. Coke, seeds, fruit, Crunchie, a TV and the denouement of the Ashes in the next few hours. Apart from being actually at the match, what could be better?

My question is soon answered. At 2.23 it starts raining.

The skies over west London are now the colour of cold rice pudding. On the screen the scoreboard lights are shining brightly in the murk, and the Australians watching in the crowd have all put on sunglasses in an attempt to persuade the umpires back on. The English fans respond with a massed chorus of 'Singing In The Rain'.

What an odd game it is. Twenty thousand fans who've paid good money for a day of pulsating sport openly celebrating the fact that no play is actually possible. And somewhere up there on the new debentures stand there'll be a solicitor from Worthing sucking on a Dorset knob and wondering if a hand-made biscuit with real butter is sufficient return on five hundred big ones.

At 2.28 there's a knock on the door. 'He's on set!' I shout to nobody in particular. But it's Gideon, and he brings news. 'I've got a driver free now, Mike. So if your wife's not feeling too good I can have you home in ten minutes. You'll have a couple of hours with her at least. We'll pick you up again around five.'

'No thanks, Gideon. I'm just fine, thanks.'

'But I thought—'

'Honestly, she'll cope, don't worry. They breed them tough in Lincolnshire.'

'It's really no bother—'

'Gideon, please, could you shut the door? The trailer's getting cold. And, Gideon?'

'Yes?'

'Could you fetch me a cup of tea and a Jammie Dodger?'

At 3.43 in the afternoon play is abandoned for the day.

At 3.43 and 10 seconds I begin frantically calling the Oval ticket office on my mobile. The game is spilling over into the

Monday! Fifth and final days of Test matches are never sold out. There's bound to be a ticket somewhere.

At 3.57 I stop pressing redial. Channel 4 is now showing a tracking shot from one of those cameras perched high on a crane, offering a bird's-eye panorama of mist and raindrops, dank rooftops and traffic-clogged streets. Most depressing of all, it zooms in on long, bedraggled queues of punters snaking round the perimeter of the ground, hoping for a seat for tomorrow's climax. All are clutching sleeping bags and tents; all have provisions for a long stay. Mark Nicholas's silky Mayfair tones are repeating the official advice on no account to turn up tomorrow if you haven't already got a ticket.

On his cloud the Bulgarian fireman shakes his head ruefully at his senior colleague. 'You have a warped sense of humour, you know that?' he says.

I have to get in tomorrow. Somehow, some way, I have to get a ticket.

Who can I call? A frantic trawl through my Filofax reveals nothing. I never realised how much till now I rely on luvvies for my social interaction. If I'd been wanting to organise a celebrity charity gala for distressed character actors at Drury Lane I'd be laughing, but now I need a sporting favour there's not a decent opening bat or left-arm chinaman to be had. Nothing. Not even Bert Kwouk.

At 5pm Gideon pops his head in again.

'Mike, good news. They're ready for you on set.'

'You mean right now?'

'Yes, right now. You've had seven hours off – I thought you'd be pleased.'

'Yes, but—'

'Good, soon as you're ready. Car outside waiting to take you to location in Barons Court. Let's go.' He sees my white knuckles gripping my mobile phone. 'Better call your wife now. Director doesn't allow mobiles on set in case they go off during a take.'

Five minutes later I'm pulling into an annexe of Hammersmith Hospital in a polished Mercedes. Ahead of me various damp technicians in parkas are erecting lamps and laying cables, while a gaggle of film extras dressed as doctors and nurses are gathered round a tea urn in the porch. I'm still frantically searching for any faint lead: scrawled messages, jotted numbers, anything or anyone.

And then I spot it. Funny, there it was in my hand the whole time.

The unique thing about your mobile phone is that it contains names and numbers of individuals, casual acquaintances, chance encounters and assorted crashing bores whom you wouldn't dream of cluttering up the pages of your address book with. People you meet in the street who seem to think that a chance encounter is an excuse to set up dinner dates stretching well into the following year.

'Let's swap mobile numbers,' they say, opening up the contact pages on their screen. 'I'll give you a ring this evening …' They won't, of course. And even if they do you won't return the call. Because you don't want to waste any more time in their company. Which is why you hadn't taken their number in the first place. In fact, you wouldn't be talking to them if you'd been nifty enough to hide in the nearest shop doorway as they approached you.

'What's he found?' says God, looking down. For the first time since He started the fun He's looking anxious.

The Bulgarian fireman squints through a pair of binoculars.

'It reads "Hendo",' he says. 'Mean anything?'

'Hendo' is one of the most respected cricket writers in the country. The love child of Boris Johnson and Bernard Ingham, he's a larger-than-life character with trenchant opinions on every facet of the game. Rarely seen without a large fedora, he's loved and feared in equal measure for his mixture of witty observation and bombast. He is also a theatre buff and expert on grand opera, which is why we'd come across one another at a barbecue given by a mutual acquaintance a year or two back. I think I recall our drunkenly exchanging phone numbers at the end of the evening.

But will he remember me? It's nearly fifteen months since the barbecue and we haven't spoken since. How will he react to a request from a man he no longer recalls for assistance in obtaining a ticket to the biggest sporting occasion since Bobby Moore lifted Jules Rimet?

I've just time to send him a text.

But simultaneously Gideon comes out through the glass frontage and opens the Mercedes door. 'We're ready for you,' he says briskly. 'Better switch that thing off, I told you the director has a thing about them … '

'Won't be a second.' No time left. My thumbs flutter desperately over the keys.

dear hendo if u hear of tix going for last rites any chance money no bar can u help mike

'This way now.' Gideon is speaking simultaneously to someone on set in his earpiece. 'I'm bringing him up now.' He opens the glass door of the hospital and gestures me inside. 'Come on,' he adds. 'Don't want to get rain on your doctor's coat.'

It'll have to do. I press Send, watch till the little envelope on the screen swooshes away into the ether and switch off my phone.

'Quick as you can, please,' says Gideon.

Ashes

The scene is a relatively straightforward one.

Martine McCutcheon has met and fallen in love with Muslim restaurateur Art Malik. But he's been the victim of a vicious attack by Martine's jealous boyfriend wielding a car jack, and now lies critically ill in a hospital ward. His life hangs in the balance. Or rather, it doesn't. The consultant surgeon knows the awful prognosis, and is about to break it to Malik's frenzied spouse. Art is going to die, perhaps today, perhaps tomorrow, certainly within six months.

'Your husband has suffered a very severe beating,' he begins gently. 'A blood vessel has erupted, filling the brain sac. There's nothing we can do. It may burst tonight, tomorrow, or next month. But when it does he will die instantly. I'm sorry.'

Martine eyes fill with the most enormous tears in the history of humankind.

'I'm afraid you have some very difficult decisions to make.'

Gideon hurries ahead to confirm my arrival for the shooting. Halfway along the linoleum the director, Robyn, a tired but friendly woman in her early forties with a gentle Edinburgh accent, stands quietly discussing the arrangements for the following day with Daphne, the executive producer and a woman cursed by a startling resemblance to wine critic Jilly Goolden.

They turn to see me. Robyn looks tired and ashen.

'Hi again, Mike. God, it seems an age since this morning. We'll be a few minutes yet, I want to do an establishing shot of Martine waiting outside the room with Art glimpsed through the glass behind her before we get to you, but don't stray too far. We're very behind and there's no overtime so I can't afford to hang around. Help yourself to coffee.'

Coffee? It's all I seem to have drunk today. Even the mention of it provokes some shudder deep within my digestive tract. She disappears back to the TV monitor and a thousand questions from the crew.

'Don't stray too far … ' I wonder whether that includes not nipping outside to check my messages? Surely I've time enough to slope off back down to the foyer and see if Hendo has responded? But even as I fumble in the lining of the coat, it becomes obvious that far more immediate concerns are about to erupt.

Suddenly the one thing I need even more than a text from Hendo is an available toilet.

I remember reading somewhere that sudden and catastrophic bowel movements can be brought on in humans by extreme anxiety or fear. Apparently prisoners about to be interrogated or threatened with violence often find themselves defecating in moments of crisis, even though five minutes before they had experienced no urges at all.

It stands to reason. I've spent the last eight hours, one could even argue the entire summer, in a state of high emotional alert. As well as the necessary pressures of filming a one-speech part on a drama on which half the crew assume I'm the hospital caretaker, I've got to deliver my speech at the fag end of the day when there's no time for retakes while my mind is solely occupied with a man in a fedora I've only ever met once and whether he's going to respond to the jumbled ramblings of an unknown madman.

And now the huge breakfast, huger lunch, five gallons of coffee and an aviary's worth of sunflower seeds has obviously tipped the balance. It all wants to come out. And my sphincter is not interested in negotiations.

But where? Every single person is gathered round the camera, including Robyn, sitting on an upturned equipment box with a pair of headphones clamped tight over her ears. Beyond her the make-up artist is still completing final checks and the camera crew are reloading the camera with a new roll of film. The only person within earshot is the producer, Daphne, idly scanning some public health notices pinned to a nearby wall.

I am going to have to make some difficult decisions.

'Daphne, do you know where the toilet is?'

Daphne is trying to memorise the early signs for the onset of meningitis. She turns distractedly and indicates for me to shush. Filming is imminent. She points her finger towards a small cubicle almost by where I'm standing. Without even stopping to thank her I heave open the door and stagger inside. Even as I'm sliding the fragile door behind me three shrill rings of an alarm bell rend the air. The cameras are about to roll.

'All quiet now please … turnover … speed … '

Within seconds I'm seated and primed for action. The last thing I remember before Vesuvius erupts is a sign pinned to the inside of the cubicle door reading, 'Please leave this toilet as you would wish to find it'.

Too late.

The relief may be profound but the noise is horrible. God knows whether they can hear it out in the corridor. I would imagine most of the residents of west London are now peering anxiously out through their lounge windows. If so, it's probably finished my chances of achieving a hot date with Martine. Still. At least it's all over. Bliss.

Operations complete, I stumble to my feet, press the flush, finish my ablutions and begin hauling up my consultant's trousers. The cistern fills noisily and at length, but with any luck I've interrupted only one take. With any luck I can leave this foetid cubicle with nothing more than a knowing smirk from the sound operator. A dab of hand-wash and all's well, Martine could eat her dinner off me. In fact, I wish she would. It's only when I give a departing glance into the bowl that I see my ordeal is far from over.

I never realised till this moment the qualities of buoyancy in your average sunflower seed. I suppose it is one of mother nature's most wonderful design skills, ensuring that the best possible distribution and pollination occurs in the jungles of Borneo and along the mighty waters of the Amazon basin.

Unfortunately in a tiny toilet cubicle with an already overworked flush only ten feet away from a film crew and separated by a pasteboard wall, what nature intended as a brilliant device becomes an acute social embarrassment.

A thin but unsightly scum is nestling on top of the now-pristine water. Certainly not As You Would Wish To Find It. And there's not even a toilet brush. That's NHS cuts for you.

I pull the flush again. But there's no improvement. Sunflowers obviously didn't get where they are today by caving in to the first obstacle they encounter on their perilous journey. While the cistern begins its laborious process of refilling once more, I press my ear to the door. I can't hear a thing.

It takes a further three flushes and nearly four minutes before the toilet is finally in a state in which I would wish to find it, by which time I've been in here nearly a quarter of an hour. Gingerly I release the bolt and peer out. With any luck they won't have heard, with any luck I can meld with the lighting boys, with any luck …

Twenty-five pairs of eyes return my gaze. Robyn the director has removed her headphones and is staring at me with a tense smile; the boom operator has placed his recording equipment on the floor and is unwrapping a toffee; Martine McCutcheon is sitting on a lighting box reading a magazine. One of the key grips is having trouble keeping a straight face. From somewhere there's a suppressed snigger.

'Everything all right, Mike?' Daphne's anxious voice startles me.

'Aahh yes, sorry, quite all right. Thank you … '

'Are you sure? We can get the unit nurse for you if you like.'

'No, it's not necessary, really.'

'Are you sure? It's really no trouble.'

'No, honestly, it's all ... um ... that is, I'm fine now, thanks.'

'Only we haven't been able to get a clean take on sound.'

'Never felt better.'

'Well, if you're sure ... ' Daphne gives a sheepish thumbs-up sign towards Robyn who clamps her headphones back on. 'OK, nice and quiet now, please, let's try and get this in one, we're now very short of time ... ' Three shrill rings of the bell, and Martine resumes her position by the porthole.

Daphne's hand taps me on my shoulder.

'Why not go out and get a breath of fresh air,' she whispers. 'It'll probably make you feel better. I'll tell them where you are.'

Thirty seconds later I'm back outside drinking in the cool fresh September air. And what's more the rain has stopped, just as the weathermen said it would.

Jesus. The weather! Hendo! The Oval!! I'd nearly forgotten. This is the opportunity I've been waiting for, a couple of minutes' dispensation before disappearing inside. Within seconds the screen is displaying its synthetic greeting. 'How are you?' it asks cheerily.

Up in the heavens God is getting bored and fractious. He's enjoyed the last few hours enormously and the incident with the seeds has been the icing on the cake as far as He is concerned. But now He's feeling sleepy.

'What do you reckon?' he says distractedly.

Bulgarian fireman puts down his binoculars. 'It's your call. And it's getting difficult to see much anyway. Poor sod, you've certainly put him through the mangle.'

God stifles a yawn. 'I've had enough of this now. Why on earth grown men want to spend their precious lifespan watching a load of blokes whacking a bit of cowhide with a stick is beyond me. Some people have got more time than sense, if you ask me.'

'There are a lot of lonely people about,' says Bulgarian fireman thoughtfully.

Down at the Hammersmith Hospital my phone bursts into

life. And it's a genuine call. Not a ringback tone, but a live enquiry, and it's another mobile. But simultaneously Gideon bursts through the main doors and beckons me towards the stairwell. 'OK, Mike, they're ready for you. Robyn's pretty stressed and she thinks we've only got time for one go at it … '

'Coming, Gideon.' The letters on my screen are silently screaming the most wonderful word in the English language: Hendo. I press the green telephone logo on the keypad and lift the phone to my ear.

'Mike, we must go please!' Gideon is now making violent shepherding motions in through the glass doors.

'Hendo!'

'Simkins—' His voice sounds slurred. In the background I can hear the noise of beer-sodden revellers.

'Mike, please, we've no time.'

'Hendo, I'm about to film, did you get my message?'

The voice on the phone is now ordering some calamari and chorizo sausages.

'Mike, please!!'

'Coming, Gideon!'

'Simkins?'

'Hendo?'

'Bloody awful message you sent me. Are you on drugs or something? It took me twenty minutes to work out what in thunder you meant … '

'MIKE, PLEASE!'

'I'm coming!!!'

'What was that?'

'Nothing, Hendo, look, I'm sorry about that—'

'Speak up, man, I can't hear you.'

'Mike, let's go!!'

'JUST A MOMENT!!!'

'Ah that's better, you'll have to keep it up. I'm in a tapas bar and it's bloody heaving.'

'Sorry, Hendo—'

'No good, I'm losing you again. Are you still there?'

'YES YES I'M HERE!'

'Let me get this right, you want a ticket for the Test tomorrow, is that it?'

'Mike, we've got to go.' Gideon is clutching me by the arm.

'Well, your luck's in. I'm with Bumble Lloyd in a tapas bar on the Embankment. He's got a spare one going. It'll be in the Sky TV hospitality box in the new grandstand, free bar, lunch thrown in, Dorset knobs on arrival, no charge, I told him what a fine fellow you were and he's only too glad to help out. Only trouble is you'll be sharing it with a load of broken-down drink-wrecked old England has-beens like him ... '

Raucous cheering breaks out in the background.

'He'll leave it at the Hobbs Gate in your name. Any good?'

'MIKE, TURN THAT PHONE OFF.'

'NO!'

'No?'

'YES!!'

'Yes?'

'YES. YES YES YES!!!'

The call cuts off. The battery's dead.

* * *

'You're looking cheerful,' says Martine McCutcheon as the make-up girl flutters about us for final checks.

'Well, the fact is I've got some good news and some bad news.'

'Oh yes? What is it?'

'Well the bad news is that your husband has a distended brain sac. He might die tonight, he might die tomorrow, but he's going to go some time in the next few months. I'm sorry.'

She smiles gently. 'And the good news?'

I lean in until I'm nearly nibbling her ear. 'I've managed to get a ticket for tomorrow at the Oval ... '

CLOSE
OF PLAY

The family gathers at Cheltenham crematorium on the appropriately named Bouncers Lane on a bright autumn morning in 2006 to scatter Mum's ashes on the grave where her parents, Bill and Alice, have lain for over fifty years. It's Tuesday 12 September, a year to the day coincidentally since Michael Vaughan lifted the tiny urn in triumph to the skies and I burst into tears and told Hendo I could never repay him and that he was a bloody good bloke, did he know that, and we embraced like children.

Since her death nearly two years ago, Mum has been living with Julia and me at our house in West Hampstead, enclosed in her brown plastic urn wrapped in a gift bag in the lounge cupboard. With another summer on the wane we've all agreed it's time now to complete the circle, which began with Mum's birth a mere half a mile from this spot in a terraced house in November 1917.

We arrive soon after eleven for the brief ceremony: Pete and his wife Jane who looked after Mum in her declining years, Geoff and his partner Avril from Brighton, and Julia, me and Mum on the 125 from Paddington. We even had a family-size bar of Galaxy on the journey down, just as a tribute.

A brisk wind is rushing down from the hills over Leckhampton and ruffling the trees on the perimeter of the graveyard. Better get on in case the weather breaks. So what to do now? Everything that needed to be said about Peggy was done at her cremation back in Ipswich in 2004. Should someone say a few words? Read a short poem? Sing a chorus of the 'The Sunshine of Your Smile'?

In the end we decide just to say goodbye. We remove the urn from the gift bag and Pete gingerly unscrews the top.

'Make sure you're up wind,' advises the accompanying official.

Up wind. Nobody's sure how to work out where that might be. Geoff licks his finger and holds it up but seems unsure how to interpret the results. Eventually we're all ready. Pete, who knew Mum nearly two decades longer than me and remembers kneeling with her in the Anderson shelter during the Blitz, prepares to conduct the solemn responsibility of shaking the contents of the urn onto the rectangle of compacted earth under which lie Bill and Alice Holliday.

'Bye-bye, Mum,' says someone. It may be me.

Pete shakes the powdered remains of Peggy Simkins out of the lip of her container and at once a steady trail of dense powder begins dropping to the ground. As it falls a fresh gust of wind scoops up some of the falling particles and carries them up into the sky, where they mingle with the clear West Country air and billow away towards the Promenade.

And as Pete lifts the tiny urn in triumph to the skies I think to myself …

I wonder if England will dare pick Panesar for the first Test at Brisbane …